Politeuphuia, Wits Common-wealth. Or, a Treasury of Divine, Moral, Historical and Political Admonitions, Similes and Sentences. For the use of Schools. Newly Corrected and Enlarged

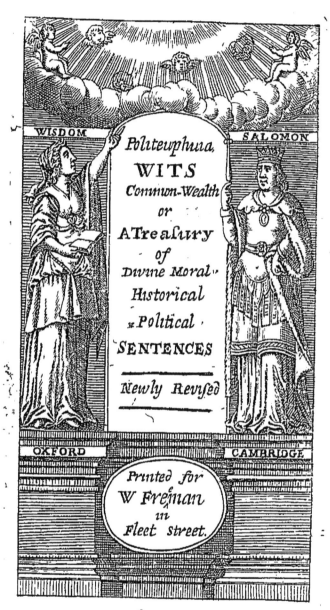

WISDOM

SALOMON

Politeuphuia,
WITS
Common-Wealth
or
A Treasury
of
Divine Moral
Historical
& Political
SENTENCES

Newly Revised

OXFORD

CAMBRIDGE

Printed for
W Freeman
in
Fleet street.

F H van Hove sculp

Politeuphuia,

WITS

Common-Wealth:

O R,

A Treafury of Divine, Moral, Hiftorical and Political *Admonitions,* *Similies* and *Sentences.*

For the USE of

SCHOOLS.

Si tibi difficilis formam natura negavit,
Ingenio formæ damna repende tuæ.

Newly Corrected and Enlarged.

LONDON,

Printed by *J. H.* for *W. Freeman* at the *Bible* againſt the *Middle-Temple-Gate,* in *Fleetſtreet,* 1707.

The PREFACE.

THE Rife and Origin of the moft part of Human Knowledge is chiefly derived from the great Variety of wholfome Inftructions, in all Profitable and Polite Literature, which our Anceftors have, with no lefs Care than Defign, preferv'd, for to enrich the Underftandings of their Pofterity : And their Doctrine having fo much Affinity with, and being fo agreeable to Reafon, and the moft Serious Faculties of Mankind,, as to afford the greateft Improvements, and yield the Happieft and moft ufeful Productions : For by means of thefe golden Remains of Antiquity, we are foon made acquainted with the Laws of Nations, the Duties of Civil Societies, and the Principles of true Religion; wherein, not only the weighty Affairs of the Government of the World, the greateft and moft important Concerns of this Life, is wholly included; but alfo, all our Intereft in that to come, has an infeparable Relation to it, and entirely depends thereon : And that the induftrious Reader might in a little Time, and without any Difficulty, reap the Benefit of what was defign'd purely for his good, we here prefent him with this New Edition of *Wits-Common-wealth*

A 3   with

The PREFACE.

with very confiderable Additions, Alterations and Improvements. Being a Magazine of Choice moral Precepts, grave Admonitions, divine Sentences, with abundance of very edifying and political Maxims for the true Regulation of Life and Behaviour. The whole containing not only useful and excellent Matter, but the Quinteffence and Marrow of what is deliver'd in the Works of the moft eminent Ancient Writers, with many Illuftrious Examples of the greateft and moft noble Vertues, together with their Rules of Patience, Humility, Juftice, &c which have been by all Civiliz'd Nations, always deferveDly celebrated and efteem'd Being, indeed, fo refin'd and clear'd from the Dregs of Paganifm, that their Doctrine might well ftrike our adulterated Profeffors of Chriftianity with Shame and Confufion, their Lives and Actions falling fo far fhort of thofe of the better Heathens, who had no other Rules to go by, than thofe of weak Reafon, and the bare Dictates of Nature What we have here collected, are laid down juft as deliver'd to us by the Ancients, in a natural, diftinct and eafie Stile, as moft profitable for the Ignorant, and moft acceptable to the Knowing The Sentences are copious in pleafing Brevity, each carrying with it a kind of lofty State and Majefty, and flowing with a delightful Elegancy, and Banqueting-like Variety, all fweeten'd with fundry Moving, lively and apt Similitudes, which if Treafur'd up in ones Breaft, will never fail to yield, tho' one was tofs'd up and down in the moft violent Tempeft of Calamity, fuch virtuous Antidotes as will fecure

cure the Soul from being discompos'd at any worldly Misfortune; and at the same time, heighten the Thoughts, and Resolutions to a generous Defiance of all Temporal Crosses whatever. What can be more satisfying than to converse with, and be advised by the wisest in all Ages, and how inestimable is the Worth and Excellency of Learning; but how inexcusable are the Errors that are hourly committed through Ignorance, which might have been with ease avoided; since you have here the plainest Directions, and the surest Guide to Knowledge, with the readiest Method to the attaining of the most commendable Qualities that are required in the perfectly honest and good? The main Design of this Treatise being to represent unto you the Loveliness of Virtue, as that alone which will make a Man happy, and withall the Odiousness of Vice, that you may avoid and abhor it. The Consequences of Vice is the Hatred of God and all good Men here, and everlasting Destruction in the World to come; whereas Virtue gains the Favour both of God and good Men in this Life, and everlasting Happiness when this Life is ended.

Ergo age, vince omnem, Miles, Virtute laborem,
Et, quantum humani possunt se tendere passus,
Arduus accelera. Sil. Ital.
Virtute præditi Cælum petunt

In

In Politeuphuian Decaſtichon.

MYſtica qui ſophiæ, cultæ quadrantia vitæ,
    Ingenii varios flores rimaris & ardes,
Intemerata legas hujus monumenta laboris,
In quo ferventem metris ſedabis orexin.
Hoc duce Mercurio, cœleſti numine plenus,
Vertice ſublimi feries arcana polorum,
Et facilè rapidas fauces vitabis Averni.
Omnia ſunt in hoc, Muſis aptiſſima ſedes.
Virtutis morumque Pharos, Cynoſura vaganti,
Ingenii, genii, mentis, rationis acumen.

A. R.

LET him who in deſire Wit's Wealth embraces,
    Here ſtand and gaze, where well behold he may
A heavenly troop of matchleſs Nymphs and Graces,
    Their ſilver arms in ſacred Fount's diſplay;
Whoſe parts all fair and equal to their faces,
    Make their naked beauty their moſt rich array.

Nor think I lead him with a vain ſuppoſe,
    Inviting him unto his reſting place,
Whence flows a river of ſmooth running Proſe,
    Whoſe ſtreams conceits (like Virgins) interlace.
Amongſt green leaves ſo grows the Damask roſe,
    So Diamonds golden Tablets do enchaſe.

M. T.

Wits

Wits Common-Wealth.

Of God

Defin. *God, the beginning of all things, the* Idea *and pattern of all good, is that Almighty Omnipotence, which wanteth beginning and ending, which, being made of none, hath by his own power created all things.*

Here God putteth to his hand, there are no men fo mighty, no beaft fo fierce, no fea fo deep, that can refift his power.

As a Prince will not fuffer that another be called a King in his Realm fo likewife God will not permit that any other in this World fhould be honoured but he only.

Without the underftanding of the Will of God by his Word, our fight is, but blindnefs, our under-ftanding ignorance, our wifdom foolifhnefs, and our devotion fraud and hypocrifie.

God will not fuffer man to have the knowledge of things to come. for if he had prefcience of his pro-fperity, he would be carelefs, and underftanding of his adverfity, he would be fenfelefs *Auguft*

God, who hath made all mortal things, hath au-thority to difpofe them even with the fame power, wherewith he hath created them.

As much do we owe unto God for the dangers from which he delivereth us, as for the great wealth and dignities whereunto he hath always raifed us.

Where Vertue doth raife to honour, there God fails not to eftablifh the dignity.

A 5   God

God is called a Well or Fountain, both becaufe he hath all good things from himfelt, and alfo for that he doth communicate from thence with his creatures without any hinderance to himfelf. for God miniftreth to all, lacking nought, and receiving nothing of any man

God in his Church is a moft bright Sun, which rifeth upon fuch as fear him, and goeth down from them that are carelefs and profane.

The treafures of vices are in us, the abundance of goodnefs in God. *Jerome*

The greatnefs of God is more feen in mercy than in punifhment

God ufeth us not as our offences deferve, but as his mercy willeth

God deals in one fort with the finner, in another manner with the juft. to the finner he pardoneth his offence, and from the juft he takes away the occafions of his fin

As an Eagle carrieth her young ones on her Wings, and as a Mother carrieth her child in her Arms. So God fupporteth his.

As a skilful Architect prov deth all things neceffary for his building : So doth God for his Creatures.

As it is impoffible with one and the fame eye to behold Heaven and Earth. fo it is as impoffible with one difordinate will to love God and the World. *Auguft*

Like as God furmounteth all other creatures, fo the remembrance of him furmounteth all other imaginations.

God is high : if thou exalteft thy felf, he flyeth from thee, but if thou humbleft thy felf unto him, he cometh down to thee.

God's Doctrine is the rule of Prudence, his Mercy the work of Juftice, and his Death the Standard of Patience. *Bern.*   The

The Refurrection of *Chrift* to the Dead is Life, to the Saints Glory, to Sinners Mercy.

Simonides, the more he ftudied to know what God was, the harder ftill it feemed unto him.

If God help, he is merciful, if not, we muft not think him unjuft

Divinity cannot be defined.

The operation of God is threefold, Creation, Formation, Confummation.

God is Eternity, and therefore not found but of fuch as continually feek him.

God is omnipotent, and can do whatfoever pleafeth him.

The Lord of Hofts is called God the Father, the Son is the image of the Father, the Father and the Son known, the Goodnefs of them both, which is the Holy Ghoft, is made manifeft. *Auguft.*

> *Unus rerum pater eft,*
> *Unus qui cuncta miniftrat.*
> *Ille dedit Phœbo radios,*
> *Dedit & cornua Lunæ.*
> *Ille homines etiam in terris*
> *Dedit, & fydera cœlo.* Boet.

Quæ Deus occulta effe voluit, non funt fcrutanda, quæ autem manifefta fecit non funt neganda: nè & in illis illicitè curiofi, & in iftis damnabiliter inveniamur ingrati Ambrof.

Of Heaven.

Defin. *Heaven is generally taken for that part of the world which is over our heads, a place full of Divine refidence, and the Land where the faithful after this Life expect their portion and inheritance*

Heaven is the feat of God, and the Earth is his Footftool.

Heaven

Heaven is the feat of Glory, the habitation of Angels, the resting-place of the Faithful, far beyond thought, and glorious beyond report.

We deem it hard to know the things on earth, and find the objects of our eyes with toil, but who can search the secrets of the Heavens? *Basil.*

Heaven is neither infinite in form nor figure, but one in nature.

Heaven, as it had its creation of nothing, so it shall be diffolved to nothing.

The difpofition and places of the Heavens are not of power to exprefs our good or bad fortunes

As Hell is the place of all horrour, fo Heaven is the haven of all reft.

Heaven is the habitation of the Elect, the throne of the Judge, the receipt of the Saved, the feat of the Lamb, the fullnefs of delight, the inheritance of the Juft, and reward of the Faithful.

From *Heaven* our *Souls* receive their fuftenance Divine.

Heaven is the Church of the Elect, the Soil of the Juft, and Field of the Faithful.

He is moft miferable that is denied to fee the Sun fhine, and he is moft accurfed to whom God denieth his heavenly favour. *Greg.*

It is hard to live well, eafie to die ill; hard to obtain Heaven, eafie to keep from thence.

None knoweth better how great is the lofs of Heaven, than they that are judged to live continually in Hell.

A good life begetteth a good death, and a good death a glorious inheritance in Heaven.

The way to Heaven is narrower than the way to Hell.

In gloria cœlefti mira ferenitas, plena fecuritas, æterna felicitas.

Eftque Dei fedes nifi terra, & pontus, & aer,
Et cœlum, & virtus? fuperos quid quærimus ultra?

Of Angels.

Defin. Angels are of an intellectual and incorporeal sub-
stance, always moveable and free, the Divine messen-
gers of the will of God, serving him by grace and not
by kind, and are partners of immortality.

ANgels at all times, and in all places, behold the
face of our heavenly Father.

Self-love, the ruine of the Angels, is the confusion
of men.

Angels are careful of mens actions, and prote-
ctours of their persons.

Angels were created of God immortal, innocent,
beautiful, good, fiee and subtil, of the essence of
God himself. *August.*

Angels have their habitation in Heaven, their eyes
fixed on the majesty of God, their tongues formed to
his praises, and themselves only in him.

Every one's Angel that hath guided him in his life,
shall at the latter day bring forth him he hath governed.

Angels intend two things; the first is the glory and
service of God, the second is the health and salvation
of his children.

Angels are the comforters, instructers and refor-
mers of men.

Angels are Tutours of the Saints, Heralds of Heaven, and Guardians of our Bodies and Souls.

The Angels exceed not in desire, desire not, because
they want not, in beholding their Creator. *Ambr.*

The Angels have charge to conduct men, wisdom to instruct men, and grace to preserve men.

Angels were the first creatures that ever God made.

Angels, wheresoever they are sent, do always behold the face of God

There are nine Orders of Angels; Angels, Arch-
angels, Vertues, Powers, Principalities, Dominions,
Thrones, Cherubins, and Seraphins.

The

The divine nature of Angels suffereth neither change nor end . for they are immutable and divine.

Angels are swift messengers to execute the wrath of God against his enemies

Every true Minister is a true Angel, and their tongues bear the Embassage of the most high God.

Angeli sic foras exeunt, ut internis contemplationis gaudiis non priventur. Greg.

Apostatæ Angelo similis efficitur homo, qui hominibus esse similis dedignatur.

Of Vertue.

Defin. Vertue is a disposition ard power of the reasonable part of the soul, which bringeth into order and decency the unreasonable part, by causing it to propound a convenient end to her own affections and passions, whereby the soul abideth in a comely and decent habit, executing that which ought to be done according to reason : briefly, it is a proportion and uprightness of life in all points agreeable to reason.

HE that desireth to be called Vertuous, it is first requisite that he be good therefore in the account of reputation, it is more worthy to be called Vertuous, than Noble or Reverend ; for that the one title descends together with Dignity, and the other is the reward of the work which we use So that it falls out in good experience, that this title of Vertue is of many men desired, but of very few truly deserved.

Vertue maketh a stranger grow natural in a strange Country, and Vice maketh the natural strange in his own Country.

Vertue is health, Vice is sickness, *petrar.*

Vertue is a stranger upon earth, but a citizen in Heaven.

Take away Discretion, and Vertue will become Vice.

Vertue is the beauty of the inward man.

Vertue laboureth like the Sun to lighten the world.

To

To forgive is no less Vertue in Princes when they be offended, than revenge is a vice in the common sort when they be wronged

Vertue goes not by birth, nor discretion by years: for there are old Fools, and young Counsellors. *Guev.*

Vertue is the Queen of Labourers, Opinion the Mistress of Fools, Vanity the Pride of Nature, and Contention the overthrow of Families.

Vertue maketh men on the Earth famous, in their Graves glorious, and in the Heavens immortal. *Chilo.*

Vertue is not obtained in seeking strange Countrys, but by mending of old errours.

Vertue is the more acceptable, by how much the more it is placed in a beautiful body.

Pythagoras, compareth Vertue to the Letter Y, which is small at the foot, and broad at the head ; meaning, that to attain Vertue is very painful, but the possession thereof passing pleasant.

A good man, though in appearance he seem needy, yet by Vertue he is rich.

Vertue is a thing that prepareth us to Immortality, and makes us equal in the Heavens. *Socrates.*

The first step to Vertue is to love Vertue in another man

Vertue, while it suffereth, overcometh.

Vertue cannot perfectly be discerned without her contraries, nor absolutely perfect without adversity.

He that remembreth his Vertue hath no Vertue to remember, seeing he wanteth humility, which is the Mother-vertue of all Vertues.

Vertue is better and more certain than any Art.

The Actions of Vertue do so much affect the beholder, that he presently admireth them, and desireth to follow them.

A man endued with Vertue, meriteth more favour than a man of much wealth.

It is no less vertue to keep things after they be gotten, than to get them. *Ovid.*

Ver-

Vertue in general is a caſtle impregnable, a river that needeth no rowing, a ſea that moveth not, a treaſure endleſs, an army invincible, a burthen ſupportable, an ever-turning ſpie, a ſign deceitleſs, a plain way faitleſs, a true guide without guile, a balm that inſtantly cureth, an eternal honour that never dieth. *Marc Aurel.*

Ipſa quidem Virtus pretium ſibi, ſoláque late
Fortunæ ſecura nitet, nec faſcibus ullis
Erigitur, plauſúve petit clareſcere vulgi.
Nil op's externæ cupiens, nil indiga laudis,
Divitiis animoſa ſuis, immotáque cunctis
Caſibus, ex alta mortalia diſpicit arce.
Hanc tamen invitam blande veſtigat, & ultro
Ambit honor, docuit totiens à rure profeſſus
Lictor, & in mediis Conſul quæſitus aratris.
　　Claud. in Conf Manlii.

Laudo factam de neceſſitate virtutem; ſed plùs laudo
illam quam eligit libertas, non inducit neceſſitas.
　　——*Virtus medio jacet obruta cæno,*
Nequitiæ naſſes candida vela ferunt.

Of Peace.

Defin. Peace is the quiet and tranquillity of Kingdoms, burying all ſeditions, tumults, uproars and factions, and planting eaſe, quietneſs and ſecurity, with all other flouriſhing ornaments of happineſs.

DEar and unprofitable is the peace that is bought with guiltleſs bloud.

They juſtly deſerve the ſword of War, which wilfully refuſe the conditions of Peace.

Peace flouriſheth where Reaſon ruleth; and Joy reigneth where Modeſty directeth.

Peace is the end of War, Honour the joy of Peace, and good Government the ground of them both.

Peace is of moſt men deſired

Concord in a City is like Harmony in Muſick.

Concord of many maketh one.

As the living members of the body united together maintain life, and divided haften death. fo Citizens in a Common-wealth by their Concord maintain the State, but by their Hatred deftroy it.

True Peace is to have Peace with Vertue, and War with Vice.

Peace asketh no lefs wifdom to conferve it, than valour to obtain it.

The colour of Peace maketh the War more fecure: for who fufpect leaft are fooneft prevented *Olaus Mag.*

Archidamia, the *Spartan* Lady, feeing her Country oppreft by the covetoufnefs of the Magiftrates, and *Pyrrhus*, triumphing in their miferies, entred the Senate-houfe with a naked fword in her hand, and in the name of all the Ladies chid the heartlefs Lords, for fuffering themfelves to live, their Country being overthrown, and they like to lofe their liberty.

Pyrrhus entring *Sicily*, poffeffed with fome hopes of Peace, afterward furprifed their Country, and enthralled the Inhabitants thereof by tyranny.

Peace from the mouth of a Tyrant is oftner promifed than performed. *Plato.*

The countenance declareth a man's inclination to Peace; and the aufterity of *Marius*'s countenance, being an infant, was ominous to *Rome* in his old age.

It is a point of godly wifdom, to be at Peace with men, at War with vices.

To rule an Eftate is a heavy burthen; but to undergo Peace is an eafie carriage.

Concord maketh fmall things mightily to increafe: but Difcord maketh great things fuddenly to decay.

To fly from Peace, which we fhould earneftly purfue, is to follow Difcord and our own deftruction.

That thing is more efteemed which is obtained by peaceful words, than that which is gotten by forcible violence.

Nemo vires fuas in pace cognofcit · fi enim bella defunt, virtutum experimenta non profunt.　　　　　　—*Pax*

——— Pax optima rerum
Quas homini noviſſe datum eſt: pax una, triumphis
Innumeris melioᵣ, pax cuſtodire ſalutem,
Et cives æquare potens——————Sil. Ital.

Of Truth.

Defin. *Truth is that certain and infallible Vertue which*
bringeth forth all goodneſs, revealeth the Creation of
the World, the power of our Creator, the eternal Crown
of Bliſs we hope for, and the puniſhment allotted for
our miſdoings: it is a vertue through which we are in-
clined to ſpeak no otherwiſe with our tongue than we
think with our heart.

TRuth ſtands not upon the tongues of men, nor
honour upon the frowns of Authority.

There is nothing ſo ſecretly hidden, but time and
truth will reveal it

Truth may be oft blamed, but never ſhamed and
Vertue, ſuppreſſed by Slander, will at laſt appear without blemiſh.

The diſſolving of a doubt is the finding of the truth.
Truth is the Law of Arts

Truth hath two champions, Wiſdom and Conſtancy.

Truth is the meſſenger of God, which every man
ought to reverence for the love of her maſter.

Truth only among all things is privileged in ſuch
wiſe, that when time ſeemeth to have broken her
wings, then as immortal ſhe taketh her force.

The pureſt Emerald ſhineth brighteſt when it hath
a foil, and Truth delighteth moſt when it is appa-
relled worſt.

The end of Grammar is to ſpeak aptly and agreea-
bly, and the end of Speech, Society, of Rhetorick,
to carry all mens minds to one opinion, of Logick,
to find out truth amidſt many falſhoods. All other
Arts do likewiſe tend to Truth.

Four

Four very good Mothers have four very bad Daughters. Truth hath Hatred, Prosperity hath Pride; Security hath Peril, and Familiarity hath Contempt.

Truth is a vertue that scaleth the heavens, illuminateth the earth, maintaineth justice, governeth Common-weals, killeth hate, nourisheth love, and discovereth secrets.

Truth is a sure pledge not impaired, a shield never pierced, a flower that never dieth, a state that feareth no fortune, and a port that yields no danger *Cicero.*

Truth is health that is never sick, a life that hath never end, a salve that healeth all sores, a sun that never setteth, a moon that is never eclipsed, an herb that is never withered, a gate that is never locked, and a voyage that never breeds weariness

Truth is such a vertue, that without it our strength is weakness, our justice tyrannous, our humility traiterous, our patience dissembled, our chastity vain, our liberty captive, and our piety superfluous.

Truth is the Centre wherein all things repose, the Card whereby we sail, the Wisdom whereby we are cured, the Rock whereon we rest, the Lamp that guideth us, and the shield that defendeth us.

Truth is the ground of Science, the scale to Charity, the type of Eternity, and the fountain of Grace.

By truth the innocent smileth before the Judge, and the Traitour is discovered before he is suspected.

Truth is a good cause, and needs no help of Oratory. and the least speech discovers the best credit.

Qui veritatem occultat, & qui mendacium prodit, uterque reus est. ille, quia prodesse non v lt, iste, quia nocere desiderat. Augustʃ.

> *Non bove mactato cœlestia numina gaudent :*
> *Sed, quæ præstanda est & sine teste, fide.*
> —— *Nolo ego te assentari mihi.*
> *Ego verum amo, Verum volo dici mihi :*
> *mendacem odi.* Plaut.

of

Of Conſcience.

Defin. *Conſcience generally is the certain and aſſured teſtimony which our ſouls carry about with them, bearing witneſs of what we ſpeak, think, wiſh, or do · it is to the wicked an Accuſer, a Judge, and an Executioner, to the godly a Comfort, Reward, and Aid againſt all adverſities.*

A Guilty Conſcience is a worm that biteth, and never ceaſeth.

The Conſcience once ſtained with innocent bloud is always tied to guilty remorſe.

An accuſing Conſcience is a worm that frets like *Seres* Wool, ſecretly and deeply, eaſily gotten, and hardly worn out

' Where the conſcience is drown'd with worldly pomp and riches, there wiſdom is turned to fooliſhneſs. .

Conſcience is the Chamber of Juſtice. *Orig*

He that frameth himſelf outwardly to do that which his Conſcience reproves inwardly, wilfully reſiſteth the Law of God.

The Conſcience is waſted where ſhipwreck is made of Faith.

A good Conſcience is the only liberty.

The Conſcience is a book, wherein our daily ſins are written.

A good Conſcience is a continual quietneſs.

Although the Conſcience of many ſeem to be ſeared with an hot iron, as if it were void of all feeling of ſin, yet at the point of death it is awakened, yea and it driveth the miſerable ſoul to deſperation.

We ſhall carry nothing with us out of this life, but either a good or bad Conſcience.

Diſcern diſcreetly, and practiſe reverently thoſe things that are good, that thine own Conſcience may be clear, and others by thy doings not offended. *Greg.* '

' A clear Conſcience needeth no excuſe, nor feareth any accuſation.

As the herb *Nepenthes*, so much commended of *Homer*, being put into wine, driveth away all sadness at a banquet : so a good Conscience being placed in us, doth abolish all tediousness of life.

None is more guilty than he whose Conscience forceth him to accuse himself.

To excuse one's self before he is accused, is to find a foul crack in a false Conscience.

Conscience beareth little or no sway where Coin brings in his plea.

The Conscience loaden with the burden of sin is his own Judge and his own Accuser.

Whenas any offence is committed through ignorance, or any other violent motion, the causes that encrease the same being cut off, penitence and remorse of Conscience presently follow.

The Philosophers count those men incurable, whose Consciences are not touched with repentance for those sins which they have committed.

There is no greater damnation than the doom of a man's own Conscience.

The violence of Conscience cometh from God, who maketh it so great, that man cannot abide it, but is forced to condemn himself.

A wicked Conscience pursueth his Master at his heels, and knoweth how to take vengeance in due time.

Nulla pœna gravior pœnâ Conscientiæ : vis autem nunquam esse tristis ? bene vive Isidor.

—Heu quantum pœnæ mens conscia donat !

—Sua quemque premit terroris imago.

Conscia mens recti famæ mendacia ridet.

Of Prayer.

Defin. *Prayer (as some Divines affirm) is to talk with God, craving by intercession and humble petition, either those things which are necessary for the maintenance of this life, or forgiveness of those sins which through frailty we commit.* THE

THE juft man's Prayer appeafeth the wrath of God.
Prayer muft be freely given, and never fold.

Prayer is the oblation of a thankful heart, and the token of a contrite and penitent mind.

Prayer is not to be attempted with force and violence of heart, but with fimplicity and meeknefs of fpirit. *Aug.*

Happy is that man, whom worldly pleafures cannot draw from the contemplation of God, and whofe life is a continual Prayer.

Prayer is the wing wherewith the foul flies to heaven, and Meditation the eye wherewith we fee God. *Amb.*

Prayer kindleth, inflameth, and lifteth the heart unto God ; and the incenfe of meditation is pleafing in his eyes

The Prayer of the poor afflicted pierceth the clouds.

Prayer is a vertue that prevaileth againft all temptation, and againft all cruel affaults of infernal fpirits, againft the delights of this lingring life, and againft the motions of the flefh *Bernard.*

Prayer begetteth confidence in the foul, confidence begetteth peace and tranquillity of confcience.

Faith joyned with Prayer maketh it more forcible, but humility coupled with it maketh it beneficial and effectual.

Vertuous and godly difpofed people do daily pray unto God for the cleanfing of the impurity of the heart, and do watch it with all diligence that they can, and labour to reftrain it that the corruption thereof burft not out either to the hurt of themfelves or others.

The *Romans* upon certain high days prayed for encreafe of wealth to the people of *Rome :* which *Scipio*, being Cenfor, changed, faying, That it was fufficient, and that they ought only to pray unto God to preferve it fuch as it was.

Thy Prayer is thy fpeech to God · when thou readeft, God fpeaketh to thee, and when thou prayeft, thou talkeft with God. *Aug*   Let

Let Prayer afcend, that Grace may defcend.

He that knoweth how to pray well, knoweth how to live well

Prayer muft be accompanied with the exercife of mortification.

No Prayer can tie the Will of God unto us, except firft of all we renounce and conquer our own Wills.

Pray in thy heart unto God at the beginning of all thy works, that thou mayft bring them to a good conclufion. *Socrat.*

Pray not to God to give thee fufficient, for that he will give to every man unasked · but pray that thou mayft be contented and fatisfied with that which he giveth thee

Heaven fhall ceafe to be, when it fhall ceafe to run and men ceafe to profper, when they ceafe to play.

The wrath and love of God follow each other, but the former is mitigated by prayer and repentance.

Prayer and Repentance bring peace to the unquiet confcience

Orans confiderare debet quid petit, quem petit, feip fum qui petit. Bern.

Hectora donavit Priamo prece motus Achilles.

Flectitur iratus voce rogante Deus.

Of Bleffednefs.

Defin. *Bleffednefs or Beatitude is the grace of God and his benefits bountifully beftowed on them that ferve him, and keep his commandments.*

TRue bleffednefs is hid from mortal eyes, and left as an object to the purer fpirits.

That man cannot be truly bleffed in whom vertue hath no place.

A man that is wife, although he fall into extreme poverty, yet is he very rich and greatly bleffed.

Bleffednefs is an outward quietnefs. *Arift.*

Bleffednefs a far off beginneth from humility.

A bleffed man cannot err.

There

There is no truer happiness in this life than that which beginneth everlasting happiness; and no truer misery than that which leadeth to everlasting misery.

The first felicity that godly men have after this life is the rest of their souls in *Christ*, the second shall be the immortality and glory of their bodies.

This is perfection and happiness, even for every thing to attain the end for which it was created, and therein to rest and be blessed.

Hateful and hapless is that happiness that traineth men from truth to insolence.

Since in every thing the excess is hurtful, the abundance of felicity is most dangerous

It is no true blessedness that hath an end.

If thou knowest all that ought to be known, thou art truly blessed.

They are to be accounted blessed, to whom fortune hath equally weighed the good with the evil.

All things truly belonging to blessedness do chiefly consist in the noble vertues of wisdom.

True blessedness consisteth in a good life and happy death. *Solon.*

Not the rich, but the wise avoid misery, and become happy and blessed.

They that think riches the cause of happiness, deceive themselves no less than if they supposed that cunning playing upon the Lute or Harp came from the Instrument, and not from Art.

Those men be truly blessed whom no fear troubleth, no pensiveness consumeth, no carnal concupiscence tormenteth, no desire of worldly wealth afflicteth, nor any foolishness moveth unto mirth.

True felicity consisteth in the good estate of the soul.

Felix anima, quæ, spreto turbine seculi, pertransiens corporis claustra, illius summi & incomprehensibilis lucis potest aliquo illustrari radio

　　　—*felix cui victa voluptas*
Terga dedit, longi quem non fregere dolores.　　Of

Of Love.

Defin. *Love is the moſt excellent effect of the Soul, whereby man's heart hath no fancy to eſteem, value, or ponder any thing in this world, but the care and ſtudy to know God: neither is it idle, but worketh to ſerve him whom he loveth : and this love is heavenly. There is alſo a love natural, and that is a poiſon which ſpreadeth through every vein, it is an herb that being ſown in the entrails mortifieth all the members, a peſtilence that through melancholy killeth the heart, and the end of all vertues.*

LOVE is the Maſter of boldneſs and confidence. *Niphus de pulch.*

Love is an unreaſonable exceſs of deſire, which cometh ſwiftly, and departeth ſlowly.

He that loveth is often deceived and blinded in that which he loveth

The love that a man getteth by his vertue is moſt permanent.

Love is full of ſpeech, but never more abundant therein than in praiſe.

A friend loveth always, a lover but for a time.

The love of beauty is the forgetting of reaſon.

Love begun in peril favoureth of greateſt delight when it is poſſeſſed.

Love inchanteth the hearts of men with unfit fancies, and layeth beauty as a ſnare to intrap vertue.

Love is a fading pleaſure mixed with bitter paſſions, and a miſery temper'd with a few momentary delights.

All bonds are little enough to hold love

Love is a vertue, if it be meaſured by dutiful choice, and not maimed with wilful chance.

Lawleſs love never endeth without loſs; nor doth the nuptial bed defiled eſcape without revenge.

Fancy is a worm that biteth foreſt the flouriſhing bloſſoms of youth.

B　　　　　　　Love

Love is not to be suppreſt by wiſdom, becauſe not to be comprehended with reaſon.

Hot love is ſoon cold, and faith plighted with an adulterous vow is tied without conſcience, and broken without care.

Love, as it is variable, ſo it is mighty in forcing effects without denial.

Cupid is not to be reſiſted without courage, but entertained with courteſie.

Love vanquiſheth Tyrants, conquereth the malice of the envious, and reconcileth mortal foes unto perfect friendſhip.

Love is a heat full of coldneſs, a ſweet full of bitterneſs, a pain full of pleaſantneſs, making the thoughts have eyes, and hearts ears, bred by deſire, nurſed by delight, weaned by jealouſie, killed by diſſembling, and buried by ingratitude.

That which with the heart is loved, with the heart is lamented.

Love is a worm, which commonly lives in the Eye, and dies in the heart.

To be free from love is ſtrange, but to think ſcorn to be beloved is monſtrous.

Love and Royalty can ſuffer no Equals.

Love being honeſt may reap diſdain, but not diſgrace.

He that feeds upon fancy may be troubled in the digeſtion.

Love never took thought, but near her life's end ; and hope of heaven had never fear of hell.

Things immortal are not ſubject to affection. *Hei.*

Affection bred by inchantment is like a flower wrought in ſilk, in colour and form moſt like, but nothing at all in ſubſtance and favour.

Love gotten by witchcraft is as unpleaſant, as fiſh taken with medicines is unwholeſome.

Love is a Chameleon, which draweth nothing in
the

the mouth but air, and nourisheth nothing in the body but the tongue.

Love breaketh the brain, but never bruiseth the brow; consumeth the heart, but never toucheth the skin; and maketh a deep scar to be seen before any wound be felt.

A man hath choice to begin love, but not to end it.

It is meet for lovers to prefer manners before money, and honesty before beauty

Lawless love without reason is the very loadstone to ruth and ruine.

Love is not satisfied with gold, but only payed with love again. *Pythag.*

Love covereth a multitude of sinful offences; and Loyalty covereth a world of infirmities.

Love-knots are tied with eyes, and cannot be untied with hands, made fast with thoughts, not to be unloosed with fingers.

To have a fair mistress in love, and want gold to maintain her; to have thousands of people to fight, and no peny to pay them, maketh your mistress wild, and your Souldiers tame.

True love is never idle, but worketh to serve him whom he loveth. *Aug.*

As Ivy in every place findeth somewhat to cleave unto, so love is seldom without a subject.

Love is threefold: the first only embraceth vertue; the second is infamous, which preferreth bodily pleasure, the third is of the body and soul. nothing more noble than the first, than the second nothing more vile, the third is equal to both. *Plato.*

Love is a cruel impression of that wonderful passion, which to be defined is impossible, because no words reach to the strong nature of it, and only they know it which inwardly do feel it. *Aurel.*

He that maketh his Mistress a Goldfinch may perhaps in time find her a Wagtail.

The

The affaults of love muft be beaten back at the firft fight, left they undermine at the fecond. *Pythag.*

He that looketh to have clear water, muft dig deep, he that longeth for fweet mufick, muft ftrain Art to the higheft, and he that feeketh to win his love, muft ftretch his labour, and hazard his life.

It falleth out in love as it doth with Vines, for the young Vines bring the moft wines, but the old is beft.

Birds are detained with fweet calls, but they are caught with broad nets Lovers are allured with fair looks, and entangled with difdainful eyes.

He that hath fore eyes muft not behold the candle; nor he that would leave his love, fall to the remembrance of his Lady · for the one caufeth his eyes to fmart, and the other procureth his heart to bleed.

Like as the fire wafteth the wood, fo fcornfulnefs confumeth love. *Hermes.*

Love can never be fully fixed, when in him that is beloved there wanteth merit

It is convenient in love to be difcreet, and in hatred provident and advifed.

Love is a frantick frenzy, that fo infects the minds of men, that under the tafte of Nectar they are poifoned with the water of *Styx.*

Love brings on lewd looks to command by power, and to be obeyed by force.

Love and Fortune favour them that are refolute

Lovers oft times proceed in their fuit as Crabs, whofe paces are always backward.

As affection in a lover is reftlefs, fo if it be perfect it is endlefs.

Love is a fweet tyranny, becaufe the lover endureth his torment willingly. *Niphus.*

The mind of a lover is not where he liveth, but where he loveth.

Love fix'd on vertue increafeth ever by continuance

The paffionate Lover if he fail, love is his Pilot,

if he walk, love is his companion, if he sleep, love is his pillow.

Love is only remedied by love, and fancy must be cured by affection. *Pyth.*

Sophocles being demanded what harm he would wish to his enemy; answered, That he might love where he was not fansied.

Iove is most fortunate where courage is most resolute.

Affections are harder to suppress, than enemies to subdue.

Lovers oaths are like fetters made of glass, that glister fair, but couple no constraint.

Love maketh a man that is naturally addicted to vice to be endued with vertue, forcing him to apply himself to all laudable exercises, that thereby he may obtain his love's favour, coveting to be skilful in good letters, that by his learning he may allure her, to excel in musick, that by his melody he may intice her, to frame his speech in a perfect Phrase that by his learning and eloquence he may perswade her, and what nature wanteth, he seeketh to amend by art, and the only cause of this vertuous disposition is love.

Love, be it never so faithful, is but a Chaos of care and fancy; though never so fortunate, is but a mass of misery. *Chilo*

Love is to be driven out by reason, not to be thrust out by force.

Amidst the natural passions of man, love is the fountain of all other.

The Lover knoweth what he doth desire, but he knoweth not what he should desire.

Love may wither by little and little, but the root will not be removed on a sudden.

It is a profit for young men, and a fault for old men, to be in love.

The best Physician to cure love is she that gave the wound.

The

The firſt ſtep to wiſdom is, not to love; the ſecond, ſo to love that it is not perceived. *Plato.*

Secret love burneth with the fierceſt flame.

As a King is honoured in his Image, ſo God in man is both loved and hated. he cannot hate man who loveth God, nor can he love God who hateth man. *Bern.*

He that gathereth Roſes muſt be content to prick his fingers: and he that will win a woman's good will muſt be content with ſharp words.

There are ſix properties in love. Self-love is the ground of miſchief, Laſcivious love, the root of remorſe, Wanton love, the cowards warfare, Pure love never ſaw the face of fear, Pure love's eyes pierce the darkeſt corners; Pure love attempteth the greateſt dangers.

Libertas quoniam nulli jam reſtat amanti,
Nullus liber erit, ſi quis amare velit.
———— *Heu quantum mentes dominatur in aquds*————
Juſta Venus!

Of Jealouſie.

Defin. *Jealouſie is a diſeaſe of the mind, proceeding from a fear that a man hath, that that thing is communicated to another which he would not have common, but private to himſelf· it is alſo bred of that love which will not ſuffer a partner in a thing beloved.*

HE that is pained with the reſtleſs torment of Jealouſie doubteth and miſtruſteth himſelf, being always frozen with fear, and fired with ſuſpicion. *Her.*

Jealouſie is ſuch a heavy and grievous enemy to the holy eſtate of matrimony, and ſoweth between the married couple ſuch deadly ſeeds of ſecret hatred and contention, as love being once raſed out with diſtruſt thereof, through envy inſueth bloody revenge.

A jealous man is ſuſpicious, evermore judging the worſt: for if his Wife be merry, he thinketh her immodeſt; if ſober, ſullen; if pleaſant, unconſtant;

if she laugh, it is lewdly , if she look, it is lightly .
yea, he is still casting beyond the Moon, and watch-
eth as the crafty Cat over the silly Mouse.

Love as it is divine with loyalty, so it is hellish with
jealousie.

Jealousie proceedeth from too much love.

The heart being once infected with Jealousie, the
sleeps are broken, and dreams prove unquiet, the
night is consumed in slumbers, thoughts and cares,
and the day in woe, vexation and misery.

The Jealous man living dies, and dying prolongs
out his life and passion worse than death , none looketh on his love, but suspicion says, This is he that
covets to be corrival in my favours, none knocks at
the door, but starting up, he thinketh them to be
the Messengers of fancy ; none talk but they whisper
of affection If she frowns, she hates him, and loves
others; if she smile it is because she hath had success
in her love . if she look frowardly on any Man, she
dissembles ; if she favour him with a gracious eye,
then, as a man possessed with a frenzy, he crieth out
that neither fire in the straw, nor love in a woman's
looks can be concealed. Thus doth he live restless,
and maketh love, that of it self is sweet, to be in tast
more bitter than gall.

Jealousie is a hell to the mind, and an horrour to the
conscience, suppressing reason, and inciting rage.

As there is no content to the sweetness in love, so
there is no despair to the prejudice of Jealousie.

As a ship in a tempest, so is the mind tost by Jealousie . the one still expecteth his wrack, the other
seeketh his own ruine

Jealousie maketh the coward stout, the bashful au-
dacious, the babler silent.

He that is jealous is like him that is sick of an ague,
and poureth in drink to augment the chilness of his
sickness. *Hip.*

There

There can be no greater Tyranny than jealousie, whereby a man continually murthereth himself living.

Jealousie begetteth revenge, revenge nourisheth jealousie.

Love is married to jealousie.

Suspicion is the mother of jealousie. *Dionysius.*

Three things breed jealousie, a mighty state, a rich treasure, and a fair wife.

Jealousie is a cruel disease, that pestereth the mind with incessant passions.

Jealousie in seeking death contemneth it, in finding it repineth thereat, not for enduring it, but because it suffereth him not to out-live revenge.

As the Crow thinks her own birds fairest, so the jealous man thinketh his own choice excellentest.

Of little Brooks proceed great Rivers, and from small sparkles of jealousie arise great flames of distemperature.

To trouble a jealous man with counsel, is to augment his pain with suspicion.

Matrimonium itâ demum tranquillè exigi potest, si uxor cæca maritus autem surdus fiat. Fæmineum genus zelotypiæ est obnoxium, & hinc oriuntur rixæ & querimoniæ: rursus marito obnoxia est uxoris garrulitas, quâ molestiâ cariturus est si surdus sit.

Of Hate.

Defin. *Hate or Envy, is a grief arising of another man's prosperity, and malignity is most commonly joined with it; whether it be the foundation of it, as some say, or one part thereof, as others would have it. This malignity or common hate is a delight and pleasure taken in another man's harm, altho' we receive no profit thereby, and it seemeth to be accidental, that is procured by a hatred or ill-will, arising of some evil affection which one man beareth to another.*

THE

T H E greateſt floud hath the ſooneſt ebb, the ſo-reſt tempeſt the ſuddeneſt calm, the hotteſt love the coldeſt end, and from the deepeſt deſire often-times enſueth the deadlieſt hate.

Hate thirſteth to ſalve his hurts by revenge.

Envy is a ſecret enemy to honour.

There is nothing that more ſpiteth a man, than to receive an injury before his enemy.

Hatred is the ſpirit of darkneſs

Hatred is blind as well as love. *Plutaich*

Envy is imagined of the Poets to dwell in a daik cave, being pale and lean, looking aſquint, abounding with gall, her teeth black, never rejoycing but in others harm, ſtill unquiet and careful, and continual-ly tormenting her ſelf.

Envy in this point may be diſcerned from hatred; the one is ſecret, the other is open

The envious man is fed with dainty meat, for he doth continually gnaw upon his own heart.

Hate hath ſundry affections, as contempt, anger, debate and ſcornfulneſs.

Envy ſhooteth at others, and woundeth her ſelf.

> Sicilian *Tyrants yet did never find*
> *Than Envy greater torment of the mind.*

A wiſe man had rather be envied for provident ſpa-ring, than pitied for his prodigal ſpending

Bavins are known by their bands, Lions by their claws, Cocks by their combs, and Envious men by their manners

Envy never caſteth her eye low, and ambition ne-ver points but always upward.

Revenge barketh only at the Stars, and ſpight ſpurns at that ſhe cannot reach.

Envy braggeth but draweth no blood, and the ma-licious have more mind to quip than might to cut

Envy

Envy is like lightning that will appear in the darkeft fog.

Very few dare ferve or follow fuch as the Prince doth hate

Much ftrangenefs breedeth hatred, and too much familiarity breedeth contempt.

The grudge, hatred and malice of them that be evil juftifieth the juftice and fentence of them that be good.

It is better to be fellow with many in love, than to be a King with hatred and envy.

Envy is blind, and can do nothing but difpraife vertue *Solon.*

As ruft confumeth Iron, fo doth envy the hearts of the envious. *Anaxag.*

An envious man waxeth lean with the fatnefs of his neighbour.

It is a fcab of the world to be envious at vertue.

Envy is the companion of mightinefs.

I do not allow of envy, but for good, faith *Evripides*, I would be envied.

Envy is the daughter of pride, the author of murther and revenge, the beginner of fecret fedition, and the perpetual tormenter of vertue

Envy is the filthy flime and impofthume of the foul, a perpetual torment to him in whom it abideth, a venome, a poifon, or quick-filver, which confumeth the flefh, and drieth up the marrow of the bones *Socrat.*

Take away envy, and that which I have is thine : let there be no envy, and that which thou haft is mine.

The envious man thinketh his Neighbour's loffes to be his gain.

Of Vices envy is the moft ancient, Pride the greateft, and Glutony the fouleft

The injured man doth oftentimes forget, but the envious man doth never fpare to perfecute.

Envy is a ficknefs growing from other mens happinefs. *Mar.Aurel.*

If any man be good, he is envied, if evil, himself is envious.

The envious bury men quick, and raise up men being dead

Hidden hatred is more dangerous than open enmity.

It is an evil thing to hurt because thou hatest but it is more wicked, because thou hast hurt, therefore to hate.

Malice drinketh up the greatest part of his own poison. *Socrat.*

That hatred is commonly most deadly which hath once been buried, and afterwards through Injury is revived.

The Injury of a friend is more grievous than the malicious hatred of an Enemy.

Envy is always ready to speak what cometh next to mind, and not that which she ought to speak.

Like as grief is a disease of the body, so is malice a sickness of the Soul

Envy is nothing else but grief of the mind at other mens prosperity. *Amb.*

Debate, deceit, contention and envy are the fruits of evil thoughts.

Envy doth always wait at vertue's elbow.

Glory in the end erecteth that which envy in the beginning seemed to depress.

Pascitur in vivis livor, post fata quiesc t.

Nulla ingenia tam prona ad invidiam sunt quàm eorum qui genus ac fortunam suam animis non aquant, qui virtutem & alienum borum oderunt.

Of Women.

Defin. *Women being of one and the self same substance with man, are what man is, only so much more imperfect, as they are created the weaker vessels.*

Wo-

Womens forrows are either too extreme, not to be redreffed, or elfe tricked up with diffimulation, not to be believed.

Who finds conftancy in a woman finds all things in a woman

Women are to be meafured, not by their beauties, but by their vertues.

Women in their wills are peremptory, and in their anfwers fharp, yet like Falcons they will ftoop to a gaudy lure.

Womens tongues pierce as deep as their eyes.

Womens eyes fhed tears both of forrow and diffimulation.

Women are wonders of nature, if they wrong not nature

Women that are vertuous are to be efteemed and honoured, but fuch as are naughty ought to be avoided and difdained.

A woman once made equal with man becometh his fuperiour *Socrat.*

Women are of right tender condition; they will complain for a fmall caufe, and for lefs will rife up into great pride.

Like as no man can tell where a fhooe wringeth him better than he that wears it, fo no man can tell a womans difpofition better than he that hath wedded her. *Marc Aurel.*

There is no creature that more defireth honour, and worfe keepeth it, than a woman

Beauty in the faces of women, and folly in their heads, be two worms that fret life and wafte goods.

Women for a little goodnefs look for great praife; but for much evil no chaftifement.

A fierce beaft and a perillous enemy to the Common wealth is a wicked woman, for fhe is of much power to do great harm. *Euripides.*

The

The Eagle, when she soareth neareft the Sun, hovers for a prey, the Salamander is moft warm when he lieth from the fire, and a woman moft heart-hollow when she is moft lip-holy.

Though women feem chaft, yet they may fecretly delight in change, and though their countenance be coy to all, yet their confcience may be courteous to fome one.

Women in mifchief are wifer than men

Women by nature are more pitiful than men, but being moved to anger they become very envious, malicious, and deceitful.

Women that are chaft when they are trufted, prove wanton when they are cauflefly fufpected.

It is the property of a woman to covet moft that which is denied her.

Virgins hearts are like Cotten-trees, whofe fruit is fo hard in the bud that it foundeth like fteel, and being ripe, put forth, is nothing but wool.

As it is natural to women to defpife that which is offered, fo it is death to them to be denied that which they demand.

Womens hearts are full of holes, apt to receive, but not to retain.

He that can abide a curft wife need not fear what company he liveth in.

Like as to a fhrewd horfe belongeth a fharp bridle, fo ought a curft wife to be fharply handled. *Plato.*

The clofets of womens thoughts are ever open, and the depth of their hearts hath a ftring that ftretcheth to their tongue's end

Women are like to Fortune ftanding upon a Globe, winged with the feathers of ficklenefs.

The rule for a Wife to live by is her Husband, if he be obedient to the Laws publick.

The eyes of women are framed by art to enamour, and their tongues by nature to enchant,

Womens

Womens faces are lures, their beauty baits, their looks nets, and their words inciting charms.

A hard-favoured woman, renowned for her Chastity, is more to be honoured than she that is inconstant, though never so famous for her beauty. *Mar. Aurel.*

Sophocles being asked, why, when he brought in the persons of women, he made them always good, whereas *Euripides* made them bad, Because I (quoth he) do represent women as they should be, *Euripides* such as they are.

A fair woman unconstant, may be resembled with the counterfeit which *Praxiteles* made of *Flora*, before the which if one stood directly, it seemed to weep, if on the left-side, it seemed to laugh, if on the right-side, to sleep.

Womens wits are like *Sheffield* knives, which sometimes are so sharp that they will cut a hair, and otherwhile so blunt that they must go to the grindstone.

If women be beautiful, they are to be won with praises; if coy, with prayers, if proud, with gifts; if covetous with promises

A woman of good life feareth no man with an evil tongue

Women often in their loves resemble the Apothecaries in their Arts, who chuse the weeds for their shops, when they leave the fairest flowers in the garden.

The wiser sort of women are commonly tickled with self love.

- The affections of women are always fettered, either with outward or inward beauty.

Womens hearts and their tongues are not relatives.

A fair woman with foul conditions is like a sumptuous sepulchre full of rotten bones.

A woman that hath been married to many can hardly please any.

An honest woman being beautiful killeth young men with her countenance. *Guevar.*   A

A woman's mind is uncertain, it hath as many new devices as a tree hath leaves : for she is always desirous of change, and seldom loveth him heartily with whom she hath been long conversant.

Trust not a woman when she weepeth, for it is her nature to weep when she wanteth her will. *Socrat.*

Silence in a woman is a special vertue.

A woman that hath no dowry to marry her, ought to have vertue to adorn her.

A woman in her wit, is pregnable; in her smile, deceivable; in her frown, revengeable ; in her death, acceptable.

A fair, beautiful and chast woman is the perfect workmanship of God, the true glory of Angels, the rare miracle of earth, and sole wonder of the world. *Hermes.*

That man that is married to a peaceable and vertuous woman, being on earth hath attained heaven ; being in want, hath attained wealth, being in woe, hath attained comfort.

Fœmina nulla bona est ; vel si bona contigit ulli,
    Nescio quo pacto res mala facta bona est.

Nisi sermonum optima femina mulieres suscipiant, & participes eruditionis virorum fiant, absurda multa pravaque consilia atque cogitationes & affectus malos pariunt. Plutarch.

Of Beauty.

Defin. Beauty is *a seemly composition of all the members, wherein all the parts with a certain grace agree together : but beauty and comliness of the mind is a convenience meet for the excellency of a man, and that where n his nature doth differ from other living Creatures : and as the outward beauty moveth and rejoyceth the eyes ; so this shining in our lives by good order and moderation, both in deed and word, draweth unto us the hearts of those men amongst whom we live.*

                          Beauty

BEauty is such a fading good, that it can scarce be possessed before it be vanished.

Beauty tameth the heart, and Gold overcometh beauty.

The greatest gift that ever the Gods bestowed upon man is Beauty; for it both delighteth the eye, contenteth the mind, and winneth good-will and favour of all men. *Anacharsis.*

Beauty is a Tyrant for a short time, the privilege of nature, a close deceit, and a solitary Kingdom.

It is a blind man's question, to ask why those things are loved which are beautiful.

The beauty of the body withereth with age, and is impaired by sickness.

The beauty of the soul is innocency and humility. *Greg.*

The fairest creature that God made was the world.

Women that paint themselves to seem beautiful do clean deface the Image of their Creator. *Ambr.*

A beautiful countenance is a silent commendation.

Beauty cannot inflame the fancy so much in a month, as ridiculous folly can quench it in a moment.

Beauty, vertue, and wealth, are three deep perswasions to make love vehement.

The more beauty is seen, the more it is admired.

In all things divisible there is something more, something less, something equal, more or less, what can be then more equal than beauty or wit? *Arist.*

The Scorpion, if he touch never so lightly invenometh the whole body, the least spark of wild fire sets a whole house on flame, the Cockatrice killeth men with his sight, the sting of love and beauty woundeth deadly, the flame of fancy, sets all the thoughts on fire, and the eyes of a Lover wounded with beauty are counted incurable.

He that is an enemy to beauty is a foe to nature.

Beauty

Beauty without honefty is like poifon preferved in a box of gold.

Beautiful women are dangerous marks for young men's eyes to fhoot at.

Chufe not thy wife by her beauty, but by her honefty : for good deeds will remain when age hath taken her beauty from her.

Pravam facit mifturam cum fapientia forma · Negleta decoris cura plus placet, & hoc ipfum quod non ornamus ornatius eft Amb.

Of Diffimulation.

Defin. *Diffimulation is an evil humour of the mind, and contrary to honefty, it is a countenance ever difagreeing from the heart's imagination, and a notorious lier, in whatfoever it fuggefteth.*

THE holieft men in fhew prove often the holloweft men in heart. *Plotin.*

The tip of the tongue foundeth not always the depth of the heart.

Where there is the greateft flourifh of vertue, there oft-times appeareth the greateft blemifh of vanity.

A counterfeit difeafe is fometimes taken away with a falfe fyrup.

It is better to have an open foe than a diffembling friend. *Pythagoras.*

Subtile Sophiftry perverteth true Philofophy.

He which dwelleth next to a Cripple will foon learn to halt : and he that is converfant with an hypocrite will foon endeavour to diffemble.

Diffembled holinefs is double iniquity.

The more talk is feafoned with fine phrafes, the lefs it favoureth of true meaning.

He that diffembleth finneth not of ignorance, but deceiveth by a colour which he himfelf knoweth to be falfe. *Origen.*

Diffemble

Diſſemble not with thy friend either for fear to diſpleaſe him, or for malice to deceive him. *Plato.*

It is far better to ſpeak the truth in a few words, than to keep ſilence with deep diſſimulation.

Deceit deſerves deceit, and the end of treachery is to have no truſt.

Craft hath need of cloaking, whereas truth is ever naked.

He that hath often been deceived with the lies of a diſſembler, will ſcarce give him credit when he bringeth a true tale. *Plato.*

The flattering of an enemy is like the melody of the Syrenes, who ſing not to ſtir up mirth, but allure unto miſhap.

The mind of a crafty diſſembler is hardned more by practice, than the hands of an Artificer by great labour.

> *Impia ſub dulci melle venena latent.*
> *Hæredis fletus ſub perſona riſus eſt.*

Of Folly.

Defin. **Folly,** *or intemperancy in our actions, is an overflowing in voluptuouſneſs, forcing and compelling all reaſon in ſuch ſort, that no conſideration of loſs or hinderance is able to ſtay or keep back him, that is, thro' long cuſtom, infected with vice from betaking himſelf of ſet purpoſe to the execution of all his deſires and luſts, as he that placeth his ſole and ſovereign good therein, ſeeking for no other contentation in any thing, but only in that which bringeth to his ſenſes delight and pleaſure.*

LATE wit and unfruitful wiſdom are the next neighbours to folly.

There can be no greater vanity in the world, than to eſteem the world, which eſteemeth no man, and to make little account of God, who ſo greatly regardeth all men. *Auguſt.*

There

There can be no greater folly in man, than by much travel to encreafe his goods, and with vain pleafures to lofe his foul. *Greg.*

It is folly to attempt any wicked beginning, in hope of a good ending.

He that is vainly carried away with all things, is never delighted with one thing.

It is a common imperfection to commit folly, but an extraordinary perfection to amend.

The importunate and the fool are brothers children. *Marcus Aurel.*

Fire is to be quenched in the fpark, weeds are to be rooted out in the bud, and folly in the bloffom.

Follies paft are fooner remembred than redreffed.

He that makes a queftion where there is no doubt, muft take an anfwer where there is no reafon.

Few vices are fufficient to darken many vertues. *Plutaich.*

He that lendeth to all that will borrow, fheweth great good-will, but little wifdom.

After rafh marriage always comes repentance.

Vanity is the Path wherein youth marcheth, and folly the Page that waits attendant upon their actions.

Pygmalion carved a Picture with his hand, and doted upon it with his heart.

Too much curiofity favoureth of felf-love; and fuch as are too familiar run into contempt.

Folly refufeth gold, and frenzy preferment: wifdom feeketh after dignity, and counfel looketh for gain.

To make the thing proper to one which before was common to all, is a true note of folly, and a beginning of difcord.

The riotous that fickneth upon a furfeit, and the fool that feedeth adverfity, can very hardly be cured. *Solon.*

The fool wanteth all things, and yet if he had them could not ufe one of them.

Some

Some be fools by nature, and some be crafty fools to get themselves a living; for when they cannot thrive by their wisdom, then they seek to live by folly.

Among the foolish he is most fool that knoweth little, and yet would seem to know much. *Aug.*

To be overcome with affections is an evident token of folly.

It is a great folly for a man to muse much on such things as pass his understanding.

Folly is the poverty of the mind.

It is meer folly to hate sin in another, and seeking to correct it, to fall into a greater sin thy self.

A fool that from base poverty is raised up to riches and worldly prosperity, is of all men most forgetful and unfriendly to his friends.

A thing done a fool knoweth; but a wise man foreseeth things before they come to pass.

The more riches that a fool hath, the foolisher he is.

The heart of a fool is in his mouth, but the mouth of a wise man is in his heart.

Instruction given to fools encreaseth folly.

Inter cætera mala hoc quoque habet stultitia, Semper incipit vivere. Seneca.

Sicut nec auris escas, nec guttur verba cognoscit: ità nec stultus sapientiam sapientis intelligit.

Of Flattery.

Defin. *Flattery is a pestilent and noisome vice: it is hardly to be discerned from friendship, because in every motion and affection of the mind they are mutually mingled together, but in their actions, they are meer contraries, for flattery dissenteth from what it seems to intend.*

HE is unwise that rather respecteth the fawning words of a flatterer, than the true love of a faithful friend. *Aurel.*

Flattery refembles Swallows, which in the Summer-time creep under every houfe, and in the Winter leave nothing behind them but dirt.

Flatterers blaze that with praife which they have caufe to blafpheme with curfes.

To flatter a wife man fhews want of wifdom in the flatterer

As no Vermine will breed where they find no warmth, no Vultures haunt where they find no prey, no Flies fwarm where they fee no flefh, no Pilgrims creep where there is no Crofs, fo there is no Parafite will lurk where he finds no gain.

He that feeketh by a plaufible fhadow of flattery to feduce a mind from chaftity to adultery, finneth againft the law of nature, in defrauding a man of his due, his honour, and his reputation. *Lactan.*

Little things catch light minds, and fancy is a worm that feedeth firft upon fennel.

White filver draweth black lines, and fweet words breed fharp torments.

It is better to fall among a fort of Ravens, than amongft flattering companions · for the Ravens never eat a man till he be dead, but flatterers will not fpare to devour him while he is alive. *Plutarch.*

Flattery is like a golden pill, which outwardly giveth pleafure, but inwardly is full of bitternefs.

Flatterers are like Trencher-flies, which wait more for lucre than for love.

Endeavour diligently to know thy felf, fo fhall no flatterer deceive thee. *Bias.*

The flatterer diligently applieth himfelf to the time, and frameth his fpeech to pleafe his mafter's humour. *Ar.*

Like as a Chameleon hath all colours fave white, fo hath a flatterer all points fave honefty

The wood maintaining fire is confumed by it; and riches, which nourifh flatteries, by them come to nothing. *Stobæus.*   He

He that truly knows himself cannot be deceived by flattery.

Flattery is like friendship in shew, but not in fruit. *So.*

To chide or flatter thy wife publickly, is the next way to make her do ill privately.

Adulatio apertis & propitiis auribus recipitur, in præcordia ima descendit : venit ad me pro amico blandus inimicus. Senec.

Sicut sumenda sunt amara salubria, ita semper vitanda est amara dulcedo. Cicero.

Of Suspicion.

Defin. *Suspicion is a certain doubtful fear of the mind, detaining the heart timorously with sundry affections and uncertain proceedings.*

IT is hard to blind suspicion with a false colour, especially when conceit standeth at the door of an enemy. *Aurel.*

Suspicious heads want no Sophistry to supply their mistrust.

Let not thine heart suspect what neither thine eyes see by proof, nor thine ears hear by report.

That man that is feared of many hath cause likewise to suspect many. *Socrates.*

Mistrust no man without cause, neither be thou credulous without proof.

Suspicion is a vertue, where a man holds his enemy in his bosom.

It is hard to harbour belief in the bosom of mistrust.

Where the party is known for a professed foe, there suspicious hate ensueth of course.

It is hard to procure credit where truth is suspected.

Suspicion is the poison of true friendship. *August.*

It

'It is better to fufpect too foon than miſlike too late.

Small acquaintance breeds Miſtruſt, and miſtruſt hinders love.

Sufpicion may enter a falfe action, but proof ſhall never bring in his plea.

Where vertue keepeth the fort, report and fufpicion may aſſail, but never ſack.

Sufpicion engendreth curioſity, backbiting, unquietnefs, factions, jealoufie, and many other miſchiefs.

Open fufpecting of others cometh of fecret condemning our felves *S. P. S.*

Where hateful fufpicion breedeth enmity, there it is hard to procure amity.

He that feareth nothing fufpecteth nothing

Fools fufpect wife-men, and wife men know fools.

When we fufpect our felves to be moſt miſerable, then is the grace of God moſt favourable. *Bernard.*

Beauty is the true glafs of divine vertue, and fufpicion the mirrour in which we fee our own noted dangers.

Sufpect the meaning, and regard not fpeeches. *Socr.*

Baniſh from thy heart unworthy fufpicion, for it polluteth the excellency of the foul.

To fufpect where there is caufe, is fufferable ; but to fufpect without caufe, is intollerable.

He that lives without offence never needs to fufpect reproof.

Caufelefs fufpicion is the next way to make him doe evil, which always before did carry a conſtant meaning *Bias.*

Octavius Auguſtus domum ſuam non ſolùm crimine, ſed ſuſpicione criminis, vacare voluit.

Sicut difficile aliquem ſuſpicatur malum qui bonus eſt : ſic difficile aliquem ſuſpicatur bonum qui ipſe malus eſt. Cicero.

Of Thoughts.

Defin. *Thought generally is all the imaginations of our brain, which, being a proposed object of the heart, maketh it continually revolve and work upon those conceits.*

THoughts of love the farther they wade, the deeper they be, and desires ended with peril favour of greatest delight.

Carry thy thoughts sealed up with silence.

Thoughts are blossoms of the mind, and words the fruits of desires. *Hermes.*

There is nothing that more shortneth the life of men than vain hope and idle thoughts.

To muse and meditate is the life of a learned man. *Cic.*

Cogitations and thoughts are the movings and travels of the soul *Arist.*

There are no colours so contrary as white and black, no elements so disagreeing as fire and water, nor any thing so opposite as mens thoughts and their words

Think from whence thou comest, blush where thou art, and tremble to remember whither thou shalt go. *Bern*

The mind is the Touch-stone of content

Thoughts are not seen, but the face is the Herald of the mind.

Who thinks before he does, thriveth before he thinks.

Thoughts and conceits are the apparel of the mind. *S P S.*

He imployeth his thoughts well that useth them rather to testifie his vertue than to nourish his displeasure

Let a Prince be guarded with Soldiers, attended by Counsellors, and shut up in Forts, yet if his Thoughts disturb him, he is miserable. *Plutarch.*

The

The Bow that ſtandeth bent doth never caſt ſtreight; and the mind that is delighted with earthly pleaſures feldom thinks on heavenly happineſs

It is an ancient cuſtom in the fancy of man to hold nothing for well done but that which he thinketh well of, although it be evil, and to eſteem nothing for evil but that which he hateth, although it be right good.

When death is at the Door, remedy is too late, and when misfortune is happened, thought of prevention is bootleſs

Cogitationes vagas & inutiles, & velut ſomno ſimiles, nè recipias, quibus ſi animum tuum oblectaveris, quàm omnia diſpoſueris teſtis remanebis.

Cogitationes ſunt improvidi animi reſpectus, & ad evagationem prona.

Of Wit.

Defin. *Wit is the firſt and principal part of the Soul, wherein the mind, the underſtanding, and the memory are contained, which are moſt neceſſary for the direction of all good and vertuous actions.*

SHarpneſs of wit is a ſpark that ſooneſt inflameth deſire. *Chilo.*

One man's will is another man's wit.

The ornaments of wit are much more fair than the badges of nobility.

A bond-man to ire hath no power to rule other men by his own wit.

Strength wanting wit and policy to rule, over-throws it ſelf. *Horace.*

That which man's ſtrength cannot bring to paſs, wit and policy will ſoon diſpatch

Wine is ſuch a wetſtone for wit, that if it be often ſet thereon, it will quickly grind all the ſteel out, and ſcarce leave a back where it found an edge.

C   There

There be three things which argue a good wit, invention, conceiving and answering.

Wit doth not commonly bend, where Will hath most force.

A good wit ill imployed is dangerous in a Common-wealth. *Demost.*

He that in these days seeketh to get wealth by wit without friends, is like unto him that thinketh to buy meat in the market without money.

As the Sea-crab swimmeth always against the stream, so doth wit always against wisdom. *Pythag.*

As a Bee is oftentimes hurt with his own honey, so is wit not seldom plagued with its own conceit.

Wit without learning is like a tree without fruit. *Arist.*

Wit, though it hath been eaten with the canker of conceit, and fretted with the rust of vain love, yet being purified in the Still of wisdom, and tried in the Fire of zeal, will shine bright, and smell sweet in the nostrils of all young novices.

Wisdom cannot be profitable to a fool, nor wit to him that useth it not.

The wit of man is apt to all goodness, if it be applied thereunto. *Diogenes*

Man's wit is made dull through gross and immoderate feeding.

Many by wit get wealth, but none by wealth purchase wit, yet both wit and wealth agree in the sympathy.

He seemeth to be most ignorant that trusteth most to his own wit. *Plato.*

By how much the interiour senses are more precious, and the gifts of the mind more excellent than the exteriour organs and instruments of the body, by so much the more is wit to be preferred before the outward proportion of lineaments.

He

He beſt perceiveth his own wit, who, though his knowledge be great, yet thinketh himſelf to underſtand little. *Plato.*

As empty veſſels make the loudeſt ſound, ſo men of leaſt wit are the greateſt bablers

Recreation of wits ought to be allowed · for when they have a little reſted, they oftentimes prove more ſharp and quick. *Seneca.*

Words wittily ſpoken do awake and revive the judgment, but great and manifeſt examples perſwade the heart

Wit in women is like oil in the flame, and either kindleth too great vertue, or too extream vanity.

Wit gotten by induſtry, though it be very hard in conceiving, yet it is not haſty in forgetting.

Quid non ingenio voluit natura liceie ?
————Nil non mortale tenemus,
Pectoris exceptis ingeniique bonis. Ovid.

Of Wiſdom.

Defin *Wiſdom is a general vertue, the Princeſs and guide of all other vertues, and that wherein the knowledge of our ſovereign good and the end of our life conſiſteth, as alſo the choice of thoſe ways by which we may come unto it.*

Wiſdom ſhineth in the midſt of anger.
It is wiſdom to think upon any thing before we execute it. *Plotinus.*

By other's faults wiſe men correct their own offences

He is wiſe that is wiſe to himſelf *Euripides*

As it is great wiſdom for a man to be Secretary to himſelf, ſo it is meer fooliſhneſs to reveal the inward thoughts of his heart to a ſtranger.

It is wiſdom to look ere we leap, and folly to doubt where no cauſe is.

It

It is more wifdom to lament the life of the Wick-ed, than the death of the Juft.

All is but lip-wifdom that wanteth experience. *S. P S.*

In many injuries, there is more fecurity and wifdom to diffemble a wrong, than to revenge it. *Alex Sev.*

There can be no greater triumph, or token of wifdom, than to conquer affections.

To the wife it is as great a pleafure to hear counfel mixed with mirth, as to the foolifh to have fport mingled with rudenefs.

Wifdom is great wealth, fparing is good getting, and thrift confifteth not in gold, but in grace.

Wifdom provideth things neceffary, not fuperfluous. *Solon*

He that enjoyeth wealth without wifdom, poffeffeth care for himfelf, envy for his neighbours, fpurs for his enemies, a prey for thieves, travel for his perfon, anguifh for his fpirit, a fcruple for his confcience, peril for his love, wo for his Children, and a curfe for his heirs: becaufe although he knows how to gather, yet he wanteth skill to difpofe what he hath gotten.

He that is too wife is a very fool.

True wifdom teacheth us as well to do well as to fpeak well.

Sapience is the foundation and root of all noble and laudable things: by her we may attain a happy end, and learn to keep our felves from everlafting pain.

It is a point of great wifdom to know to what purpofe the time beft ferveth.

Wifdom is a tree that fpringeth from the heart, and beareth fruit in the tongue.

A wife man is never lefs alone than when he is a-lone. *Ambr.*

The firft point of wifdom is to difcern that which is falfe. the fecond, to know that which is true. *Lacte-*

Wif-

Wifdom is the food of the foul.

A wife man's Country is the whole world.

Wifdom garnifheth riches, and fhadoweth poverty. *Socrat.*

Liberality knoweth not the circumftances how to give, if wifdom bend not the courfe by a right compafs.

A valiant mind, forward in wit, and not guided by wifdom, runneth into many inconfiderate Actions

Wifdom is wealth to a poor Man

Many things imperfect by nature are made perfect by wifdom.

Of all the Gifts of God, wifdom is moft pure: fhe giveth goodnefs to good people, fhe pardoneth the wicked, fhe maketh the poor rich, and the rich honourable, and fuch as anfeignedly embrace her fhe maketh like unto God *Hermes.*

Juftice without wifdom is refolved into cruelty, temperance into fury, and fortitude into tyranny *Cic.*

Wifdom reformeth abufes paft, ordereth things prefent, and forefeeth things to come.

We can in no fort behave our felves more prudently, than by confidering how we may deal prudently.

A man of perfect wifdom is immortal, and one of an in feeing underftanding fhall abound in wealth: fo that a wife man fhall live ever to purchafe, and purchafe ever to live.

It is not poffible for that man to obtain wifdom, and knowledge which is in bondage to a woman. *Marc. Aurel.*

Wifdom was begot by nature, nourifhed by experience, and brought forth by learning, who like a Midwife putteth nothing in the mind, but delivereth and enfranchifeth the over-burthened memory .

Power and magnanimity in a young Souldier is combated by old age, and taken prifoner by wifdom.

The only mother of extream mischief, and first original of wars, was worldly wisdom.

Wisdom is like a thing fallen into the water, which no man can find except he search at the bottom

Oculorum est in nobis sensus acerrimus, quibus tamen sapientiam non cernimus. quàm illa ardentes amores excitaret sui, si videretur! Cicero.

Primus ad sapientiam gradus est, seipsum noscere quod ut omnium difficillimum est, ità longè utilissimum

Of Sermons

Defin. *Sermons are speech or talk commonly used of divine matters and holy Scriptures, conferring either with God, or of God.*

Ermons are testimonies of obedience, and obedience to the Word of God is the mother of all vertues.

Sermons consist of three heads, Reprehension, Admonition and Comfort.

Sermons are the utterance of Angels from the mouths of good men.

A good man's Sermons are Lances to a bad man's Conscience, and balm to a penitent Sinner

Honesty is the true beauty of the soul, and Sermons the excellency of a good tongue

Four things issue from Sermons, Prudence, Temperance, Fortitude and Justice

Orations did ever prevail amongst the ignorant, so should Sermons amongst Christians.

Sermons gilt with words and not matter, are like Images, that painted seem fair, but being looked into are found earth.

Sermons adorn men with wisdom, and give them knowledge of things past and things to come

Sermons rain down knowledge and understanding, and bring to heaven those which follow them.

All

All the life of man which expreſſeth a worthy end conſiſteth in contemplation and action, hearing of Sermons and imitating them.

The vertue of wiſdom proceedeth from know ledge, and reaſon is gotten by hearing of Sermons.

The knowledge of good and evil cometh by hearing the word of God preached. *Baſil.*

Science is a dead knowledge of things and cannot exchange the will to follow the known good but Sermons are beams proceeding from that true Sun, which doth not only illuminate the underſtanding, but alſo kindleth the fire of zeal in men's hearts *Amb*

The vertue of Sermons among other vertues is like the vertue of Sight among the five Senſes.

Sermons have three eyes, Memory, Underſtanding and Prudence.

Preachers in their Sermons reſemble Heralds declaring the meſſage of their Maſter.

Quantò magis quiſque in ſacris eloquiis aſſiduus fuerit, tanto ex eis uberiorem intelligentiam capit. Bern.

Omnia ſunt hominum ſubito fluitantia motu,

   Tempus in æternum vox unet una Dei.

Of Memory

Defin. *Memory is that which preſerveth underſtanding, and keepeth faſt thoſe things heard and learned, it is the mother of the Muſes, the treaſure of knowledge, the hearing of deaf things, and the ſight of the blind.*

THE Memory of man is like a net, which holdeth great things, and letteth the ſmall come through. *Solon.*

Before thou ſleep, apparel remembrance with what thou haſt ſaid and done waking

No man ought to make his memory rich by ſearching out the ſecrets of God. *Bernard.*

There is a Divine Memory given of God, in which Casket the Jewels of wisdom and science are lockt. *August.*

Memory is the Mother of the Muses.

It is folly to remember that by which we forget our selves.

Themistocles was of so great Memory, that he defired to be taught the art of forgetfulnefs.

Boaft not of the remembrance of ill, but rather be forry for bearing that load in thy Memory.

Memory is an enemy to reft, and the chronicle of our misfortunes. *Aniel.*

Remembrance of good things is the key which unlocks happy Memory.

Memory is the foul's treafury, and thence fhe hath her garment of adornation.

Never trouble thy head with remembrance of idle words, but apply thy wit to underftand deep meanings.

Writing is the tongue of the hand, and the Herald of Memory

Whatfoever thou bequeatheft to Memory, fuffer it to fleep with her; after employ it, and it will have better ability.

Surfeits and cold confound Memory. *Galen.*

The beft remembrance is to think well, fay well, and do well: all other are fuperfluous.

Memory doth temper profperity, mitigate adverfity, keeps youth under, and delights age *Lactan.*

The remembrance of our old iniquities ought to work new repentance.

It is great wifdom to forget other mens faults, by remembring our own offences. *Socrat.*

The firft Leffon that *Socrates* taught his Scholars was, *Reminifcere.*

Memoria non eft futurorum, nec præfentium, fed præteritorum, unde fenfus eft præfentium, opinio feu fides futurorum & memoria præteritorum. Arift.

Memoria

Memoria eſt ſignataium reium in mente veſtigium.
Cicero.

Of Learning.

Defin *Learning is the knowledge and underſtanding of the Arts and Sciences, ſhe is alſo the mother of veitue and perfection.*

IF a Governour or Captain be void of wiſdom and learning, civil policy cannot be maintained, martial diſcipline wanteth hei greateſt ſtay, and courage pioveth raſhneſs.

Learning in a Soulder is an armour of never-tainted proof, and a wounding dart unreſiſtible. *Vegetius.*

Learning was the firſt founder of weals publick, and the firſt Crown of Conqueſt.

Learning addeth to Conqueſt perpetuity, when Fortune's Sun ſetteth at the firſt ſhining.

He that laboureth to inſtruct the mind with good and laudable qualities, and vertues and honeſt diſcipline, ſhall purchaſe praiſe with men, and favour with God. *Auguſt.*

Learning is the diſplay of Honour, and Humility is ſiſter unto true Nobility · the latter being as needfull in a houſholdei, as the other in a man of arms is profitab'e.

It neither favoureth of learning, nor can be approved of wiſdom, to give over-much credit to things which ſtand without reaſon.

The conqueſt of *Timotheus* won by Oratory and ſweet words was good, ſo were the victories of *Democriths* effected with the ſword. but in an abſolute Commander let both the one and the other be reſident.

In all thy conqueſts have ſovereign regard to Learning, for therein was *Alexander* ienowned, who in his conqueſt of *Thebes* ſold all the free men (Prieſts only excepted) and in the greatneſs of the Maſſacre

C 5
not

not only gave charge for the saving of *Pindarus* the Poet, but also himself saw both him, his house and family undammnified.

Learning is the temperance of youth, the Comfort of old age, standing for wealth upon poverty, and serving for an ornament to riches *Cicero.*

The most learning and knowledge that we have is the least part of that we be ignorant of *Plato*

Those men are in a wrong opinion that suppose learning to be nothing available to the government of the common-wealth.

Sleep and labour are enemies to learning

It is less pain to learn in youth, than to be ignorant in age *Solon.*

Man's understanding seeth, heareth, and liveth, all the rest is blind and deaf, wanting reason *Plato.*

He is much to be commended that to his good bringing up addeth vertue, wisdom and learning.

False Doctrine is the leprosie of the mind.

Be sober and chast among young folk, that they may learn of thee, and among old folk serious, that thou maist learn of them

Nature without learning is blind. *Plato.*

A man cannot be better accompanied than among wise men, nor better spend his time than in reading of Books.

Good learning can neither be taken away nor spent.

Learning maketh young men sober, and comforteth old men, it is wealth to the poor, and treasure to the rich *Arist.*

It is no shame for a man to learn that he knoweth not, of what age soever he be. *Isocrates.*

Of all things the least quantity is to be born, save of learning and knowledge, of which the more that a man hath, the better he may bear it

Learn by other men's vices how filthy thine own are

An opinion without learning cannot be good *Sen*

Doctrine

Doctrinæ radices amaræ, fructus dulces, Bion.

Vita hominis sine literis mors est, & vivi hominis sepultura. Cicero.

*Inter cuncta leges, & percunctabere doctos
Qua ratione queas traducere leniter ævum.* Horat.

Of Knowledge.

Defin. *Knowledge is that understand which we have
both of our Creator, and of his works and will, and of
our own selves, it is the store-house of all wisdom, and
the beginning of our salvation*

Knowledge is of such a quality, that the more a man knoweth, the more he encreaseth his desire to know

The knowledge of all things is profitable, but the abuse of any thing is uncomely

To know and not be able to perform, is a double mis-hap. *Solon.*

Experience with instruction is the best way to perfection.

It is more to know how to use the victory, than to overcome.

He that wanteth knowledge, science and nurture, is but the shape of a man, though never so well beautified with the gifts of nature.

Alexander the Great, made so great account of knowledge and learning, that he was wont to say, he was more bound to *Aristotle* for giving him learning, than to his Father *Philip* for his life, sith the one was momentary, and the other not to be blotted out with oblivion

Learning and knowledge is of good men diligently sought for; and carefully kept in their bosoms, to the end that thereby they may know sin, and eschew the same and know vertue, and attain unto it for if it be not applied thereunto of them that have it, she leaveth in them her whole duty undone. *Plato.*

Perfect

Perfect hearing is a great help in a man to obtain knowledge *Isocrates.*

In war Iron is better than Gold, and in man's life knowledge is to be preferred before riches. *Socrates.*

The *Ægyptians* accounted it a most intolerable calamity to endure but for three days the darkness which God sent unto them by *Moses*. how much more ought we to be afraid when we remain all our life in the night of ignorance?

Doubtfulness and Untruth are the daughters of ignorance.

Above all things we should have a care to keep the body from diseases, the foul from ignorance, and the City from sedition. *Pythag.*

The best knowledge is for a man to know himself. *Sociates.*

He that well knoweth himself esteemeth but little of himself, he considereth from whence he came, and whereunto he must go, he regardeth not the vain pleasures of this brittle life, but extolleth the law of God, and seeketh to live in his fear. But he that knoweth not himself is ignorant of God, wilfull in wickedness, unprofitable in his life, and utterly graceless at his death. *Macrob.*

The understanding and knowledge of vain men is but beast-like to those that are possessed with the heavenly Spirit, which are secret and hid, and when as they speak and utter their knowledge, all other ought to be silent

Knowledge seemeth to be a thing indifferent both to good and evil.

Socrates thanked God only for these three things : first, that he had made him a man, and not a woman ; secondly, that he was born a *Grecian*, and not a *Barbarian*, thirdly, that he was a *Philosopher*, and not unlearned. esteeming the gifts of Nature and Fortune of no value, unless they be beautified with the gifts of the mind.   Ex-

Experience is the Miſtreſs of Age.

Cunning continueth when all other worldly wealth is waſted.

He that knoweth not that which he ought to know is a brute beaſt among men. he that knoweth no more than he hath need of, is a man among brute beaſts and he that knoweth all that may be known is a God among men. *Pythag.*

He is ſufficiently well learned that knoweth how to do well and he hath power enough that can refrain from doing evil *Cicero.*

To lack knowledge is a very evil thing, to think ſcorn to learn is worſe : but to withſtand and repugn the truth againſt men of knowledge teaching the truth, is worſt, and fartheſt from all grace.

No ſcience is perfect that is not grounded on infallible principles. —

Solon, who was taught by much experience and reading, wrought many things for the profit of the weal publick.

A man that is rich in knowledge is rich in all things, for without it there is nothing , and with it what can be wanting ? *Solon.*

Endeavour thy ſelf to do ſo well, that others may rather envy at thy knowledge than laugh at thy ignorance.

Licet omnes ſcientiæ nobiles ſunt, tamen divina eſt nobilior, quia ejus ſubjectum eſt nobilius. Ariſt.

Of Eloquence.

Defin. *Eloquence or Oratory is an art which teacheth the laudable manner of well-ſpeaking; it is the ornament of the brain, and the gilt ſometimes to an evil-reputed matter.*

THE ſpeech of a man is a divine work, and full of admiration: therefore we ought at no time to pollute our tongues with vile and filthy talk.

Bre-

Brevity is a great praise of Eloquence. *Cicero.*

Speech is the nourishment of the soul, which only becomes odious and corrupt by the wickedness of men *Isocrates.*

It is a special vertue to speak little and well.

Silence is a sweet Eloquence. for fools in their dumbness are accounted wise

Many through Eloquence make a good matter seem bad, and a bad matter seem good

Eloquence hath a double fountain the one internal, proceeding from the mind, called the Divine guide, the other external, uttered in speech, called the messenger of conceits and thought. *Cicero*

Internal Oratory aims at friendship towards a man's self, respecting only the mark of vertue, through the instructions of Philosophy.

External Eloquence aims at friendship towards others, causing us to speak and teach whatsoever is fruitful and profitable for every one.

Internal speech maketh a man always agree with himself, it causeth him never to complain, never to repent, it maketh him full of peace, full of love and contentation in his own vertue, it healeth him of every rebellious passion which is disobedient to reason, and of all contentions between Wit and Will.

External carrieth with it all the force and efficacy to perswade.

Eloquence is made by air, beaten and framed with articulate and distinct sound, yet the reason thereof is hard to be comprehended by humane sense. *Quin.*

Words are the shadows of works, and Eloquence the ornament to both.

When the Lips of perfect Eloquence are opened, we behold, as it were in a Temple, the goodly similitudes and images of the soul.

It is not so necessary that the Orator and the Law should agree in one and the same thing, as it is re-
                                              quisite

quifite the life of a Philofopher fhould be conformable with his doctrine and fpeech.

Eloquence is a profeffion of ferious, grave and weighty matters, and not a play conftantly uttered to obtain honour only.

All Oratory ought to have reafon for a foundation, and the love of our neighbour for a mark to aim at.

The tongue is a flippery inftrument, and bringeth great danger to thofe that either neglect or de le it.

If Eloquence be directed with a religious underftanding, it will fing us a fong tuned with all the concords of true harmony of vertue

Eloquence ought to be like gold, which is then of greateft price and value when it hath leaft drofs in it.

A dry and thirfty ear muft be watred with Eloquence, which is good to drink and that Eloquence, grounded upon reafon only, is able to content and fatisfie the hearing

The goodlieft affembly in the world is where the Graces and Mufes meet together.

Unprofitable Eloquence is like Cyprefs trees, which are great and tall, but bear no fruit.

Babling Orators are the thieves of time, and compared to empty veffels, which give greater found than they that are full

The tongue by Eloquence ferveth both to perfect and inftruct others, and likewife to hurt and corrupt others.

There be two only times for a man to fhew Eloquence the one, when the matter is neceffary, the other, when a man fpeaketh that which he knoweth.

Great men ought to be confiderate in their fpeech, and to be eloquent in fententious words, of another phrafe than that of the vulgar fort, or elfe to be filent, wanting the vertue of Eloquence. *Guevar*

Men ought to be more confiderate in writing than in fpeaking, becaufe a rafh and indifcreet word may,
be

be corrected prefently, but that which is written can no more be denied or amended but with infamy.

Oratory is the fpur to arms, for the eloquent Oration of *Ifocrates* was the firft trumpet that gave *Philip* an alarm to the *Afian* wars, which *Alexander* his fon without intermiffion ended.

Ut hominis decus eft ingenium, fic ingenii lumen eft eloquentia. Cicero.

Orationis facultas præcipuum naturæ humanæ bonum eft.

Of Poetry.

Defin. *A Poet was called* Vates, *which is as much as Divine Fore feer, or Prophet and of this word* Carmina, *which was taken for* Poefie, *came this word* Charm, *becaufe it is as a divine inchantment to the fenfes, drawing them by the fweetnefs of delightful numbers to a wondrous admiration The Greeks derive a Poet from this word* ποιεῖν, *which fignifieth to make, and we following it, call a Poet a maker · which name how great it is, the fimpleft can judge, and Poetry* Ariftotle *calleth an art of imitation, or, to fpeak metaphorically, a fpeaking picture.*

Witty Poems are fit for wife Heads, and examples of honour for fuch as triumph in vertue.

Think thy felf to be a good Oratour and Poet, when thou canft perfwade thy felf to do that which thou oughteft.

A King ought now and then to take pleafure in hearing and reading of Comedies, becaufe thereby he may perceive and hear many things done in his Realm, which otherwife he fhould not know. *Few*

Poetry quickneth the wit, fweetneth the difcourfe, and tickleth the ear.

Poetry applied to the praifes of God knitteth the foul unto him, foundeth the fenfes, moderateth griefs, and tempereth hatred. *Guevar.*

Art

Art is taught by Art, but Poetry only is the gift of God.

As the seal leaveth the impreſſion of his form in wax ; ſo the learned Poet ingraveth his paſſions ſo perfectly in mens hearts, that the hearer almoſt is transformed into the author.

A corrupt ſubject defraudeth Poetry of her due · praiſe.

A true Poet in his lines forgetteth profane pleaſure, but approveth doctrine.

Love heateth the brain, and anger maketh a Poet. *Juvenal.*

Poetry is another nature, making things ſeem better than they are by nature·

Impious Poets make themſelves contemptible.

It was written of *Socrates* that he was ill-brought up to Poetry, becauſe he loved the truth.

He which firſt invented the Iambick verſifying, to bite and quip, was the firſt that felt the ſmart thereof.

Eaſe is the nurſe of Poetry   *S P. S.*

Poets are born, but Orators are made.

O ſacer & magnus vatum labor ! omnia fato
Eripis, & donas populis mortalibus ævum.
  Carmina quam tribuent, fama perennis erit.

Of Admiration.

Defin. *Admiration is a paſſion of the ſoul which by a ſudden apprehenſion exalteth the powers and makes them as in a trance ſleeping in judgment of the preſent object, thinking all things to be wonderful that it beholdeth.*

THey are unfortunate Princes that neither will be taught to admire themſelves, nor wonder at their faults. *Pet.*

In vain is he fortified with terrour that is not guarded with love and admiration.

They

They should lift to do leaft that may do what they will, either in art or admiration.

He that will lofe a friend to be rid of a foe, may be admired for his policy, but not for his charity.

Princes, for all their admirations, buy their quiet with wrongs.

It is better for a few eyes to make a little river, than for all fights to infer an admiration

Realms get nothing by change, but perils and admiration.

Depth of words, height of courage, and largenefs of magnificence, get admiration.

Some by admiring other mens vertues become enemies to their own vices. *Bias.*

Wifdom doth prefer and admire the unjuſteſt peace before the juſteſt war.

It is a fign of a malicious mind, not to admire the man that is worthy of admiration. *Marc. Aurel.*

He that from a man of ſtrength and admiration takes away his right, augmenteth his ſtrength, and gives him more right.

Over fhadowing providence blinds the fharpeft and moſt admired counfels of the wife, that they cannot difcern their nakednefs. *Hermes.*

Admire with love, and love with joy in the midſt of woe *S. P S*

Ill-perfwading want, wronged patience, loofenefs and force, are the breeders of Civil wars and admiration

Men wholly ufed to war wonder at the name of peace

They which are brought up in admiration and blood think it beſt fifhing in troubled waters.

The weather-like vulgar are apt to admire every thing, and ready to turn as often as the tide. *S ciat*

It were a wonder beyond wonder, if injuſtice fhould keep what impiety hath gotten.

An

An eafie-yielding zeal quickly is overcome with admitting of gravity's Eloquence

It 's no wonder that the armed power doth either find right, or make right; for what may he not that may what he will?

Admiratio peperit Philofophiam.

Adm ratio qua magna eft non puet verba, fed filen-tium.

Nil admirari prope res eft una, Numici,
Solique, qua poffit hominem fervare beatum. Hor.

Of Schools.

Defin. *A School is the nurfery of learning, or the ftore-houfe from whence the mind fetcheth inftruGtions and riches, adorning the Soul with mental vertues and divine knowledge.*

Tyranny is vile in a School-mafter: for youth fhould rather be trained with courtefie than compulfion

Becaufe youth by nature is wild, therefore fhould School-mafters break them by gentlenefs.

That child is grofs-witted, which being throughly School-taught continues ftill barbarous.

Women prove the beft School mafters, when they place their delight in inftruGtions,

Women ought to have as great intereft in Schools as men, though not fo foon as men, becaufe their wits being more perfeGt, they would make mens reputations lefs perfeGt

Two things are to be regarded in Schools and by School-mafters. firft, wherein Children muft be taught, next, how they fhould be taught

Grammar is the door to Science, whereby we learn to fpeak well and exaGtly

Education is a fecond nature, and the principles learnt in Schools the beft education.

The

The nature of man is like a pair of Balance, guided by School-rules and custom.

If the royalleſt-born creature have not his nature refined with School-rudiments, it is groſs and barbarous.

A Phyſician's ſtudy is the School of Philoſophy. *Muſonius.*

Nature not manured with knowledge bringeth forth nothing but thiſtles and brambles.

Nature in ſome ſort is a School of decency, and teacheth rules of honeſt civility.

The Beſt wiſdom is to know a man's ſelf: and learning and Schools firſt bring that knowledge.

Man's nature, being the inſtinct and inclination of the ſpirit, is better by School rudiments.

The want of School-doctrine is the firſt corruption of nature.

Lions are tamer than men, if Doctrine did not bridle them.

Schools tame Nature, and tamed Nature is perfect Vertue.

Every good beginning cometh by nature, but the progreſs by School-education.

Courage and greatneſs is as much aſpired to in Schools as from Nature.

Educatio eſt prima, ſecunda, tertia pars vitæ: ſine qua omnis doctrina eſt veluti armata injuſtitia.

——Nunc adhibe puro
Pectore verba, puer, nunc te melioribus offer.
Quo ſemel eſt imbuta recens ſervabit odorem
Teſta diu. Horat.

Of Ignorance.

Defin. *Ignorance is that defect which cauſeth a man to judge of evil things, to deliberate worſe, not to know how to take the advantage of preſent good things, but to conceive ill of whatſoever is good in man's life.*

IT

IT proceedeth of a light judgment to credit all things that a man heareth, and to do all things that he seeth. *Socrat.*

Ignorance hath always the boldest face.

To abound in all things, and not to know the use of them, is plain penury.

It is a great shame for an old man to be ignorant in the knowledge of God's law.

Idleness engendreth ignorance, and ignorance engendreth errour.

There is nothing worse than to live beastly, and out of honest order · and the greatest and most evident cause thereof is the sin of ignorance, which is an utter enemy to knowledge. *Plato.*

Through want of wit cometh much harm, and by means of ignorance much good is left undone.

Where there is no capacity, there perswasions are in vain. *Socrates.*

To rule without regard, to urge without reason, and to laugh immoderately, are manifest signs of ignorance.

Ignorance in adversity is a blessing, in prosperity a scorn, in science a plague.

He that knoweth not how much he seeketh, doth not know when to find that which he lacketh.

There can be no greater ignorance than presumption.

Ignorance is no excuse for faults, sith we have power of knowledge.

It is better to be unborn than untaught. for ignorance is the root of misfortune *Plato.*

Ignorance is never known to be ignorance, till it be matched with knowledge.

The ignorant man hath no greater foe than his own ignorance, for it destroyeth where it liveth. *Lactan.*

He is an ignorant Musician that can sing but one song; but he is more accursed that knoweth no vertue.   Igno-

Ignorance is a dangerous and spiritual poison, which all men ought warily to shun *Greg.*

Ignorance is a sickness of the mind, and the occasion of all errours.

The soul of man receiving and comprehending the divine understanding conducteth all things rightly and happily, but if she be once joyned with ignorance, she worketh clean contrary and the understanding is unto the soul as the sight to the body. *August.*

From their lewd mother ignorance issue two daughters, Falshood and Doubt.

Ignorance believeth not what it seeth.

He that is ignorant in the truth, and led about with opinions, must needs err.

Ignorance is a voluntary misfortune.

Ignorance is the mother of errour.

The harder we receive our health, because we were ignorant that we were sick

From small errours, not let at the beginning, spring oft-times great and mighty mischiefs.

The chiefest cause and beginning of errour is, when men imagine those things to please God, which please themselves, and those things to displease God wherewith they themselves are discontented

An errour begun is not to be overcome with violence, but with truth.

Custom, though never so ancient, without truth, is but an old errour *Cyprian*

He that erreth before he knows the truth ought the sooner to be forgiven. *Cyprian.*

A wilful-minded man is subject to much errour.

Unicum est bonum scientia. & malum unicum ignorantia.

Imperitiam comitatur temeritas.

Of Goodneſs.

Defin. Goodneſs is that which includeth in it ſelf a dig-
nity that ſavoureth of God and his works, having a
perpetuity and ſtedfaſtneſs of godly ſubſtance.

Goodneſs in general makes every one think the
ſtrength of vertue in another, whereof they find
the aſſured foundation in themſelves. *Plato.*

As oft as we do good we offer ſacrifice.

It is too much for one good man to want

A man may be too juſt and too wiſe, but never too
good *Socrat*

The humour of youth is ever to think that good
whoſe goodneſs he ſeeth not.

Theie is no good unleſs it be voluntary.

A good man's wiſh is ſubſtance, faith and fame ,
Glory and grace according to the ſame

A man is not to be accounted good for his age, but
for his charitable actions.

He may worthily be called good who maketh other
men fare the better for his goodneſs.

Thou canſt not be perfectly good when thou hateſt
thine enemy , what ſhalt thou then be when thou hateſt him that is thy friend ? *Socrates.*

There is no greater delectation and comfort to a
good man, than to be ſeen in the company of good
men *Plato*

The farther a good man is known, the farther his
veitues ſpread, and root themſelves in men's hearts
and remembrance

Whatſoever is right and honeſt and joyned with
vertue, that alone is only good

He that is mighty is not by and by good ; but he
that is good is preſently mighty. *Iſocrates.*

The goodneſs that proceedeth from an ignorant
man is like the herbs that grow upon a dunghill.

Riches

Riches will decay, profperity may change . but goodnefs doth continue till death.

The more our grace and goodnefs doth increafe, the more our fouls addrefs themfelves to God. *Ba-fil.*

As God is all goodnefs, fo loveth he all good things, as Righteoufnefs and Vertue, and hateth Vice and Wickednefs.

The goodnefs of the foul is the moft principal and chiefeft goodnefs that can be. *Plato.*

Vir bonus & prudens (qualem vix reperit unum
Millibus è cunctis hominum confultus Apollo)
Judex ipfe fui totum fe explorat ad unguem.
Difficile eft hominibus perfuadere, bonitatem propter
ipfam diligendam. Cicero.

Of Comfort.

Defin *Comfort is an eafe, help, or confolation in our troubles and adverfities, which disburthening the mind, reftores it to calm and quiet patience*

COmfort in extremity healeth many wounds, pacifieth the difcontented heart, and governeth the mind

Troubles are but inftructions to teach men wit: for by them thou mayft know falfhood from faith, and thy trufty friend from thy traiterous foe.

Defpair not when all worldly means are done : for God will raife thee, if thou truft in him. *Auguft.*

Grieve not at Afflictions, for they are the rods wherewith God beateth his children.

There is nothing grievous, if the thought make it not fo.

Art thou backbited? rejoyce, if guiltlefs, if guilty, amend.

Be not difcontented at the lofs of children, for they were born to die.

There

There is nothing the world can take away, becaufe the world giveth nothing · fame perifheth, honours fade, wealth decayeth. only true riches is our conftancy in all cafualties. *Aurel.*

All things are vanity which are under the Sun, all things continual labour and travel · what hath a man to mourn for then, when all things he can lofe in this life are but fading and miferable?

That comfort is vain that taketh not away the grief. *Plato.*

To a mind afflicted with forrow the beft remedy is, to defer counfel until the party be more apt to take confolation. *Marc. Aurel.*

Let not forrow over much moleft thee, for when thou haft wept thy worft, grief muft have end.

Wrong is the trial of thy patience.

Sicknefs is the prifon of the body, but comfort the liberty of the foul. *Plato.*

The beft comfort to a Mifer is to behold the overflow of his wealth.

The fufpectlefs, the temperate, and the wife men are never uncomfortable.

By forrow the heart is tormented, by comfort, when it is half dead it is revived.

Sad fighs write the woes of the heart; and kind fpeeches comfort the foul in heavinefs.

Affurance puts away forrow, and fear poifons comfort. *Stobæus.*

He that will be truly valiant muft neither let joy nor grief overcome him for better not to be, than to be a bond-flave to paffion.

He that coveteth comfort without forrow muft apply his wit in following wifdom

To friends afflicted with forrow, we ought to give remedy to their perfons, and confolation and comfort to their heart.

The multiplying of comfort is the affwaging of cares. *Solon.*

In the midst of all thy cares let this be thy chiefest comfort, hard things may be mollified, strait things may be loosened, and little things shall never grieve him that can handsomely bear them.

Sorrow seldom taketh place in him that abstaineth from four things : that is, from hastiness, wilful frowardness, pride and sloth.

Mala de te loquuntur homines, sed mali : non de te loquuntur, sed de se.

Flebile principium melior fortuna sequuta est.

Of Patience.

Defin. *Patience is an habit that consisteth in sustaining stoutly all labours and griefs for the love of honesty : it is that excellent good thing that keepeth the tranquility of our spirit as much as may be in adversities : and not to complain of that which is uncertain.*

PAtience is a voluntary adventuring of hard things for the desire of vertue. *Socrates.*

The remedy of injuries is, by continual patience to learn to forget them. *Pub.*

He is worthy to be counted courageous, strong and stout, who doth not only with patience suffer injuries, rebukes and displeasures done unto him, but also doth good against those evils. *Arist.*

Better it is to offer thy self in triumph, than to be drawn to it by dishonour. *Appian.*

It is a special sign of heroical magnanimity to despise light wrongs, and nothing to regard mean adventures.

It is good to forbear to talk of things needless to be spoken but it is much better to conceal things dangerous to be told.

Patience is so like to fortitude, that it seemeth she is either her sister or her daughter.

The

The common fort do take revenge for their credit, but noble minds forgive for their vertue.

Patience without comfort brings peril of confumption

It is a pleafant tarrying that ftayeth from evil doing.

The end of patience is the expectation of promifes.

That is to be born with patience, which cannot be redreffed with carefulnefs.

It is not merit to fuffer perfecutions, if we have no patience therein.

It is more fafety to forget an injury, than to revenge it. *Aurel.*

The fweeteft falve for mifery is patience, and the only medicine for want is content.

Patience is the beft falve againft love and fortune.

To fuffer infirmities, and diffemble mifhap; the one is the office of a conftant fick man, the other of a conftant States man.

To be difcreet in profperity, and patient in adverfity, is the true motion and effect of a vertuous and valiant mind. *Cicero.*

Quintus Fabius, after he had been Conful, difdain'd not to march under the Enfigns of other Confuls.

Patience being oft provoked with injuries, breaketh forth at laft into fury.

It is good for a good man to wifh the beft, to think upon the worft, and patiently to fuffer whatfoever doth happen.

Humility, patience and fair fpeech are the pacifiers of wrath and anger.

He feemeth to be perfectly patient that in his fury can fubdue his own affections.

Patience and Perfeverance are two proper notes whereby God's children are truly known from Hypocrites, Counterfeits and Diffemblers. *Auguft.*

In

In suffering of afflictions patience is made more strong and perfect.

The troubles that come of necessity ought to be born with boldness and good courage.

The best way for a man to be avenged is to contemn injury and rebuke, and to live with such honesty and good behaviour, that the doer of wrong shall at last be thereof ashamed, or at the least lose the fruit of his malice, that is, he shall not rejoyce, nor have glory of the hinderance and damage. *Plato.*

———*Serpens, sitis, ardor, arenæ,*
Dulcia virtuti; gaudet patientia duris.
Leniter ex merito quicquid patiare ferendum est.

Of Friendship.

Defin. *Friendship is a perpetual community of will, the end whereof is fellowship of life; and it is framed by the profit of a long continued love. Friendship is also an inveterate and ancient love, wherein is more pleasure than desire.*

FRiendship is a perfect consent of things appertaining as well unto God as to man, with benevolence and charity.

Friendship in good men is a blessing, and stable connexing of sundry wills, making of two persons one, in having and suffering and therefore a Friend is properly called a second self, for that in both men is but one mind and possession, and that which more is, a man rejoyceth more at his friend's good hap than he doth at his own. *Aurel.*

True and perfect friendship is to make one heart and mind of many hearts and bodies.

It is the property of true friends to live and love together. but feigned friends fly from a man in time of trial.

Friendſhip judgeth without partiality, and affection winketh at apparent follies.

A friend's love cannot be recompenſed with riches, when for his friend he putteth his life in jeopardy.

To diſſwade a man in a courſe of honour, were not the part of a friend, and to ſet one forward in folly, is no diſcretion in a man

Friends meeting after long abſence are the ſweeteſt flowers in the garden of true affection.

The love of men to women is a thing common and of courſe, but the friendſhip of man to man is infinite and immortal. *Plato.*

The tellowſhip of a true friend in miſery is always ſweet, and his counſels in proſperity are always fortunate.

Friendſhip, being an equity of reciprocal good-will, is of three kinds, the one of neighbourhood, the other hoſpitality, the laſt love. *Ariſt.*

Love is confirmed either by gifts, or ſtudy of vertue then groweth it from a paſſion to a perfect habit, and ſo leaveth the name of Love, and is called Friendſhip: which no time can violate.

We ought to uſe a friend like gold, to try him before we have need

He is a true friend, whoſe care is to pleaſure his friend in all things, moved thereunto by a meer good-will which he beareth unto him. *Ariſt*

It is no ſmall grief to a good nature to try his friend *Eurip.*

To beg a thing at a friend's hand, is to buy it.

Perfect amity conſiſteth in equality and agreeing of the minds.

A friend unto a friend neither hideth ſecret, nor denieth money.

The want of friends is perilous, but ſome friends prove tedious.

The

The words of a friend joyned with true affection give life to the heart, and comfort to a care-oppressed mind. *Chilo.*

No defigning man can be a true friend.

Friends ought always to be tried before they are trusted, left shining like a Carbuncle, as if they had fire, they be found when they be touched to be without faith.

Good-will is the beginning of friendship, which by use causeth friendship to follow.

If thou defirest to be thought a friend, it is necessary that thou do the works that belong unto a friend.

Among friends there should be no cause of breach; but with a diffembler no care of reconciliation.

He is a friend indeed that lightly forgetteth his friend's offence.

Proud and scornful people are perilous friends.

Friendship ought to be founded on equalness: for where equality is not, friendship cannot long continue, *Cicero.*

Where true friends are knit in love, there sorrows are shared equally.

Friends must be used as Muficians tune their strings, who finding them in difcord do not break them, but rather by intention or remiffion frame them to a pleafant confent.

In Mufick there are many difcords, before they can be framed to a Diapafon and in contracting of good will, many jars before there be eftablished a true and perfect friendship.

A friend is in profperity a pleafure, in adverfity a folace, in grief a comfort, in joy a merry companion, and at all times a fecond felf.

A friend is a precious Jewel, within whofe bofome he may unload his forrows, and unfold his fecrets

As fire and heat are infeparable, fo are the hearts of faithful friends. *Arift.*

He

He that promiseth speedily, and is long in performing is but a slack friend.

Like as a Physician cureth a man secretly, he not seeing it. so should a good friend help his friend privily, when he knoweth not thereof

The injury done by a friend is much more grievous than the wrongs wrought by an enemy.

Friendship is given by nature for help to vertue, not for a companion of vices.

Friendship ought to resemble the love between man and wife, that is, of two bodies to be made one Will and Affection.

The property of a true friend is, to perform more than he promiseth; but the condition of a dissembler is, to promise more than he meaneth to perform.

Great profers are meet to be used to strangers, and good turns to true friends.

If thou intend'st to prove thy friend, stay not till need and necessity urgeth thee, lest such trial be not only unprofitable and without fruit, but also hurtful and prejudicial

The opinion of vertue is the fountain of friendship.

Feigned friends resemble Crows, that fly not but toward such places where there is something to be fed upon.

He that seeketh after a swarm of friends commonly falleth into a wasp's nest of enemies.

Friendship oftentimes is better than consanguinity.

A friendly admonition is a special point of true friendship.

It is best to be praised of those friends, that will not spare to reprehend us, when we are blame-worthy.

He that will not hear the admonition of a friend, is worthy to feel the correction of a foe.

He which goeth about to cut off friendship, doth even as it were go about to take the Sun from the world. *Cicero.*

D 4

There is no more certain token of true friendship, than is consent and communicating of our cogitations with another. *Cicero.*

Unity is the essence of amity.

He that hath no friend to comfort him in his necessity, lives like a man in a Wilderness, subject to every beast's tyranny. *Bias.*

Believe after trial, and judge before friendship.

The fau't which thou sufferest in thy friend, thou committest in thy self.

Shew faithfulness to thy friend, and equity to all men. *Protag*

No wise man will chuse to live without friends, although he have plenty of worldly wealth.

Though a wise man be contented and satisfied with himself; yet will he have friends, because he will not be destitute of so great a vertue

There be many men that want not friends, and yet lack true friendship.

Never admit him for thy friend, whom by force thou hast brought into subjection.

He is not meet to be admitted for a faithful friend, who is ready to enter amity with every one

Admit none to be thy friend, except thou first know how he hath dealt with his other friends before: for look how he hath served them, so will he likewise deal with thee.

The agreement of the wicked is easily upon a small occasion broken, but the friendship of the vertuous continueth for ever. *Hermes.*

As mighty floods, by how much they are brought into small rivers, by so much they lose of their strength · so friendship cannot be amongst many without abating the force thereof. *Plato*

Be slow to fall into friendship, but when thou art in, continue firm and constant. *Socrates.*

Illud

Illud amicitiæ quondam venerabile nomen
Proſtat, & in quæſtu pro meretrice ſedet.
Amicitiâ majus nil dedit natura, nec rarius
Vive ſine invidia, molleſque rigloiius annos
Exige, amicitias & tibi junge pares. Ovid.

Of Temperance.

Defin. *Temperance is that light which driveth away round*
about her the darkneſs and obſcurity of paſſion. ſhe is
of all the vertues moſt wholeſome, for ſhe preſerveth
both publickly and privately humane ſociety, ſhe lifteth
up the ſoul miſerably thrown down in vice, and reſtoreth
her again into her place. It is alſo a mutual conſent
of the parts of the ſoul, cauſing all diſorder and unbrid-
led affections to take Reaſon for a rule and direction.

Temperance calleth a man back from groſs affections and carnal appetites, and letteth him not to
exceed, neither in fooliſh nor in ungodly ſorrowing.
Solon.

A young man untemperate and full of carnal affection quickly turneth the body into age and feeble
infirmities. *Anaxagoras.*

He cannot commend temperance that delighteth
in pleaſure, nor love government that liketh riot

Conſtancy and temperance in our actions make
vertue ſtrong.

Men muſt eat to live, and not live to eat.

In private families Continence is to be praiſed, in
publick Offices, Dignity.

Intemperance is the fountain of all our perturbations.

The pride of the fleſh is to be curbed and reſtrai-
ned with the ſharp bit of Abſtinence. *Ariſt.*

The moderation of the mind is the felicity thereof.

Frugality is the badge of diſcretion, Riot, of intemperance.

He

He that is not puffed up with praise, nor afflicted with adversities, nor moved by slanders, nor corrupted by benefits, is fortunately temperate.

He that fixeth his whole delight in pleasure can never be wise and temperate.

Temperance by forbearing to be revenged reconcileth our enemies, and by good government conquers them.

Temperance is rich in most losses, confident in all perils, prudent in all assaults, and happy in it self. *Her.*

It is not temperance which is accompanied with a fearful mind. but that is true Temperance where the heart hath courage to revenge, and reason power to restrain the heart.

Trim not thy house with Tables and Pictures, but paint and gild it with Temperance. the one vainly feedeth the eyes, the other is an eternal ornament which cannot be defaced. *Epictetus.*

Temperance is so called, because it keepeth a mean in all those things which belong to the delighting of the Body. *Arist.*

Temperance crieth, *Nè quid nimis. Solon.*

The parts of Temperance are Modesty, Shamefac'dness, Abstinence, Continency, Honesty, Moderation, Sparingness and Sobriety. *Plato.*

Justice may not be without Temperance, because it is the chief point of a just man to have his soul free from perturbations

Heroical vertues are made perfect by the mixture of Temperance and Fortitude; which separated become vicious.

A temperate man which is not courageous quickly becometh a coward and faint hearted.

Temperance is the mother of all duty and honesty.

In Temperance a man may behold Modesty without any perturbation of the soul.

Temperance compelleth men to follow reafon, bringeth peace to the mind, and mollifieth the affections with concord and agreement. *Socrates.*

He is worthy to be called a moderate perfon who firmly governeth and bridleth (through reafon) the vice of fenfuality, and all other grofs affections of the mind. *Aurel.*

Nihil reperiri poteft tam eximium, quàm iftam virtutem moderatricem animi, temperantiam, non laterē in tenebris, neque effe abditam, fed in luce. Cicero.

Non poteft temperantiam laudare is qui ponit fummum bonum in voluptate: eft enim temperantia libidinum inimica.

Of Innocency

Defin. *Innocency is an affection of the mind fo well framed that it will hurt no man either by word or deed, a tower of brafs againft flanderers, and the only balm or cure of a wounded name, ftrengthening the confcience, which by it knoweth its own purity.*

THere can be no greater good than Innocency, nor worfe evil than a guilty Confcience.

The Innocent man is happy, though he be in *Phalaris's* Bull. *Cicero*

Great callings are little worth, if the mind be not content and innocent.

The heart pricked with defire of wrong, maketh fick the innocency of the foul.

Riches and honour are broken Pillars, but innocency is an unmoving Column.

Innocency and pruduce are two anchors, that cannot be torn up by any tempeft.

Innocency will be your beft guard, and your integrity will be a Coat of Mail unto you.

Innocency, to God is the chiefeft incenfe· and a confcience without guile is a facrifice of the fweeteft favour. *Aug.*

Inno-

Innocency, being ſtopped by the malignant, taketh breath and heart again to the overthrow of her enemies. *Cicero*

As fire is extinguiſhed by water, ſo innocency doth quench reproach

Ot all treaſures in a Common-wealth, the innocent man is moſt to be eſteemed

Innocency is in ſome ſort the effect of Regeneration. *Bern*

Religion is the ſoul of innocency, moving in an unſpotted conſcience

Innocency is built upon Divine Reaſon.

Humane happineſs conſiſteth in innocency of the ſoul and uncorrupt manners

All innocency conſiſteth in mediocrity, as all vice doth in exceſs

Innocency is a good which cannot be taken away by torment *Marc. Aurel*

Innocency is the moſt profitable thing in the world; becauſe it maketh all things elſe profitable

Innocency, Palm like, groweth in deſpite of oppreſſion.

Beauty is a flower ſoon withered, health is ſoon altered, ſtrength by incontinence abated, but innocency is divine and immortal.

Innocency is an aſſured comfort, both in life and death.

As length of time diminiſheth all things; ſo innocency and vertue increaſe all things

The fear of death never troubleth the mind of an innocent man *Cicero*

Age breedeth no defect in innocency, but innocency is an excellency in Age.

Nature, Reaſon and Uſe, are three neceſſary things to obtain innocency by. *Lactan.*

Ut Nepenthes herba addita poculis omnem convivii triſtitiam diſcutit, ità bona mens inſita nobis omnem vitæ ſolicitudinem abolet. *Integer*

Integer vitæ, fcelerifque purus,
Non eget Mauri jaculis, &c. Horat.

Of Kings.

Defin. *Kings are the fupreme Govei nours and Rulers over*
States and Monai chies, placed by the hand of God,
to figure to the world his almighty power. If they be
vertuous they are the bleffings of the Realm, if vici-
ous, fcourges allotted for then fubjeéts iniquities.

THE Majefty of a Prince is like the lightning
from the Eaft, and the threats of a King like
the noife of thunder

Kings have long arms, and Rulers large reaches.

The life of a Prince is the rule, the fquare, the
frame and form of an honeft life, according to the
which their fubjeéts frame the manner of their lives,
and order their families and rather from the Lives of
Princes do fubjeéts take their patterns and examples
than from their Laws.

Subjeéts follow the example of their Princes, as,
certain flowers turn according to the Sun. *Horace.*

Princes are never without Flatterers to feduce
them, Ambition to deprave them, and Defires to corrupt them. *Plato.*

It belongeth to him that governeth to be Learned
the better to know what he doth, Wife, to find out
how he ought to do it, Difcreet, to attend and take
opportunity; and Refolute in the aétion of Juftice,
without corruption or fear of any

It is neceffary for Princes to be ftout and alfo rich:
that by their ftoutnefs they may proteét their own,
and by their riches reprefs their enemies.

It is better for a Prince to defend his own Country
by Juftice, than to conquer another's by tyranny.

That Prince who is too liberal in giving his own
is afterwards through neceffity compelled to be a
Tyrant, and to take from others their right.

As

As Princes become Tyrants for want of Riches, so they become vicious through abundance of Treasure. *Plu.*

When an unworthy man is preferred to promotion, he is preferred to his own shame.

The Prince that is feared of many must of necessity fear many.

The word of a Prince is faith royal.

Princes must not measure things by report, but by the way of conscience. *Socrat.*

It behoveth a Prince or Ruler to be of such zealous and godly courage, that he always shew himself to be a strong wall for the defence of the truth.

The Prince's palace is like a common fountain or spring to his City or Country, whereby the common people by the cleanness thereof be long preserved in honesty, or by the impureness thereof are with sundry vices corrupted.

A King ruleth as he ought, a Tyrant as he listeth; a King to the profit of all, a Tyrant only to pleasure a few. *Arist.*

A King ought to refrain the company of vicious persons. for the evil that they commit in his company is accounted his. *Plato.*

Rulers do sin more grievously by example than by act; and the greater governances they bear, the greater account they have to render, if in their own precepts and ordinances they be found negligent.

Not only happy, but also most fortunate is that Prince, that for righteousness of Justice is feared, and for his goodness beloved.

The greater that a Prince is in power above others the more he ought to excel in vertue above others.

When Princes most greedily do prosecute vices, then their Enemies are busie in weaving some web of deadly danger. *Olaus.*

Princes

Princes by charging their Kingdoms with unjuſt Tributes, procure from their Subjects a wilful denial of due and moſt juſt payments.

He that poſſeſſeth an Empire, and knoweth not how to defend it, may loſe his poſſeſſion before he knows who offended him.

It little profiteth a Prince to be Lord of many Kingdoms, if on the other part he become bond ſlave to many vices.

It appertaineth unto Princes, as much to moderate their own pleaſures, as to give orders for matters of importance.

Children born of Kings are compoſed of precious maſs, to be ſeparated from the common ſort. *Plat.*

Malice and Vice taking their full ſwing through the career of the power and liberty which wicked Princes yield unto them, do puſh forward every violent paſſion, make every little choler turn to murther or baniſhment, and every regard and love to rape and adultery, and covetouſneſs to confiſcation.

A Kingdom is nought elſe than care of another's ſafety. for *Antiochus* told his ſon *Demetrius*, that their Kingdom was a noble ſlavery.

Self-love is not fit for Princes, nor Pride an ornament meet for a Diadem.

Kings and Princes do loſe more in the opinions they hold, than in the reaſons they uſe.

It is no leſs diſcredit to a Prince to have deſtroyed many of his Subjects, than it is to a Phyſician to have killed many of his Patients.

Kings, as they are men before God, ſo are they Gods before men. *Lactan.*

It is very requiſite that the Prince live according to that law himſelf, which he would have executed upon others. *Archi.*

It becometh a King to take good heed to his Counſellors, in noting who ſcoth his luſts, and who intend
tend

tend the publick profit ; for thereby fhall he know the good from the bad. *Plutarch.*

The ftrength of a Prince is the friendfhip and love of his people

That King fhall beft govern his Realm that reigneth over his People as a Father doth over his Children. *Agefil*

So great is the perfon and dignity of a Prince that in ufing his power and authority as he ought, he being here among men upon earth, reprefenteth the glorious eftate and high Majefty of God in heaven. *Amb.*

It is requifite for all thofe who have rule and governance in a Common-weal under their Prince, to know the bounds of their ftate, and the full effect of their duty ; that by executing juftice they may be feared, and by fhewing mercy they may be loved. *Lactan.*

It is requifite for Princes to place fuch men in authority as care leaft for it, and to keep them from government that prefs forward to it.

Except wife men be made Governours, or Governours become wife men, mankind fhall never live in quiet, nor vertue be able to defend her felf. *Plato.*

He that would be a Ruler or Governour, muft firft learn to be an obedient fubject . for it is not poffible for a proud and covetous minded fubject to become a gentle and temperate Governour. *Alex Severus.*

When rule and authority is committed unto a good man, he doth thereby publifh his vertue, which before lay hid . but being committed to an evil man, it miniftreth boldnefs and licence to him, to do that evil which before he durft not do

Animata imago Rex putandus eft Dei.
Nulla fides regni fociis omnifque poteftas
Impatiens confortis erit.

Of

Of Nobility.

Defin. *Nobility is a glittering excellency proceeding from Ancestors, and an honour which cometh from ancient Linage and Stock: it is also a praise that proceedeth from the deserts of our Elders and Fore-fathers. And of this nobleness there are three sorts : the first bred of vertue and excellent deeds, the second proceedeth from the knowledge of honest discipline and true sciences ; the third cometh from the Scutcheons and Arms of our Ancestors, or from riches.*

Nobility is of more antiquity than possessions. *Cicero.*

The time of our life is short, but the race of Nobility and Honour everlasting. *Cicero.*

Nobleness of birth is either universal, or particular. the first, to be born in noble and famous Countries; the latter, to come of noble Progenitors. *Arist.*

Nobility is best continued by that convenient means whereby it rose.

He is not to be held for Noble that hath much, but he that giveth much.

It is requisite for him that is Noble born to take heed of Flatterers, for they will be ready daily to attend his person for profit's sake.

Nobility is a title quickly lost. for if riches forsake it, or vertue abandon it, it streightway becometh as a thing that had never been.

Whatsoever thy Father by his worthiness hath deserved belongs not to thee, it is thine own desert that must make thee noble.

Vertue and Nobleness can never be seen in a man, except he first put away his Vices.

He that defendeth his Country by the sword deserveth honour, but he that maintaineth it in peace meriteth more honour.

The

The Nobility which we receive from our Ancestours, becaufe it cometh not from our felves, is fcarcely to be counted our own.

To come of noble parentage, and not to be endowed with noble qualities, is rather a defamation than a glory.

Noble perfons have the beft capacities. for whether they give themfelves to goodnefs or ungracioufnefs, they do in either of them fo excel, as none of the common fort of people can come any thing nigh them. *Cic.*

True Nobility confifteth not in dignity, linage, great revenues, lands or poffeffions, but in wifdom, knowledge and vertue, which in man is true Nobility, and that Nobility bringeth man to dignity.

True Nobility is not after the vulgar opinion of the common people, but is the only praife and furname of vertue.

Omnes boni femper Nobilitati favemus, & quia utile eft Reipublicæ nobiles homines effe dignos majoribus fuis, & quia valere debet apud nos clarorum hominum benè de Republica meritorum memoria etiam mortuorum. Cicero.

——Nobilitas fola eft atque unica virtus.

Of Honour.

Defin. *Honour is a paffion of the foul, a mighty defire, naturally coveted of all creatures, yet many times miftaken, by unacquaintance with vertue*

HOnour and glory labour in miftruft, and are born Fortune's bond-flaves.

Honour is the firft ftep to difquiet, and dominion is attended with envy. *Guevar*

The faith of a Knight is not limited by value, but by honour and vertue.

Honour is the fruit of Vertue and Truth.

Honour,

Honour, Glory and Renown is to many perfons more fweet than life.

It is the chiefeft part of honour for a man to joyn to his high office and calling the vertue of affability, lowlinefs, tender compaffion and pity · for thereby he draweth unto him, as it were by violence, the hearts of the multitude. *Olaus Magnus.*

The greater the perfons be in authority that commit an offence, the more foul and filthy is the fault.

It better becometh a man of honour to praife an enemy, than his friend.

Happy is that Country whofe Captains are Gentlemen, and whofe Gentlemen are Captains.

Honour is no privilege againft infamy.

A man ought not to think it honour for himfelf to hear or declare the news of others, but that others fhould declare the vertuous deeds of him.

To attain to honour, Wifdom is the Pole-ftar, and to retain it, Patience is neceffary.

The next way to live with honour, and die with praife, is to be honeft in our defires, and temperate in our tongues.

The conditions of honour are fuch, that fhe enquireth for him fhe never faw, runneth after him that flies from her, honours him that efteems her not, demandeth for him that wills her not, giveth to him that requires her not, and trufteth him whom fhe knoweth not.

Noblemen enterprifing great things, ought not to employ their force as their own mind willeth, but as honour and reafon teacheth. *Niphus.*

High and noble hearts which feel themfelves wounded, do not fo much efteem their own pain, as they are angry to fee their enemies rejoyce.

The Captain which fubdueth a Country by intreaty, deferveth more honour than he that overcometh it by battel.

Honour

Honour without quiet hurteth more than it doth profit.

He that regards his reputation must second all things to his honour.

The heavens admit but one Sun, and high places but one Commander.

Men in authority are eyes in a State, according to whose life every private man applieth his manner of living.

It is not the place that maketh the person, but the person that maketh the place honourable, *Cicero.*

There is more honour purchased in pleasuring a foe, than in revenging a thousand injuries.

Where Hate bears sovereignty, Honour hath no certainty.

Honour is brittle, and riches are blossoms, which every frost of fortune causeth to wither.

Better it is for the honourable to be praised for many foes foiled, than for many barns filled.

A man having honour, and wanting wisdom, is like a fair tree without fruit.

Exiguum nobis vitæ curriculum natura circumscripsit, sed honoris cursus sempiternus.

Is honos videri solet, qui non propter spem futuri beneficii, sed propter magna merita claris viris defertur & datur. estque non invitamentum ad tempus, sed perpetuæ virtutis præmium.

Of Liberality.

Defin. *Liberality is an excellent use of those benefits which God putteth into our hands for the succouring of many. which vertue is altogether joyned with justice, and ought to be guided by moderation and reason.*

Bounties best honour is to help the poor; and happiness, to live in good mens thoughts.

True bounty is never tied to suspect.

Liberality is approved by two fountains; the one is a sure judgment, the other is an honest favour.

That man is only liberal which destributeth according to his substance, and where it is most needful. *Thales.*

The whole effect of bounty is in love.

Who in their bounty do begin to want, shall in their weakness find their friends and foes.

He is called a liberal man which according to his revenues giveth freely, when, where, and to whom he should.

He that may give, and giveth not, is a clear enemy; and he that promiseth forthwith, and is long before he performs, is a suspicious friend. *Aurel.*

Gifts make beggars bold, and he that lends must lose his friend, or else his mony, without heed.

Bounty hath open hands, a zealous heart, a constant faith in earth, and a place prepared in heaven.

He never gives in vain that gives in zeal.

They that are liberal doth with-hold or hide nothing from them whom they love, whereby love increaseth, and friendship is also made more firm and stable.

As liberality maketh friends of enemies, so pride maketh enemies of friends.

Liberality and thankfulness are the bonds of concord *Cicero.*

A liberal-minded man can never be envious.

Bounty, for giving frail and mortal things, receives immortal fame for his reward.

The deeds of the liberal do more profit the giver than benefit the receiver.

Liberality in a noble mind is excellent, although, it exceed in the term of measure.

A liberal heart causeth benevolence, though sometimes through misfortune ability be wanting

It is a token of righteousness to acknowledge heaven's liberality, and to give praises to God for so great benefits. *Bern.* The

The office of Liberality confifteth in giving with judgment. *Cicero.*

That liberality is moft commendable which is fhewed to the diftreffed, unlefs they have deferved that punifhment : for good deeds beftowed upon undeferving perfons are ill beftowed.

The beft property in a King is, to let no man excel him in Liberality. *Agefil.*

Extra fortunam eft quicquid donatur amicis,
Quas dederis folas femper habebis opes. Ovid.

Liberalitate qui utuntur, benevolentiam fibi conciliant & (quod aptiffimum eft ad quietè vivendum) charitatem.

Of Benefits.

Defin. *Benefits are thofe good turns which are received either by defert, or without defert, tending to our happinefs of Life, or amendment of Manners.*

IT is a great commendation to the giver, to beftow many benefits upon him which deferveth well, and defireth nothing.

He that mindeth to give muft not fay, Will you have any thing?

If thou promife little and perform much, it will make thy benefits to be the more thankfully received. *Aurel.*

He that knoweth not how to ufe a benefit doth unjuftly ask it.

He receives a benefit, in the giving thereof, who beftows his gift on a worthy man

He bindeth all men by his benefits, who beftoweth them upon fuch as do well deferve them.

The liberal man doth daily feek out occafion to put his vertue in practice *Cicero.*

The memory of a benefit doth foon vanifh away, but the remembrance of an injury fticketh faft in the heart.

He

He is a conquerer which beſtoweth a good turn, and he vanquiſhed which receiveth it.

As the Moon doth ſhew her light in the World which ſhe receiveth from the Sun : ſo we ought to beſtow the benefits received of God to the profit and commodity of our neighbour.

This is a law that ſhould be obſerved betwixt the Giver and the Receiver ; the one ſhould ſtreightway forget the benefit beſtowed, and the other ſhould always have it in remembrance. *Solon.*

It becometh him to hold his peace that giveth a reward, far better than it becometh him to be ſilent that receiveth a benefit.

He that doth thankfully receive a benefit, hath paid the firſt penſion thereof already.

He that thinks to be thankful doth ſtraightway think upon recompence.

That gift is twice doubly to be accepted of, which cometh from a free hand and a liberal heart.

It behoveth a man in receiving of benefits to be thankful, tho' he want power to require them. *Aur.*

A benefit well given recovereth many loſſes.

The remembrance of a good turn ought to make the Receiver thankful.

Nor gold, nor ſilver, nor ought we receive, is to be accounted a benefit, but the mind of him which giveth.

He giveth too late who giveth when he is asked. *Plautus.*

Ita ſunt omnes noſtri cives :
Si quid benè facias, levior plumâ gratia eſt.
Si quid peccatum eſt, plumbeas nas gerunt.
Beneficium nec in puerum nec in ſenem conferendum eſt :
in hunc, quia perit antequam gratiæ referendæ detur
opportunitas , in illum, quia non memin t.

Of Courtesie.

Defin. Courtesie is a vertue which belongeth to the couragrous part of the soul whereby we are hardly moved to anger. Her office and duty is, to be able to support and endure patiently those crimes which are laid upon her. not to suffer her self to be hastily carried to revenge, nor to be easily spurred to wrath, but to make him that possesseth her mild, gracious, and of a staid and settled mind.

Courtesie in Majesty is the next way to bind affection in duty.

As the tree is known by his fruit, the gold by the touch, and the bell by the found. so is man's birth by his benevolence, his honour by his humility, and his calling by his courtesie.

Many more were the enemies that *Cæsar* pardoned than those he overcame.

The noblest conquest is without bloudshed.

Courtesie bewaileth her dead enemies, and cherisheth her living friends.

The courteous man reconcileth displeasure, the froward urgeth hate.

Proud looks lose hearts, but courteous words win them. *Ferdin*

Courtesie covereth many imperfections, and preventetn more dangers.

It is a true token of Nobility, and the certain mark of a Gentleman, to be courteous to strangers, patient in injury, and constant in performing what he promiseth.

As the peg straineth the Lute-strings, so courtesie stretcheth the heart strings.

Courtesie is that vertue, whereby a man easily appeaseth the motions and instigations of the Soul caused by choler.

Courtesie draweth unto us the love of strangers, and good liking of our own Country men.

He that is mild and courteous to others receiveth much more honour than the party whom he honoureth. *Plut.*

They lie who say that a man must use cruelty towards his Enemies, esteeming that to be an Art only proper to a noble and courageous man. *Cicero.*

Mildness and courtesie are the characters of an holy soul, which never suffereth innocency to be oppressed.

It becomes a noble and strong man to be both courageous and courteous, that he may chastise the wicked, and pardon when need requireth. *Plato.*

The rigour of Discipline directing Courtesie, and Courtesie directing Order, the one will set forth and commend the other, so that neither Rigour shall be rigorous, nor Courtesie dissolute.

As it belongeth to the Sun to lighten the earth with his beams, so it pertaineth to the vertue of a Prince to have compassion, and to be courteous to the miserable *Arist*

Satis est homines imprudentiâ lapsos non erigere, urgere vero jacentes, ac præcipitantes impellere, certè est inhumanum. Cicero.

Of Justice.

Defin *Justice is Godliness, and Godliness is the knowledge of God: it is moreover, in respect of us, taken for an equal description of right and of laws.*

Justice allots no privilege to defraud a man of his patrimony.

Justice is a vertue that gives every man his own by even portions.

Delay in punishment is no privilege of pardon.

E   Justice

Juſtice is the badge of Vertue, the ſtaff of Peace, and the maintenance of Honour. *Cicero.*

It is a ſharp ſentence that is given without judgment.

Good mens ears are always open to juſt mens prayers. *Baſil.*

Not the pain, but the cauſe maketh the Martyr. *Ambroſe*

The office of a Juſtice is to be given for merit, not for affection.

A publick fault ought not to ſuffer a ſecret puniſhment

Juſtice and Order are the only preſervers of worldly quietneſs.

The parts which true Juſtice doth conſiſt of are in number ſeven, Innocency, Friendſhip, Concord, Godlineſs, Humanity, Gratefulneſs, and Faithfulneſs

Juſtice is painted blind, with a veil before her face not becauſe ſhe is blind, but thereby to ſignifie, that Juſtice, though ſhe do behold that which is right and honeſt, yet will ſhe reſpect no perſon.

In *Athens* were erected certain images of Judge without hands and eyes; to ſhew that Judges ſhould neither be corrupted with bribes, nor by any perſon drawn from that which is right and law. *Quint*

A good Judge is true in word, honeſt in thought and vertuous in his deeds; without fear of any but God, without hate of any but the wicked.

There are two kinds of injuſtice · the one is of ſuch as do wrongfully offer it, and the other is of thoſe who, although they be able, yet will they not defend the wrong from them unto whom it is wickedly offered. *Cicero.*

He that politickly intendeth good to the Commonwealth may well be called juſt. but he that practiſeth only for his own profit is a vicious and wicked perſon.

A good

A good Magiſtrate may be called the Phyſician of the Common-wealth.

He is a good Judge that knoweth how and where to diſtribute.

He that flieth judgment, confeſſeth himſelf to be faulty. *Marc. Aurel.*

The Judge himſelf is condemned, when the guilty perſon is pardoned.

As a Phyſician cannot ſee every ſecret grief, but upon revealment may apply a curing medicine for the hidden diſeaſe: ſo many can diſcover a miſchief which the Magiſtrate ſeeth not, but the Magiſtrate alone muſt remedy the ſame.

A Juſtice ought to do that willingly which he can do, and deny that modeſtly which he cannot do.

As there is no aſſurance of fair weather, untill the sky be clear from clouds · ſo there can be in no Common-wealth a grounded peace and proſperity, where are no informers to find out offences, as well as Magiſtrates to puniſh Offenders.

Philoſophers make four ſorts of Juſtice: the firſt Celeſtial, the ſecond Natural; the third Civil, the fourth Judicial.

Juſtice is a perfect knowledge of good and evil agreeing to natural reaſon. *Ariſt*

Juſtice is a vertue of the mind, rewarding all men according to their worthineſs.

Wiſdom and Eloquence without Truth and Juſtice are a *Panurgy*, that is to ſay, a guile or ſlight, ſuch as Paraſites uſe in Comedies, which ſtill turneth to their own confuſion.

Covetouſneſs and wrath in Judges is to be hated with extreme deteſtation.

Celeſtial Juſtice is a perfect conſideration and dutiful acknowledging of God.

Natural Juſtice is that which all people have in themſelves by Nature.

Judicial

Judicial Juſtice depends upon Law, made for the commodity of a Common-weal.

Juſtice is a meaſure which God hath ordained amongſt men upon earth, to defend the feeble from the mighty, the truth from falſhood, and to root out the wicked from among the good. *Lactan.*

Every man in general loveth Juſtice, yet they all hate the execution thereof in particular. *Cicero.*

Fortitude without wiſdom is but raſhneſs, wiſdom without Juſtice is but craftineſs, Juſtice without temperance is but cruelty; temperance without Fortitude is but ſavageneſs.

Equity judgeth with lenity, laws with extremity.

Hatred, love and covetouſneſs cauſe Judges oftentimes to forget the truth, and to leave undone the true execution of their charge.

It is better for a man to be made a Judge among his enemies than among his friends for of his enemies he ſhall make one his friend, but among his friends ne ſhall make one his enemy.

Juſtice by the Poets is feigned to be a Virgin, and to have reigned among men in the golden age, who being by them abuſed, forſook the World, and returned to the Kingdom of *Jupiter*

Juſtitia ſine prudentia plurimum poterit, ſine juſtitia nihil valebit prudentia.

Titius juſtitiæ nulla eſt capitalior peſtis quàm illi qui tum, dum maximè fallunt, id agunt ut boni viri videantur. Cicero.

Of Law.

Defin. *The Law is a ſingular reaſon imprinted in nature, commanding thoſe things that are to be done, and forbidding the contrary. It is divided into two parts, that is, the Law of Nature, and the Law written. The Law of Nature is a ſenſe of feeling, which every one hath in himſelf, and in his conſcience, whereby he diſcerneth between good and evil, as much as ſufficeth*

to take from him the cloak of Ignorance, in that he is
reproved even by his own witnefs The Law written
is that which is divided into Divinity and Civility.
the firft teaching Manners, Ceremonies and Judgments;
the latter, matters of Policy and Government.

THE vertues of the Law are four, to bear fway,
to forbid, to punifh, and to fuffer

The precepts of the Law may be comprehended
under thefe three points; to live honeftly, to hurt
no man wilfully, and to render every man his due
carefully. *Arift.*

Whatfoever is righteous in the Law of man, the
fame is alfo righteous in the Law of God. For every
Law that by man is made muft always be confonant
to the Law of God.

The Law is a certain Rule proceeding from the
mind of God, perfwading that which is right, and
forbidding that which is wrong.

Evil Judges do moft commonly punifh the purfe,
and fpare the perfon.

Judges ought to difpatch with fpeed, and anfwer
with patience.

Law and wifdom are two laudable things, for
the one concerneth Vertue, and the other Good conditions.

The Law was made to no other end, but to bridle fuch as live without Reafon and Law

A true and faithful heart ftandeth more in awe of
his fuperiour, whom he loveth for fear, than of his
Prince, whom he feareth of love

An evil cuftom being for continuance never fo
ancient, is nought elfe than the oldnefs of errour.
Lactantius.

How many more Taverns, fo many more drin-
kers, the number of Phyficians, the increafe of difeafes, the more account that Juftice is made of,

the more suits : so the more Law, the more corruption. *Plato.*

The heart, understanding, counsel and soul in a Common-wealth, are the good Laws and Ordinances therein used. *Cicero.*

To restrain punishment is a great errour in government.

It becometh a Law maker not to be a Law breaker. *Bias.*

Those Countries must needs perish where the Common Laws be of none effect.

Those Cities in which there are no severe Laws for the punishing of sin, are rather to be counted forests for Monsters, than places habitable for men. *Plato.*

Four things belong to a Judge, to hear courteously, to answer wisely, to consider soberly, and to give judgment without partiality. *Socrates.*

A man ought to love his Prince loyally, to keep his Laws carefully, and to defend his Country valiantly.

Chiefly three are to be obeyed and reverenced ; one God, one King, and one Law.

Four customs are more pleasant to be recounted than profitable to be followed; the liberty of neighbours, the gallantness of women, the goodness of wine, and the mirth and joy at feasts.

Laws are like Spiders Webs, which catch the small Flies, and let the great break through

The Lawyer that pleads for a mighty man in a wrong matter must either forget the Truth, or forsake his Clients Friendship.

The most necessary Law for a Common-wealth is that the people among themselves live in peace and concord, without strife or dissention. *Cicero.*

Laws do vex the meaner sort of men, but the mighty are able to withstand them.

The Law is a strong and forcible thing, if it get a good Prince to execute it.

The

The Law that is perfect and good would have no man either condemned or justified, until his cause be throughly heard and understood as it ought.

An evil Law is like the shadow of a Cloud, which vanisheth away so soon as it is seen.

——*Jus sæpe vi opprimitur.*
Quid faciunt leges ubi sola pecunia regnat ?
Aut ubi paupertas vincere nulla potest ?
Turpe reos emptâ miseros defendere linguâ ;
Non benè cælestis Judicis arca patet.

Of Counsel.

Defin. Counsel is an holy thing it is the sentence or advice which particularly is given by every man for that purpose assembled it is the key of certainty, and the end of all doctrine and study.

THere is no man so simple but he can give counsel, though there be no need. and there is none so wise of himself, but he will be willing to hear counsel in time of necessity.

It is the chief thing in the world to give good counsel to another man, and the hardest for a man to follow the same himself.

Take no counsel of a man given wholly to the world, for his advice will be after his own desire. *Pythag*

Make not an envious man, a drunkard, nor him that is in subjection to a woman, or thy counsel; for it is impossible for them to keep close thy secrets

Good counsel may properly be called the beginning and ending of every good work.

It is requisite for a man to consult and determine all things with himself, before he ask the counsel or advice of his friend

He that doeth nothing without good advice, needs not repent him after the deed. *Bias.*

It

It is better to prefer the stedfast counsel of advised policy, than the rash enterprise of a malapert boldness.

Counsel doth more harm than good, if the giver thereof be not wife, and he which receiveth it very patient

Counsel is to be given by the wife, and the remedy by the rich.

In counsels we must be hard to resolve, and constant to perform

He that useth many counsels is not easily deceived

In time of necessity a wife man will be glad to hear counsel.

As it is the part of a wife man wifely to consult and give counsel, so it is the duty of a wary man heedfully to conceive, and uprightly to judge *Guevar.*

It is an easie thing for a man being in perfect health to give counsel to another that is sick, but it is hard for the sick man to follow that counsel. *Becanus.*

The greatest benefit that one friend can do for another is, in weighty matters to succour him with good counsel.

Parvi sunt foris arma, nisi est consilium domi.

Non viribus, aut velocitatibus, aut celeritate corporum res magne geruntur, sed consilio, authoritate, & prudentiâ. Cicero.

Of Precepts.

Defin. *Precepts are any Rules, Orders or Methods, which by instruction lead us either to a good conversation, or to a happiness of life, being grounded upon the grace of God and his Word.*

IF thou talk, keep measure in thy communication for if thou be too brief, thou shalt not be well understood; if too long, thou shalt be troublesome to the hearer, and not well born in mind. *Protag.*

Thanks

Thanks wox old as foon as gifts are had in poffeffion.

He that refufeth to buy counfel good cheap, fhall buy repentance dear.

Mock no man in mifery, but take heed by him how to avoid the like misfortune

Begin nothing before thou know how to finifh it.

Think that the weakeft of thy eremies is ftronger than thy felf.

Defire not that of another which thou thy felf being asked wouldft deny. *Pythag*

Give no vain or unmeet gifts, as armour to a Woman, books to a Plough man, or nets to a Student.

If thou beftow a benefit, keep it fecret, but if thou receive any, publifh it abroad

Give at the firft asking. for that is not freely given which is often craved

Take in good worth whatfoever happeneth, and upbraid no man with his misfortune.

Labour not to inform him that is without reafon, for fo fhalt thou make him thine enemy.

Be neither hafty, angry, nor wrathful; for they be the conditions of a fool.

Fear to hazard that for the gain of momentary pleafure, which being once loft, can never be recovered. *Auguft.*

Efteem not a fading content before a perpetual honour.

Apparel thy felf with Juftice, and cloath thy felf with Chaftity, fo fhalt thou be happy, and thy works profper

Fear to commit that which thou oughteft to fear.

Forget not to give thanks to them that inftruct thee in learning, nor challenge unto thy felf the praife of other mens inventions.

Attempt not two things at once, for the one wil hinder the other.

E 5   Be

Be not flack to recompence them who have done thee good.

Be rather too much forward, than too much negligent.

Be not fuperfluous in words, for they do greatly deface the authority of the perfon

Let Vertue be thy life, Valour thy love, Honour thy fame, and Heaven thy felicity

Be not led away with every new opinion, for it is the only way to bring to errour.

Let not thy Liberality exceed thy Ability.

Let not the eye go beyond the ear, nor the tongue fo far as the feet. *Plato.*

Chufe rather to live folitary, than in the company of a wicked woman.

Beware of pride in profperity, for it will make thee impatient in the time of adverfity.

Neither fuffer thine hands to work, thy tongue to fpeak, nor thine ears to hear that which is filthy and evil. *Hermes.*

Be not fecure, left want of care procure thy calamity, nor be too careful, left penfive thoughts opprefs thee with mifery.

Speak no more to a ftranger in private than thou wouldft have publickly known.

Hazard not thy hap on another's chance

Be always one to thy friend, as well in adverfity as profperity.

Behold thy felf in a Looking-glafs and if thou appear beautiful, do fuch things as become thy beauty: but if thou feem foul, then perform with good manners the beauty that thy face lacketh. *Socrates.*

Chufe thy wife rather for her wit and modefty, than for her wealth and beauty.

Keep fecretly thy mif-hap, left thy enemy wax joyful thereat.

Keep

Keep whatfoever thy friend committeth unto thee as carefully as thou wouldſt thy own.

If thy parents grow poor, ſupply their want with thy wealth, if froward with age, bear patiently with their imperfections

Honour them that have deſerved honour.

Live and hope, as if thou ſhouldſt die immediately.

Never praiſe any unworthy perſon becauſe he hath worldly wealth

Tell no man afore hand what thou intendeſt, for if thou ſpeed not in thy purpoſe, thou ſhalt be mocked. *Soci ites.*

Never wiſh for thoſe things that cannot be attained.

Rather chuſe to purchaſe by perſwaſion, than to enjoy by violence.

Strive not in words with thy parents, although thou tell the truth.

Haunt not too much thy friend's houſe, for fear he wax weary of thy often coming: neither be too long abſent, for that cauſeth a ſuſpicion of thy true friendſhip.

Fly from the filthy pleaſures of the fleſh as thou wouldſt fly from the ſting of a Serpent.

Give to a good man, and he will requite it but if thou give to an evil man he will ask more *Anaxag*

Receive not the gifts that an evil-minded man doth profer unto thee.

If thou intend to do any good, defer it not till the next day, for thou knoweſt not what chance may happen the ſame night to prevent thee *Olaus Mag.*

Give not thy ſelf to pleaſure and eaſe, for if thou uſe thy ſelf thereunto, thou ſhalt not be able to ſuſtain the adverſity which may afterwards happen.

To a man full of queſtions make no anſwer at all. *Plato.*

Take good heed at the beginning to what thou granteſt, for after one inconvenience another followeth.   If

Be not flack to recompence them who have done thee good.

Be rather too much forward, than too much negligent.

Be not fuperfluous in words, for they do greatly deface the authority of the perfon

Let Vertue be thy life, Valour thy love, Honour thy fame, and Heaven thy felicity.

Be not led away with every new opinion, for it is the only way to bring to errour.

Let not thy Liberality exceed thy Ability.

Let not the eye go beyond the ear, nor the tongue fo far as the feet *Plato.*

Chufe rather to live folitary, than in the company of a wicked woman.

Beware of pride in profperity, for it will make thee impatient in the time of adverfity.

Neither fuffer thine hands to work, thy tongue to fpeak, nor thine ears to hear that which is filthy and evil. *Hermes.*

Be not fecure, left want of care procure thy calamity, nor be too careful, left penfive thoughts opprefs thee with mifery.

Speak no more to a ftranger in private than thou wouldft have publickly known.

Hazard not thy hap on another's chance

Be always one to thy friend, as well in adverfity as profperity

Behold thy felf in a Looking-glafs: and if thou appear beautiful, do fuch things as become thy beauty: but if thou feem foul, then perform with good manners the beauty that thy face lacketh. *Socrates.*

Chufe thy wife rather for her wit and modefty, than for her wealth and beauty.

Keep fecretly thy mifhap, left thy enemy wax joyful thereat.

Keep whatfoever thy friend committeth unto thee as carefully as thou wouldft thy own.

If thy parents grow poor, fupply their want with thy wealth, if froward with age, bear patiently with their imperfections

Honour them that have deferved honour.

Live and hope, as if thou fhouldft die immediately.

Never praife any unworthy perfon becaufe he hath worldly wealth.

Tell no man afore hand what thou intendeft, for if thou fpeed not in thy purpofe, thou fhalt be mocked *Socrites*

Never wifh for thofe things that cannot be attained.

Rather chufe to purchafe by perfwafion, than to enjoy by violence.

Strive not in words with thy parents, although thou tell the truth.

Haunt not too much thy friend's houfe, for fear he wax weary of thy often coming: neither be too long abfent, for that caufeth a fufpicion of thy true friendfhip.

Fly from the filthy pleafures of the flefh as thou wouldft fly from the fting of a Serpent

Give to a good man, and he will requite it· but if thou give to an evil man he will ask more *Anixag*

Receive not the gifts that an evil-minded man doth profer unto thee.

If thou intend to do any good, defer it not till the next day, for thou knoweft not what chance may happen the fame night to prevent thee. *Olaus Mag.*

Give not thy felf to pleafure and eafe: for if thou ufe thy felf thereunto, thou fhalt not be able to fuftain the adverfity which may afterwards happen.

To a man full of queftions make no anfwer at all. *Plato.*

Take good heed at the beginning to what thou granteft, for after one inconvenience another followeth.   . . . If

If thou doubt in any thing, ask counfel of wife men, and be not angry, although they reprove thee.

Live with thine underlings as thou wouldft thy betters fhould live with thee, and do to all men as thou wouldft be done unto

Boaft not of thy good deeds, left thy evil deeds be alfo laid to thy charge

Perform thy promife as juftly as thou wouldft pay thy debts for a man ought to be more faithful than his oath. *Auc*

If thou do good to an ill difpofed perfon, it fhall happen to thee as it doth to thofe who feed other men's dogs, which bark as well at their feeder as at any other ftranger.

Never fpread thy table to Tale-bears and Flatterers, nor liften with thine ears to murmuring peop'e *Bias*

Be not like the Boulter, which cafteth out the flower, and keepeth the bran.

Si vis ab omnibus cognofci, da operam ut à nemine cog-nofcaris

Nulli te facias nimis fodalem,
Gaudebis minus, & minus dolebis.

Of Confideration.

Defin *Confideration or judgment is that which properly ought to be in every Magiftrate obferving the tenour of the Law · it is the extinguifher of controverfies, and bringer forth of happy counfels and agreements.*

Confideration is the enemy to untimely attempts *Solon.*

There is no Needle's point fo fmall, but it hath its compafs neither is there any Hair fo flender, but it hath its fhadow.

He is not to be accounted rich who is never fatisfied, nor happy, whofe ftedfaft mind in quiet poffeffion of vertue is not eftablifhed.   The

The confideration of pleafures paſt greatly augments the pain prefent.

No man doth fo much rejoyce at his Profperity prefent, as he that calleth to mind his miſeries paſt. *Chilo*

It is a benefit to deny fuch things as will hurt him that asketh them.

The pardon may well be granted, where he that hath offended is afhamed of his fauit.

Wife men will always confider what they ought to do, before they conclude any thing

In any affairs whatfoever, theie is no greater fafety, than foundly to confider into whofe hands men commit their caufe. *Juſtin.*

We muſt think with confideration, confider with acknowledging, acknowledge with admiration, admire with love, and love with joy in the midſt of woe *S. P. S.*

Not fo hard is the invention in getting, as the difpofitios in keeping when it is gotten. *Ovid.*

Men lofe many things, not becaufe they cannot attain them, but becaufe they dare not attempt them. *Pythag.*

As a veſſel favoureth always of the fame Liquor wherewith it was firſt feafoned . fo the mind retaineth thofe Qualities in age wherein it was trained up in youth *Horace.*

Confideration is the root of all noble things, for by her we do attain to the end of all our hopes.

True confideration is the Tutor both to action and fpeaking.

The haters of confideration never profper in their actions.

Confideration is an honour, to the meaneſt, and improvidence a fhame in a Prince.

Good confideration ought to be had before we give credit for fair tongues oftentimes work great mifchief.   Gir-

Circumfpect heed in War is the caufe of fcap'ng many dangers in peace.

The caufes bringing circumfpection are fear, care, neceffity and. affliction.

Feai afflicteth, caie compelleth, neceffity bindeth. affliction woundeth

Be circumfpect to fhew a good countenance to all, yet enter not into familiarity with any, but only fuch whofe converfation is honeft, and whofe truth by trial is made trufty. *Archim.*

Sudden truft brings fudden repentancc.

Qui fua metitur pondera, ferre poteft.

———Verfato diu quid ferre recufant,

Quidque valent humeri Horace.

Of Office

Defin. *Office or Duty is the knowledge of man concerning his own nature, and the contemplation of Divine nature, and a labour to benefit our felves and all other men : it is alfo taken for authority to rule*

MAn's life may not be deftitute of office, becaufe in it honefty confifteth.

Office is the end whereat vertue aimeth, and chiefly when we obferve things comely.

The firft office of duty is to acknowledge the Divinity.

Office is ftrengthened by zeal, and zeal makes opinion invincible.

We muft fear a diffembling Officer, becaufe he delights in a tyrannous office.

The office of a wife man ever prefers confideration before conclufion.

In doing nothing but what we ought, we deferve no greater rewards than what we bear about us. *Chryf.*

To know evil is an office of profit, but to do evil is a sin of indignity.

Upon the Anvil of upbraiding is forged the office of unthankfulness.

It is an office of pity, to give a speedy death to a miserable and condemned creature *Bias.*

Love, Sufficiency and Exercise, are the three beauties which adorn Offices.

Old men well experienced in Laws and Customs, ought chiefly to be chosen Officers

It is not meet that man should bear any authority which with his money seeketh to buy another man's office.

The buyers of offices sell by retail as dear as they can that which they buy in gross.

No point of Philosophy is more excellent than Office in publick affairs, if Officers do practice that which Philosophers teach.

Where offices are vendible, there the best-monied ignorants bear the greatest rule.

They which sell offices, sell the most sacred things in the world, even Justice it self, the Commonwealth, Subjects and the Laws.

He is only fit to rule and bear office who comes to it by constraint and against his will

' The office of a Monarch is continually to look upon the Law of God, to engrave it in his soul, and to meditate upon his Word.

Officers must rule by good Laws and good Examples, judge by Providence, Wisdom and Justice; and defend by Prowess, Care and Vigilance. *Agesil.*

Pericula, labores, dolores etiam, optimus quisque suscipere mavult, quàm deserere ullam officii partem. Cicero.

Sigismundus Romanorum Imperator dicere solitus est, Nullâ nobis militiâ opus esset, si suas quique civitates Praetores caeteríque Magistratus moderatè justéque gubernarent.

Of

Of Anceſtours

Defin *Anceſtours are our forefathers, the reputed firſt be-*
ginners of our names and dignities; from whom we
challenge a lineal deſcent of Honour, proving our ſelves
of their ſelf ſubſtance.

TRue Nobility deſcending from Anceſtry proves
baſe, if preſent life continue not the dignity
Of it.

What can the vertue of our Anceſtry profit us, if
we do not imitate them in their godly actions?

Great merits ask great rewards, and great Anceſtours vertuous iſſues.

As it is more common to revenge than to reward,
ſo it is eaſier to be born great than to continue great.
Stobæus.

It is miſerable to purſue the change, which gains
nothing but ſorrow, and the blot of Anceſtry.

The thing poſſeſt is not the thing it ſeems, and
though we be great by our Anceſtours, yet we forget our Anceſtours. *Suet*

The ſhifting of Chambers changeth not the diſeaſe; and the exchange of Names exchangeth not Nature and Anceſtry.

Ambition, which chiefly comes from Anceſtours
being got to the top of his deſires, cuts of the mean
by which he did climb.

From our Anceſtours come our names, but from
our Vertues our report

Mercenary faith is diſcontented with every occaſion,
and new ſtart up glory with an old fame.

When greatneſs cannot bear it ſelf, either with Vertue or Anceſtry, it overthrows it ſelf only with the
weight of it ſelf

Many troubled in conſcience for diſgracing their
names with raſh acts, in cold bloud repent their diſ-
honours.   The

The bafe iffue of ignoble Anceftry will lofe their troths to fave their lives

Might will make his Anceftours whom he pleafeth.

The event of things is clofed up in darknefs, and though we know what our Anceftours were, we know not what we fhall be.

The longer we delay the fhew of vertue, the ftroger we make prefumptions that we are guilty of bafe beginnings.

Stemmata quid faciunt ? quid prodeft (Pontice) longo
Sanguine cenferi, pictofque oftendere vultus
Majorum, & flantes in curribus Æmilianos ? Juv.
——*Genus, & proavos, & qua non fecimus ipfi,*
Vix ea noftra voco. Ovid.

Of War.

Defin. *War is of two forts, Civil and Foreign. Civil*
War is the overthrow of all Eftates and Monarchies,
and the feed of all kinds of evil in them, even of thofe
that are moft execrable : it begetteth want of reve-
rence towards God, difobedience to Magiftrates, cor-
ruption of Manners, change of Laws, contempt of Ju-
ftice, and bafe eftimation of learning and Science. Fo-
reign War is that which Plato calleth a more gentle
contention, and is then only moft lawful, when it is
for true Religion, or to procure the continuance of
peace.

THere is nothing more unconftant than War, did not patience make it ftable, and true hope fuc-cefsful.

War for excellency (as that between *Euripides* and *Xenocles*) is pleafing in the fight of all men.

Than War there is nothing more neceffary for the breach of Friendfhip by diffenfion ftrengtheneth the powers of Love in her new conjunction.

War

War is moſt lawful when it is warranted by the Word, either to defend a man's own right, or to repulſe the enemies of God. *Laſtan.*

Diverſity of Religion is the ground of Civil War in ſhew, but it is Ambition in effect.

War ought to be deliberately begun, but ſpeedily ended.

Affairs of War muſt be deliberated on by many, but concluded on by a few.

The effects of War are covetous deſires, the fall of juſtice, force and violence. *Epict.*

War was only ordained to make men live in peace.

In the ſack of a Town have an eſpecial care to preſerve the honour of Ladies and Maids from the violence of unruly Soldiers.

Have an eſpecial care to whom you commit the Government of an Army, Town, or Fort: for love doth much, but money doth more.

Entring into thy Enemie's Camp, let all things of uſe and baggage follow thee at thy back; but thine enemy coming upon thee, let the ſame be brought into the middle of the Army.

Where thou mayſt conquer with money, never uſe arms; and rather chuſe to overcome thine enemies by policy than fight.

In places of danger, and in troubleſome times, ever double the number of thy Sentinels.

Neceſſity makes War to be juſt. *Bias.*

Nulla ſalus bello, pacem te poſcimus omnes.

Incerti ſunt exitus pugnarum, Marſque eſt communis, qui ſæpe ſpoliantem jam & exſultantem evertit & percutit ab abjecto. Cic.

Of Generals in War.

Defin. *Generals are the Heads and Leaders of Armies, and they ought to be great, magnanimous and conſtant in all their doings, free from defects of raſhneſs and cowardice.*

THE Tent of the General is the pure river running through the Army, by whoſe ſoundneſs all the Soldiers are preſerved and made ſtout. but if he be impure or corrupted, the whole Hoſt is infected.

Unleſs wiſe and valiant men be choſen Generals, the old Chaos will return, and vertue die at the feet of confuſion.

He that will be a commander in Armies, firſt let him be commanded in the ſame; for an ambitious Soldier will never make a temperate conductor.

A wiſe General muſt not only forecaſt to prevent ſuch evils as he hears of, but alſo be circumſpect to foreſee ſuch ills as may happen beyond expectation. *Demoſt.*

A General, after the battle ended, muſt have a circumſpect care how he praiſeth one Captain more than another

A General ought not to bring all his forces to battel at once, unleſs it be upon great advantage. *Olaus.*

It is very needful for a General to know the humour and diſpoſition of his adverſary's General whom he fighteth againſt.

The Oration of a General gives courage to Cowards and baſe minded Soldiers. *Vegetius*

A coverous General purchaſeth to himſelf more hate than love.

A General muſt not be ignorant of ſuch things as are neceſſary in a journey.

Captains muſt be valiant, as deſpiſing death, confident, as not wonted to be overcome, yet doubtful by their preſent feeling, and reſpectful by that they ſee already.

A

A Captain's feet ought to be steddy, his hands diligent, his eyes watchful, and his heart resolute.

It is requisite for a General to know all Advantages of the place where the Battel should be fought.

It proveth oft the ruine of an Army, when the General is careless, and maketh no account of his enemies proceedings.

It is dangerous for the person of the General to follow his flying enemy.

It behoveth that the General be always lodged in the midst of the Camp.

A General or Captain in danger ought to change his habit or retire. *Ferdin.*

The death of a General, or his being in danger, must be dissembled, for fear it procure the loss of the battel.

A good General should ever be like a good Shepherd, looking into the want of his Soldiers, and providing all things necessary to comfort them. *Basil.*

Let a General give to honour a renowned burial, in how mean a person soever it did inhabit, for honour after death encourageth as much as wealth in life. *Vegetius*

If thou beest a Commander in Armies, despise not the poor, for honour's birth issueth from the womb of desert.

The whole scope of a General's thoughts should be to win glory and amplifie renown, loathing to be a plague or scourge of affliction, seeking by Conquest to erect, not by Victory to confound *Cæsar*

The Trophy of a General is his own conscience, and his Valour is his Tomb's treasury.

Commanders in Arms should not be chosen for their age or riches, but for their wisdom and valour

A General or chief Governour must be wise to command, liberal to reward, and valiant to defend.

There

There are eight conditions that a General ought to
have, to avoid unjuſt wrongs, to coṛreᴄt blaſphe-
mers, to ſuccour innocents, to chaſtiſe quarrellers, to
pay his ſouldiers, to defend his people, to provide
things neceſſary, and to obſerve faith with enemies.

Ducis in conſilio poſita eſt vertus militum.
Optimus ille dux, qui novit vincere, & victoria uti.
Ipſe manu ſua pila gerens, præcedit anheli
Militis ante pedes , monſtrat tolerare labores
Non jubet. Lucan.

Of Policy.

Defin. *Policy is a word derived of the Greek word* Po-
liteia, *which is a Regiment of a City or Common-*
wealth, and that which the Grecians, *call Political*
Government, the Latins *call the Government of a*
Common-wealth, or of a Civil Society This word Policy *hath been taken among the Ancients ſometimes*
for a Burgeſs, which is the enjoying of the Rights and
Privileges of a Town; ſometimes for the order and
manner of life uſed by ſome political perſon , and ſome-
times the order and eſtate whereby one or many Towns
are governed, and politick affairs are managed and
adminiſtred.

POlicy is a neceſſary friend to Proweſs.
    That War cannot be proſperous where enemies
abound and money waxeth ſcant.

No man ought to give that treaſure to any one in
particular, which is kept for the preſervation of all.

It is greater commendation to obtain honour by
policy and wiſdom, than to have it by deſcent

That Country may above all other be counted happy, where every man enjoyeth his own labour, and
no man liveth by the ſweat of another Body.

Of right that Common-wealth ought to be deſtroyed, which of all other hath been counted the
flower

flower of vertue, and after becometh the filthy fink of vice.

There can be no greater danger to a Common wealth, nor no like flander to a Prince, as to commit the charge of men to him in the field, which will be first ready to command, and laft ready to fight.

What Power and Policy cannot compafs, Gold both commands and conquers. *Ariftippus.*

He that getteth by conqueft doth much ; but he that can well keep that which he hath gotten doth more.

Money and Soldiers are the ftrength and finews of War. *Agefil.*

It is better to prevent an inconvenience by breaking an oath, than to fuffer injury by obferving of promife.

Warlike feats are better learned in the fields of *Africk*, than in the beautiful Schools of *Greece.*

It is better to have men wanting money, than money wanting men. *Themift.*

The authority of a Common-wealth is impaired when the buildings be ruinated.

In proof of Conqueft men ought to profit themfelves as much by policy as by power.

There are no Common-weals more loofe than thofe where the common people have moft liberty. *Cicero.*

A Policy is foon deftroyed by the pride men have in commanding and liberty in finning

In Common-weals fuch fhould be more honoured who in time of peace maintain the State in tranquility, and in the fury of war defend it by their labour and magnanimity.

A Monarch is beft in a well governed State.

A certain man urging the popular eftate to *Lycurgus*, was thus anfwered by him, firft ordain thou fuch a Government in thine own Common-weal.

Becaufe

Becaufe many cannot fitly govern, therefore it is moft neceffary that one fhould be made Sovereign. *Homer*

The Oracle of *Apollo* at *Delphos* being demanded the reafon why *Jupiter* fhould be the chief of Gods, fith *Mars* was the beft Soldier, made this anfwer; *Mars* is valiant, but *Jupiter* is wife concluding by this anfwer, that policy is of more force to fubdue than valour.

One *Neftor* is more to be efteemed than ten fuch as *Ajax.*

Strength, wanting wit and policy to rule, overthroweth it felf. *Horace.*

Publica res ad privatum commodum trahi poteft, dummodo ftatus publicus non lædatur. Cicero.

Diu apparandum eft bellum, ut vincas celerius.

Of Courage

Defin. *Courage is a fiery humour of the Spirits kindling the mind with forwardnefs in attempts, and bearing the body through danger and the hardeft adventure.*

Courage and Courtefie are the two principal points which adorn a Captain

Courage confifteth not in hazarding without fear, but in being refolutely-minded in a juft caufe. *Plut.*

The talk of a Soldier ought to hang at the point of his Sword.

The want of courage in Commanders breeds neglect and contempt among Soldiers.

Faint-hearted Cowards are never permitted to put in their plea at the Bar of Love

Courage conquers his enemy before the field be fought.

Fortitude is a knowledge inftructing a man, how with commendation to adventure dangerous and fearful things, and in taking them in hand to be nothing terrified. *Socrat.* The

The courage of a man is seen in the resolution of his death.

Fortitude is the fairest blossom that springs from a noble mind.

Fortitude is the mean between fear and boldness

There is not any thing hard to be accomplished by him that with courage enterpriseth it *Cicero*.

Courage begun with deliberate constancy, and continued without change, doth seldom fail

It cannot be accounted courageous and true victory, that bringeth not with it some clemency. *Bias*.

To conquer is natural, to pity, heavenly.

It is more courage to die free, than to live captive. *Leosth*.

Bias holding wars with *Iphicrates* King of *Athens*, falling into the hands of his enemies, and his soldiers fearfully asking what they should do, he answered, Make report to those that are alive, that, I die with courage fighting, and I will say to the dead, that you scape cowardly flying.

Courage adventureth on danger, conquereth by perseverance, and endeth with honour.

There is nothing that maketh a man of more fortitude, or sooner great and mighty, than the trial of a perverse fortune, nor any thing that breedeth more stability of faith and patience, than the exercise of adversities.

Heat is the instrument, anger the whetstone of fortitude.

Courage contemneth all perils, despiseth calamities, and conquers death.

Courage depending on mediocrity hath audaciousness for one, and fear for his other extreme.

As fortitude suffereth not the mind to be dejected by any evils, so temperance suffereth it not to be drawn from honesty by any allurements.

Courage

Courage is the Champion of Juſtice, and never ought to contend but in righteous actions. *Epict.*

Thunder terrifieth children, and threatnings fear fools, but nothing diſmayeth a man of courage and reſolution.

Courage is a wiſe man's coat, and cowardiſe a fool's cognizance.

——Ignavum eſt, peritura parcere vitæ.
Quemcunque magnanimum videris, miſerum neges.
Rebus anguſtis animoſus, atque fortis appare. Hor.

Of Fame.

Defin. *Fame is but an echo, and an idle humour of report, which running from ear to ear, conveyeth through the world the tidings of truth and falſhood.*

THere is no ſweeter friend than Fame, nor worſer enemy than Report.

It is a part of good fortune to be well reported of, and to have a good name. *Plot.*

It is no ſmall pleaſure to have a good name, and yet it is more frail than any glaſs *Eraſmus.*

A good life is the readieſt way to a good name.

Deſire to be famous, but firſt be careful to purchaſe fame with credit.

There is no kind of miſhap more infamous than for a man to loſe his good name, and to be ill reported of amongſt all men for his bad dealing.

As the ſhadow doth follow the body, ſo good deeds accompany fame *Cicero*

Fame is the ſpeedy Herald to bear news.

Fame riſeth up like a bubble, continueth like a ſhadow, and dies in the boſome of time

Nothing is more famous in a Prince than the love of his Subjects, nor any thing more famous in Subjects than obedience.

F

Fame

Fame is like the turning wheel, that never ſtayeth; like the burning ſlame, that quickly quencheth, like the Summer-fruit, that ſoon withereth.

A good report ſhineth moſt clearly in the deepeſt darkneſs.

If thou deſire to be well ſpoken of, then learn to ſpeak well of others, and when thou learneſt to ſpeak well, then learn likewiſe to do well: ſo ſhalt thou be ſure to get a worthy name.

Our good name ought to be more dear unto us than our life.

Beauty conquers the heart, gold conquers Beauty, but fame ſubdues, and goes beyond them both.

To fly from Fame or Deſtiny is of all things moſt impoſſible.

Keep the fame thou haſt honeſtly gotten, for it is a jewel ineſtimable.

A rumour raiſed of nothing ſoon vaniſheth, and the end of it is nothing elſe but to make the innocency of him who is ſlandred to be more admired. *Eraſmus.*

Honeſtus rumor alterum eſt patrimonium.

Actum præclarè cum iis eſt, quorum virtus, nec oblivione eorum qui ſunt, nec reticentiâ poſteriorum, ſepulta eſſe poterit. Cicero.

Of Rage.

Defin. *Rage is a ſhort fury, the inflammation of the blood, and alteration of the heart: it is a deſire of revenge or regardleſs care of friends, an enemy of all reaſon, and as uneaſie to be guided by another as a furious Tyrant.*

RAge or anger, if it be but a ſmall time deferred, the force thereof will be greatly aſſwaged; but if it be ſuffered to continue, it increaſeth more and more in miſchief, until by revenge it be fully ſatisfied.   Whilſt

Whilft Rage hath run his courfe, forbear to fpeak; fol many men in their anger will give no ear to reafon.

Anger is the firft entrance to unfeemly wrath. *Py-thag.*

Wrath proceedeth from the feeblenefs of courage, and lack of difcretion.

Women are fooner angry than men, the fick fooner than the healthy, and old men fooner than young men. *Hermes.*

The ireful man is more mifgoverned than he whom loathfome drunkennefs detains

The raging perturbations of the mind do punifh reafon, and blind the fight of wifdom, *Anax.*

What ragingly and rafhly is begun, doth challenge fhame before it be half done

Grief never leaves a wrathful man weaponlefs.

Anger is foon buried in a wife man's breaft.

Anger and Power meeting together in one man, are of more force than any thunderbolt.

Flee from the furious in his wrath, and truft not to the fair tongue of thine enemy.

He overcometh a ftout enemy that overcometh his own anger. *Chilo.*

What in private perfons is termed Choler, in great men is called Fury and Cruelty

Anger fpringeth from injury done unto us, but hatred oftentimes is conceived of no occafion. *Arift.*

Wrath and Revenge take from man the mercy of God, and deftroy and quench the grace that God had given him.

He beft keepeth himfelf from anger that always doth remember that God looketh upon him *Plato.*

As fire, being kindled but with a fmall fpark, worketh oft-times great hurt and damage, becaufe the fiercenefs thereof was not at the firft abated . fo anger, being harboured in the heart, breaketh forth oft-times into much cruelty.

The

The angry man meditating upon mifchief, thinketh that he hath good counfel in hand.

Wrath is a defire to be revenged, feeking a time or opportunity for the fame. *Lact.*

As difordinate anger is a fault, fo is fometimes the want of a moderate choler, or rather hatred of vice.

Anger is the finew of the foul, for that it ferveth to increafe valour, being moderate and temperate. *Plato.*

Anger makes a man to differ from himfelf.

There is no falfe counfel to be taken from the mouth of an angry man. *Anax*

Anger is like unto a cloud, that maketh every thing feem bigger than it is.

Rafh judgment maketh hafte to repentance.

Anger confifteth in habit and difpofition, but wrath in deed and effect.

Like as green wood, which is long in kindling, continueth longer hot than the dry, if it hath once taken fire. fo commonly it falleth out, that the man feldom moved to anger is more hard to be pacified in his anger than he that is quickly vexed.

If thou have not fo much power as to refrain thine anger, yet diffemble it, and keep it fecret, and fo by little and little thou mayft happily forget it.

Wrath and rigour lead fhame in a leafe. *Ifoci at.*

In correction be not angry · for he that punifheth in his rage, fhall never keep that mean which is between too much and too little.

Hafty and froward fpeeches beget anger, anger being kindled begetteth wrath, wrath feeketh greedily after revenge, revenge is never fatisfied but in blood-fhedding.

As he that loveth quietnefs fleepeth fecure; fo he that delights in ftrife and anger paffeth his days in great danger.

It

It is good for a man to abstain from anger, if not for wisdom's sake, yet for his own bodily health's sake.

He that is much subject to wrath, and hunteth after revenge, quencheth the grace that God hath given him, and commits through rage and fury more horrible offences than can afterwards be reformed.

Ira feras mentes obsidet, eruditas præterlabitur.
——Pone vesano's, precor,
Animi tumores, téque pietate refer Sen.
——Diis proximus ille est,
Quem ratio non ira movet. Simpl.

Of Cruelty.

Defin. *Cruelty is commonly taken for every extreme wrong · it is the rigorous effect of an evil disposed will, and the fruit which is reapt from injustice*

CRuelty hath his curses from above; but courtesie is graced with the title of commendation.

Where lenity cannot reclaim, there severity must correct.

It is as great cruelty to spare all, as to spare none.

Tyrants use trial by arms, but the just refer their causes to the arbitrament of the Laws.

To pardon many for the offence of one, is an office of Christianity, but to punish many for the fault of one appertaineth properly to Tyrants.

It is amongst evils the greatest evil, and in Tyrants the greatest tyranny, that they of themselves will not live according to Reason and Justice, neither will they consent that Malefactors should receive punishment

It is more profit for a Prince that is a Tyrant, that his Common wealth be rich, and his Palace poor, than the Common-wealth to be poor, and his own Palace rich.

He

He never ferveth gratefully, who by violence is fubject to another.

The woman that holdeth in her eye moft cruelty, hath often in her heart moft diſhoneſty

The Captain that is bloody minded and full of revenge is either ſlain by his enemies, or ſold by his Soldiers.

Cauſeleſs cruelty never ſcapes long without revenge.

With the ireful we muſt not be importunate to crave pardon, but to deſire that revenge may be deferred.

Tyranny amongſt many other evils, is moſt wretched in this, that his friends dare not counſel him.

He that ſhews himſelf cruel towards his ſervants, doth manifeſtly declare that his will is good to puniſh others alſo, but he wanteth authority

Private cruelty doth much hurt, but a Prince's anger is an open War.

Victory ſhould not thirſt after blood, nor the gain of conqueſt induce a man to cruelty. *Sopho.*

A cruel Prince over a rebellious Nation, is a great vertue warring with a world of wickedneſs.

Nulla vobis cum tyrannis eſt ſocietas, ſed ſumma diſtractio, neque eſt contra naturam ſpoliare eum, quem honeſtum eſt necare.

Of Fear.

Defin. *Fear is two-fold, good and evil. Good fear is that which is grounded upon a good diſcourſe of reaſon and judgment, ſtanding in awe of blame, reproach and diſhonour, more than death or grief. Evil fear is deſtitute of reaſon, it is that which we call Cowardlineſs and Puſillanimity, always attended on with two perturbations of the ſoul, Fear and Sadneſs. It is alſo the defect of the vertue of Fortitude.*

THE fear and reverence of one God is more worth than the ſtrength of all men.

No

No man can be juft without the fear and reverence of the Lord.

Fear dependeth upon love, and without love it is foon had in contempt.

If thou be ignorant what fin is, or knoweft not vertue, by the fear and love of God thou mayft quickly underftand them both. *Socrates.*

He that feareth God truly, ferveth him faithfully, loveth him intirely, prayeth unto him devoutly, and diftributeth unto the poor liberally

Wicked men wanting the fear of God, are haunted of evil to their own overthrow and deftruction. *Boetius.*

It is the property of a Servant to fear his Mafter with hatred, but a Son feareth his Father for love. *Amb.*

Neither ftrength nor bignefs are of value in a fearfull body.

They that defire to be feared, needs muft they dread them of whom they be feared.

Fear is the companion of a guilty confcience

A Mafter that feareth his Servant is more fervile than the Servant himfelf.

It is a deadly fear to live in continual danger of death.

It is a mere folly for a man to fear that which he cannot fhun.

It is a natural thing in all men to leave their lives with forrow, and to take their death with fear.

To demand how many, and not where the enemies be, is a fign of a cowardly fear

Fear followeth hope, wherefore if thou wilt not fear, hope not. *Æfculap.*

It many times happens, that the parties not willing to joyn in love, do confent and agree together in fear.

It is far better to fear thy choice, than to rue thy unhappy chance. F 4 He

He that feareth every tempest is not fit to be a traveller.

The sword dispatcheth quickly, but fear tormenteth continually.

Fear standeth at the gates of the ears, and putteth back all perswasions. *Plato.*

The more a man fears, the sooner he shall be hurt.

Too much fear opens the door to desperation.

He that through his cruelty is much feared of other men, walketh in small assurance of his own life.

The fear of death to a wicked person is of greater force to trouble than the stroke it self.

A fearful man never thinks so well of any man's opinion as he doth of his own conceit, and yet he will be ready to ask counsel upon every trifling cause.

It is a lamentable thing to be old with fear, when a man is but young in years.

It becometh not a Commander in Arms to be a man of a fearful disposition. *Olaus.*

The law of fear was melted in the mould of the love of Christ. *August.*

-It is the property of a wise man, with a quiet mind patiently to bear all things, never dreading more than he needs in adversity, nor fearing things not to be feared in time of prosperity. but those things which he hath, he honestly enjoyeth, those things which he possesseth not, he doth not greatly covet.

It becometh a wise man to be heedful, but not to be fearful, for base fear bringeth double danger. *Vegetius.*

It is requisite for all men to know God, and to live in his fear. But such as worship God for fear lest any harm should happen unto them, are like them that hate Tyrants in their heart, and yet study to please them, because they would in quiet keep that they possess.

Multos

———Multos in summa pericula mifit
Venturi timor ipse mali: fortissimus ille est,
Qui promptus metuenda pati, si comminus instent,
Et differre potest. ———
   ———Nos maximus omnia cogit,
Quæ possunt fieri, facta putare timor.

Of Famine.

Defin. *Famine is a vehement hungry desire of eating, as*
thirst is of drinking, which (as Galen *saith in the*
third Book of Natural Faculties) filleth and choaketh
the stomach with evil and noisome humours, and dissol-
veth and destroyeth the strength thereof it begetteth
loathsomness, and filleth all the body full of outrage-
ous and filthy diseases.

BArren *Scythia* is Famine's Country, and the place
of her abode the steril and fruitless top of mount
Caucafus.

Famine and dearth do thus differ. Dearth is that,
when all thofe things that belong to the life of man,
for example, meat, drink, apparel, lodging, and other
things, are rated at a high price.

Famine is, when all thefe neceffaries before named are not to be got for money, though there be
store of money

God is the efficient caufe of Famine, and fins the
impulfive or forcing caufes, which the holy Scripture
fetteth down to be thefe, Atheifm, Idolatry, Contempt of God's Word, private Gain, Perjury and Oppreffion, Covetoufnefs, Cruelty, Pride, Drunkennefs
and Surfeiting, and neglect of Tithe-paying.

After Famine cometh the Peftilence.

In the time of Famine, Mice, Dogs, Horfes, Affes,
Chaff, Pelts, Hides, Saw-duft, have been ufed for
good fuftenance, and at the laft Man's flefh; yea,
that which is not to be fpoken without trembling, the

Moe-

Mothers have been conſtrained (through hunger) to eat their own children. *Joſeph.*

Whenas *Hannibal* beſieged *Caſilinum,* a City in *Italy ,* in the City, by reaſon of extreme ſcarcity, a Mouſe was ſold for two hundred pieces of money, and yet he that ſold it died for hunger, and the buyer lived. *Plin*

Fate forbiddeth Famine to abide where Plenty dwelleth.

Famine is like to the eating and devouring Ulcer, called the *Eſthiomenus,* called of the Courtiers (who commonly more than others are ſubject thereunto) the Wolf, which ulcerateth the skin, and eateth the fleſh to the very bones.

Famine is more intolerable than the Peſtilence or the Sword : therefore when God gave *David* his choice of theſe three evils, he choſe the Peſtilence, as the eaſieſt to be endured.

Darius, when in flight he had drunk puddle-water, polluted with dead carkaſſes, ſaid, that he never drank any thing more pleaſant. the reaſon was, becauſe he always before uſed to drink e'er he was a-thirſt. *Curtius.*

Artaxerxes, whenas in a certain flight he had nothing to feed on but dry Figs and brown Bread, Good God, quoth he, what pleaſant food have I never taſted of till now !

   Cibi condimentum eſt fames ; potionis ſitis.

   —— *Neque enim Cerere nq e famémque*
Fata coire ſinunt. O vid.

   Fames omnia expugnat.

Of Ruine.

Defin. *Ruine is the overthrow or utter ſubverſion of all manner of eſtates, making glorious things inglorious, and bringing well-ordered ſhapes into a Chaos of all deformity.*

                                    When

WHen Law-breakers are reftored, and judgment cancelled, then every one knoweth that his ruine is at hand, without any hope of fafety

Soldiers get fame by ruine, honour by fcars, and praife by clemency.

Over the greateft beauty hangs the greateft ruine.

A little water cannot quench a great fire, nor a little hope eafe a great mifery.

The beft deferts are commonly ruined by bafe neglects and ill rewarding.

He that hath not tafted misfortune, hath tafted no fortune.

He that fees another man's ruine muft fear his own mifery.

He that hath but one eye muft fear to lofe it ; and he that hath but one vertue muft die e'er he ruine it.

When the heart is environed with oppreffion, then the ears are fhut up from hearing of good counfel.

The ruines of time are the monuments of mortality.

Ruine is a friend to folitarinefs, a foe to company, and heir to defperation

The greateft ruine of the body is nothing to the leaft ruine of the foul.

Ruined hearts live with tears in their eyes, and die with mirth in their looks.

Security puts away ruine, and fear hinders gladnefs.

He that will be reputed valiant, muft let neither chance or grief difmay him.

The ftudy of wifdom is the readieft ruine of grief and vexation.

Many friends affwage many misfortunes.

Counfel in trouble gives fmall comfort, when help is paft remedy.

It is good for a man in the midft of profperity to fear a ruine, and in the midft of adverfity to hope for better fucceedings.

Of

Of all creatures man is the most apt to fall, because being weakest he undertakes the greatest actions.

Prosperity is more hurtful than adversity, in that the one may be more easily born than the other forgotten

Omnia sunt hominum tenui pendentia filo;
   Et subito casu, quæ valuêre, ruunt.
Suis & ipsi Roma viribus ruit. Horace,

Of Fortune.

Defin *Fortune is nothing else but a feigned device of man's spirit, and a mere imagination w.thout truth.*

EXteriour actions are tied to the wings of Fortune. *Plato.*

No man is so perfectly grounded in any degree of estate, but that he may be made subject to chance and alteration of life.

To a man whom fortune doth not favour, diligence can little avail. *Marc. Aurel.*

Fortune hath no power over discretion. *Solon.*

To him that is fortunate every Land is his Country.

There is no greater check to the pride of Fortune, than with a resolute courage to pass over her crosses without care. *S. T. M*

Fortune flies, and if she touch Poverty, it is with her heel, rather disdaining their want with a frown, than envying their wealth with disparagement.

Fortune is so variable, that she never stayeth her wheel, nor ever ceaseth to be turning of the same. *Soc.*

Fortune sheweth her greatness, when such as be of small value are advanced to the possession of mighty things.

The gifts of Fortune are transitory, tied to no time, but the gifts of Nature are permanent, and endure always.

Little

Little advantageth it that the mind be generous, and the body warlike, if he that taketh arms be unfortunate, for the hour of happy fortune is more worth than all the policies of war.

Every man is the workman of his own fortune, and fashioneth her according to his manners. *Socrat.*

He that will live happily, must neither trust to good fortune, nor submit to bad; he must be prepared against all assaults.

The World may make a man unfortunate, but not miserable; that is from himself

Fortune is the only rebellious handmaid against vertue. *Plut.*

Fortune did never shew her self noble, but unto a mind that was generous and noble.

Fortune is constant in nothing but inconstancy *Aurel.*

Fortune is like *Janus*, double faced, as well full of smiles to comfort, as of frowns to discourage.

Fortune ever favours them that are most valiant; and things the more hard, the more haughty *Cicero.*

The changes of Fortune and end of life are always uncertain. *Pacuvius*

Fortune in no worldly things is more uncertain than in war *Olaus*

A valiant man never loseth his reputation, because Fortune faileth him, but because courage dieth in him.

No man is unhappy, but he that esteems himself unhappy, by the base reputation of his courage.

There can be no man more unhappy than he to whom adversity never happened. *Stobæus.*

To be humble in the height of Fortune, stays the deceit of her wheel in turning.

By the excessive gain of wealthy men Fortune was first made a Goddess,

Thou shalt sooner find good Fortune, than keep it.

Fortune is unconstant, and will quickly require again what she hath before bestowed upon thee. *Thales.*

Fortune

Fortune is not fully pacified when she hath once revenged.

That is not thine own which Fortune hath given thee. *Socrat.*

Thou provokest fortune to anger, when thou sayest thou art happy.

Fortune is to great men deceitful, to good men unstable, and to all that are high, unsure.

A happy man shall have more Cousins and Kins folks than ever he had friends either by his Father or Mother's side. *Thales.*

When Fortune cometh suddenly with some present delight and pleasure, it is a token that by her flattering us she hath made ready her snares to catch us *Aur.*

Through Idleness, negligence, and too much trust in Fortune, not only men, but Cities and Kingdoms, have been utterly lost and destroyed.

Fortune delighteth not so much to keep under the vanquished, as to bridle and check the Victors.

Fortune is as brittle as the glass, and when she shineth, then she is broken in pieces.

In great perils it is better that men submit themselves unto reason, than recommend themselves to Fortune.

Fortune is exceeding slippery and cannot be held of any man against her own will.

Fortune is never more deceitful than when she seemeth most to favour.

Fortuna multis dat nimis, satis nulli
  Nulli tam bona est fortuna, de qua non possit queri.
Passibus ambiguis fortuna volubilis errat:
  Et manet in nullo certa tenaxque loco
Sed modo læta manet, vultus modo sumit acerbos,
  Et tantum constans in levitate sua est. *Ovid.*

Of Riches

Defin. *Riches of the Philosophers and Poets are called the goods of* Fortune, *under which are comprehended Plate, Money, Jewels, Lands and possessions in abundance. They are according to their use good or bad: good, if they be well used, bad, if they be abused.*

Riches are good, when the party that possesseth them can tell how to use them.

Riches rightly used breed delight, pleasure, profit and praise, but to him that abuseth them, they procure envy, hatred, dishonour and contempt. *Plaut.*

As the greater we see our shadow, the nearer we draw towards night, so must we fear lest the more that we our selves abound in wealth, the farther off truth and the light estrange themselves from us.

A rich man is either wicked of himself, or heir of a wicked man. *Jer.*

As poverty is not meritorious,—if it be not born with patience: so riches are not hurtful, unless they be abused.

It commonly happeneth that those men which enjoy most wealth are most vexed with the greedy desire of getting more, and mightily molested with fear lest they should lose what they have already gotten. *August.*

If you live by great persons which have not a sense of Religion, the less you take notice of them, the better.

The greatest riches in the world to a good man is his soul and reason, by which he loveth righteousness, and hateth iniquity.

There is no man more willing to become surety for another than he that is in want.

He hath riches sufficient, that needeth neither to flatter nor borrow. *Solon.*

Rich

Rich men without Wifdom and Learning are cal
led fheep with golden fleeces.

The more that a miferable man encreafeth in ri
ches, the more he diminifheth in friends, and aug
menteth the number of his enemies. *Anaxag.*

Rich men have need of many Leffons to inftruct
them to do well. *Philip.*

Rich men through excefs, idlenefs, and delicious
pleafures, are more grofs in conceit than poorer perfons.

Thofe riches are to be defpifed which are loft with
too much liberality, and ruft with niggardly fparing.

Where the rich are honoured, good men are little
regarded.

It worketh great impatience in a rich man to be
fuddenly decayed and faln into poverty.

He hath moft that coveteth leaft.

Great abundance of riches cannot of any man be
both gathered and kept without fin. *Erafmus.*

There be three caufes that chiefly move mens
minds to defire worldly wealth. The one is the love
of riches, eafe, mirth and pleafure. Another is the de
fire of worfhip, honour and glory. The third is the
doubtfulnefs and miftruft of wicked and faithlefs
men, who are too much careful for their own living
here in the world, and think all they can get too
little to fuffice them. *Solon.*

Sufficient is the fure hold which keepeth wife men
from evil works.

Upon a covetous-minded man riches are ill beftow
ed, for he is neither the warmer cloathed, the better
fed, or any thing in fhew the more wealthy for them.

If thou know how to ufe money, it will become thy
handmaid, if not, it will become thy Mafter. *Diod*

Small expences often ufed confume great fubftance
in fhort fpace.

No man is rich by his birth, for all men are born
naked. He

He that delights only in riches, delights in a dangerous pleasure.

Men should live exceeding quiet, if these two words [Mine and Thine] were taken away. *Anaxag.*

It is better to have a man without money, than money without a man. *Themist.*

Plato would have both Plenty and Poverty to be banished his Common wealth the one, because it causeth pleasure, idleness and ambition, the other, because it maketh men aoject, seditious, and given to all filthy lucre

Silver commands Peasants, and Gold controls Princes.

Money is the sinews of war, and the keys to unlock hidden secrets.

Plenty begetteth want, for he that hath much needs much.

O thou insatiable hunger of gold and silver! what is it that thou dost not compel the souls of men to buy and sell? *Tully.*

It is against nature, that we should increase our own riches and substance, with the spoil of other men's wealth.

He that hoardeth up money taketh pains for other men.

It's a rare miracle for money to lack a Master. *Bias.*

As the touch stone trieth gold, so gold trieth the hearts of men.

He is rich that lives content with his Estate

Multa loquor : quidvis nummis præsentibus opta,
Et veniet; clausum possidet arca Jovem.

Difficile est virtutes eum revereri, qui semper secundâ fortunâ sit usus.

Of Change.

Defin. *Change is generally any alteration, either of times, states, studies, opinions, or any other faculty whatsoever.*

THE

THE whole world is nothing but a fhop of change, for riches we exchange poverty, for health ficknefs, for pleafure forrow, for honour contempt; briefly, it is nothing elfe but change, whatfoever chanceth unto us.

There is no change more certain than the change of life to death. *Crates.*

There is no better change, than for a man that hath been lewd to become honeft, and for a woman that hath been as lafcivious as *Lais*, to wax as re pentant as *Magdalen.*

The unftaid and wandering minded man is never wife.

Who changeth peace for War, hath all miferies laid open to his eye, his Goods fpoiled, his Children flain, his Wife ravifhed, his Cattle driven away, briefly, himfelf made moft miferable to behold his unhappinefs.

Change doth avert the good, and erect the bad, prefer the faithlefs, and confound defert.

Change feldom brings better chance, but very of ten worfe.

The day by courfe changeth to night, the night likewife changeth to day, the Summer to Winter, Youth to Age, and Profperity to Adverfity.

Nothing is lighter than the Change of time, nor any thing more certain.

All things by nature, in the univerfe, are fubject to Alteration and Change How much below a man then is it, when any thing doth happen, to be di fturbed, or wonder, as if fome ftrange thing had hap- pened?

Nature by change produceth her increafe

He that by change of fortune mounteth higher than ye fhould, muft arm himfelf with patience, to defcend lower than he would.

Change in all matters, except they be mifchievous, is moft dangerous. *Xenoph.*   Change

Change of honour is envie's mark.

He is no-where that is every-where.

That plant never profpereth that is often removed. *Seneca.*

Change and inconftancy fpring from lightnefs of the mind. *Greg.*

What was done, is done again all things do change, yet under the Cope of heaven there is no new thing. *Sirac*

Every thing holds the name of the place whence it cometh, yet all things feel change howfoever it cometh.

As there is nothing more certain than the change of life, fo there is nothing more uncertain than the time when it will change.

Good things quickly pafs away, and worfe fucceed. *Seneca.*

The pureft thing that is may be changed betwixt evening and morning.

What by deftiny is decreed, man cannot change or prevent.

The change of opinions breeds the change of States, and continual alterations fet forward fubverfions.

Cùm fortuna manet, vultum fervatis, amici :
    Cùm cecidit, turpi vertitis ora fugâ.
Clariffimæ olim urbes nunc nihil funt, quæ nunc maxi-mè fuperbiunt, eandem aliquando fortunam experientur. Demoft.

Of Poverty.

Defin. *Poverty is a tribulation, or want of fuch neceffary things as belong to our lives and eftates, through which we are brought to a mif-hap and mifery.*

AS Kings have honour to countenance their actions, fo poor men have honefty to direct their lives.

Poverty is as glad to creep to credit as dignity, and the humble thoughts that fmoke from a poor

man's

man's cottage are often as fweet a facrifice to the gods as the perfumes in the palace of a Prince.

There is no greater poverty upon a man than to want wifdom, whereby he fhould know how to govern himfelf. *Plato.*

There is no fault in poverty, but their minds that fo think are faulty.

Poverty is a branch of Temperance, and Penury a compendious obfervation of the Laws. *Stobæus.*

If thou wilt live after nature, thou fhalt never be poor, if after thine own opinion, thou fhalt never be rich.

Poverty is the mother of Health.

Poverty is the miftrefs of Philofophy.

The miferable lack of the poor man, and the fuperfluous fubftance of the rich man, move much difcord among the people

A noble mind refufeth no danger, if once he perceiveth himfelf affaulted with poverty.

Poverty caufeth good mens children to be vertuous, fo that they attain to that by vertue which others come unto by riches

Riches are painful to fools, and poverty pleafant to the wife.

He never accounted of profperity, that hath not before been pinched with poverty

He is not poor that hath little, but he that defireth much. *Bias.*

To live poorly and honeftly, is better than to live richly and wickedly.

Poverty is the father of innumerable infirmities.

Adverfity is the trial of the mind, and mif hap the balance of the thought.

Adverfity overcome is the higheft Glory, and willingly undergone, the greateft Vertue.

Poverty is the mother of Ruine.

Neceffity is a fore penance, and extremity is as hard to bear as death.

Need teacheth things unlawful. *Senec.* Poverty

Poverty, Want, Extremity and Misfortune, are all easie to be born, if they be tempered with Content. *Thales.*

To write to our better, is of necessity ; to write to our equal, is of will, to write to our inferiour, is of pure vertue .

The rich doth revenge himself with Arms, the poor with tears. *Guevar.*

It is some comfort in misery, to know the worst of our mis-haps. *S. P. S.*

In adversity rich men should give remedy, and wise men minister comfort by good counsel.

It is a thing very common unto a man afflicted, to seek the company of another in like trouble.

There is no man in so wretched a condition, but he hopeth to grow better . neither is there any man so set aloft, but he may doubt a sudden fall. *Isocrates.*

He ought not to be dismayed, that from a high e-state is descended to a low degree; neither ought he to glory or grow proud, that from a base estate is advanced to promotion.

As riches are the mother of pleasure and delight, so poverty is the nurse of sorrow and calamities.

Want is the enemy to desire.

In all estates a mean must be observed · to live wa-rily increaseth treasure, but to live wastfully causeth poverty. *Protag.*

Poverty is no hindrance to wisdom.

Poor men are shrubs, that by their baseness escape many blasts, when high and tall Cedars are shaken.

Where poor intreat and cannot obtain, there rich men command and will be obeyed. *Sever.*

Mis hap is the true touch-stone of friendship, and adversity the trial of friends.

Happy is that mis hap whereby we pass into greater perfection.

Poverty that contenteth is great riches.

Care

Care not for poverty, fith no man liveth fo bafely as he was born. *Saluft.*

It is given only to a wife man to be content in poverty.

Suffer that with patience which thou canft not avoid, and be not difpleafed at thy poor eftate.

The beggar's crutch ferveth him both to lean upon and to fight withall.

Patiently fhould that be born which no ftrength can overcome, nor counfel avoid · whether it be poverty to pinch the body, or adverfity to crofs the mind.

Poverty poffeffed in fafety, is better than great riches enjoyed with much fear.

When a man is plagued with poverty and ficknefs, both joyned together, without any fuccour or eafement, then rifeth in him an intolerable grief, a fire not able to be quenched, a forrow without remedy, and a tempeft full of wrecks.

Poverty is a vertue of it felf. *Diog.*

He liveth in a moft wretched eftate of beggary that is not endued with many good qualities.

Si ad naturam vivas nunquam eris pauper, fi ad opinionem, nunquam eris dives. Exiguum natura defiderat opinio immenfum. Seneca

———— *O vitæ tuta facultas*
Pauperis, anguftique laris ! O munera nondum
Intellecta Deûm !
Paupertas æquanimiter toleranda eft ; nam fic facientes reddunt ipfam levem.

Of Banifhment.

Defin. *Banifhment is a putting away or driving out of any man, either from the place where he ought and fhould inhabit, or from the place where he took delight and defired to dwell.*

FOR fin was man thruft out of Paradife into the world, therefore his life in it is a banifhment.

No banifhment is fweet, but the banifhment of a righteous foul from the prifon of a world-wearied body. *Stob us.*

Banifhment is there, where no place is for vertue. *Cicero.*

The banifhed man without a houfe to dwell in, is like a coarfe without a grave to reft in.

It is better for a man to be banifhed his country with wife men, than to live there ftill amongft fools.

He that denieth himfelf to his country is in banifhment already.

Wherefoever a man lives well, there is his country. *Cicero.*

A chaft eye exileth licentious looks.

Good fortune attends not every great Eftate, nor evil chance every exiled perfon.

To ftuff thy Coffers with Coin, is to commit thine honour to exile. *Marc. Aurel.*

True happinefs is never had till after death, nor exile welcome but in death.

It is a needlefs queftion to ask a fick man if he be willing to have his health; or an exile if he would be called from banifhment.

Death and banifhment come foon enough, if flow enough.

There is more forrow in lofing a man's own Country, than joy in conquering a world of other Nations. *Themift.*

Sweet is reft after long Pilgrimage, and great is the comfort that a banifhed man takes at tidings of his recalment.

It is the nature of a man to love thofe things deareft which are banifhed fartheft from him

He that in the morning is proud of his poffeffions, may happen ere night to be banifhed from his pleafure.

Beauty

Beauty and youth once baniſhed are never repealed.

The comfort of Fugitives is, that there be many Fugitives.

Care followeth a fugitive perſon, even as a ſhadow follows the body.

Exilium terribile eſt iis quibus quaſi conſcriptus eſt habitandi locus, non iis qui omnem orbem terrarum unam urbem eſſe ducunt. Cicero.

Privari pati iâ magnum malum eſt, ſed majus re quàm ſermone

Of Abſence and Preſence

Defin. *Abſence is the departing or loſs of a friend, or any other object wherein we take delight. and Preſence is the continual company of the party with whom we deſire to be converſant.*

ABſence in love makes true love more firm and conſtant. *Niphus.*

We never know how profitable the preſence of a friend is, until we have felt the want by his abſence for a time.

The abſence of friends is the preſence of griefs. *Bias.*

As contraries are known by contraries; ſo the delight of preſence is known by the evil of abſence.

Man ſeparated from money, is like a ſoul ſeparated from a body.

The grief of unwiſhed abſence is worſe than the wounds of a ſtubborn lance.

A tedious preſence decays love, and a long abſence forgets true familiarity.

Abſence puts off happineſs, and time alters reſolutions.

When thought abſents it ſelf from truth, the ſoul preſents her ſelf to ſin. *Demoſt*

The evils got by abſence Wiſdom cureth.

Take heed of ſpeaking ill of the abſent.

The

The folitary man is either a God or a Beaft.

Life and faith once abfented never return.

The faireft prefence is but a dunghill covered over with white and purple.

Infamy is never abfent from Arrogancy. *Diogenes.*

Men gain their defires by travel, fuftain them by thought, and are abfent from them by annoyance. *Ar.*

The prefence of one day blameth the abfence of another, but the laft fhall give judgment of all that is paft.

The abfence of punifhment is no pardon of tranf-greffions.

Non una eadénique moleftia eft rerum præfentium & abfentium. Eurip.

Diftantia loci non feparat amicitiam, fed operatiorem.

Of Acts.

Defin. Acts are the monumental deeds of our lives, and our actions are the enfigns by which we are known, alfo the perfectnefs of our good and evil living.

ALL the praife of the inward vertue confifteth in the outward action. *Cicero.*

An action without reafon, and a reafon without an action, are both alike imperfect.

Action is the ready entrance into Contemplation.

A filent deed is better than an unprofitable word.

Neither can good words colour a black action, nor bad words deprave a good action

Shape beautifies an image, and good actions commend a man.

Actions are by fo much more manifeft than words, by how much the eyes are furer witnefles than the ears

It is an argument of too much weaknefs, to remember what fhould have been done.

In action a man doth not only benefit himfelf, but profit others. *S. P. S.*

G   Cod

God would never have delivered a foul into the body which hath arms and legs, (only inftruments of action) but becaufe it was intended the mind fhould employ them.

There muft not only be in a man a mind of charity, but alfo diftributing hands. *Amb.*

Action is the matter of vertue and honour.

By the actions of a good man we adjudge always the excellencies of his life.

An imperfect man by one perfect good action gains a liberal name of goodnefs.

Speech is one of the greateft actions which makes manifeft the prudent vertue of the foul.

All new actions feem fair, though they be like a painted woman.

To keep a friend certain is a harder matter than to get a friend. *Ovid.*

Prefumptuous boldnefs is a bafe action in the eyes of thy betters.

So love as thou mayft hate, fo hate as thou mayft love, and both without challenge.

The end of every thing is the trial of the action.

Confcientia benè actæ vitæ, multorúmque benefactorum recordatio, res jucundiffima eft.

Exercitationes virtutum in omni ætate mirificos afferunt fructus

Of Praife.

Defin. *Praife is an exalting, or a lifting up to honour, either the good parts we behold in others, or thofe excellencies with which our eyes (tickl'd by delight) are enamoured.*

There be many that in words are ready to praife that which is good, but few that in works are willing to follow the fame.

It is better to be praifed for true-fpeaking, than to be honoured for flattering and lying.

For

For a man to praise too much his own writings, is nothing else but to give men occasion to speak evil both of him and his works

As it is seemly for a Philosopher and a wealthy man to praise the profits of Peace; even so in his mouth it is uncomely to prate of the perils of War.

Perfect praise and felicity consisteth in a contented life and happy death. *Solon*

Praise-bestowed on an unworthy person is a manifest sign of flattery

Praise is a poison to an ambitious man, for it leadeth him beyond the scope of honesty.

Nothing deserveth commendation unless it be vertuous.

Praise encourageth the spirit to do great and mighty things, and nourisheth true vertue where it is begun.

Commendations make the labour light, the wit studious, and the hope rich.

Three things are commendable in a Scholar, silence in his tongue, diligence in reading, civility in his behaviour.

He which often praiseth one abuseth himself, confirmeth an errour, and proveth in the end a Liar: and he which is praised becometh a great deal more vain. *August.*

Praise is the hire of Vertue *Cicero.*

Too much praise is a burthen.

Amongst all the praises of *Lucullus*, he deserveth most by this answer, I had rather, said he, deliver one *Roman* from the hands of an enemy, than enjoy all the riches of mine adversaries.

Pompey being grown to the height of his fortune, and exalted by many praises and victories, was thus prettily checkt at his departing out of *Athens* : *Quantùm hominem te esse nôsti, eatenus es Deus*

He that praiseth a man openly will not stick to flatter him secretly. *Diog.*

To do good to the poor is a double praise, becaufe a double facrifice, one to God, another to man.

Moft praife-worthy is a good nature that can amend a bad nature.

Vertues beget praife, and praife begets honour and authority.

Nothing is more uncertain than praife: for what one day gives us, another day takes away from us.

It is a greater praife to help the helplefs, than to maintain the needlefs.

The doing what we ought deferves no praife, becaufe it is our duty. *Auguft.*

If another man praife thee, yet remember thou to be thine own judge.

All things that are good have ever the pre-eminence in praife and comparifon.

As the fhadow followeth the body, fo praife followeth vertue. *Seneca.*

To be praifed of evil men is as evil as to be praifed for evil-doing.

Neither praife any thing that is not commendable, neither difpraife that which is praife-worthy.

The praife of our Anceftours is a light to their pofterity. *Saluft.*

When they offered to *Titus* a crown of gold, together with great praifes, for taking *Jerufalem*, he faid that he himfelf was not the author thereof, but God.

Never challenge unto thy felf the praife of another man's inventions *Marc. Aurel.*

He that praifeth any man becaufe he is a Gentleman, praifeth his Parents alfo.

As they which praife unwillingly feem to have but little themfelves: fo they which praife other men flenderly feem defirous to be praifed themfelves. *Juft.*

It is a point of flattery to praife a man to his face.

Be neither too hafty to praife, nor too forward to difcommend any. *Anax.*

There

There is no day so clear, but it hath some clouds; nor' any praise so complete, but it is subject to the scandal of the envious.

Si laus allicere nos ad rectè faciendum non potest, nec metus quidem a fœdissimis factis potest avocare, Cicero.

Laus ubi nova oritur, etiam vetus admittitur.

Laudare sua, & aliena vituperare nemo debet.

Of Aid.

Defin. *Aid generally is any relief or succour chiefly in an extremity, and is the greatest upholder of ability when it is most weak and desperate.*

SOrrow is so hard of belief, that it refuseth all aid, imagining truth to be dreams, and dreams to be truth.

Fatal is the aid that brings us to the ascent of a crown, from whence men come not down, but fall down.

Sorrow makes silence her best aid and her best orator.

The shew of injustice aids and aggravates despight. *Hermes.*

The multitude, which look not into causes, rest satisfied with any thing which is aided by the Laws

Fear casteth too deep, and is ever too wise, if it be not aided by some resolution.

One man is born to help another as far as ability will serve.

To help the weak is charity, and to aid the mighty, presumption *Greg.*

A doubtful-minded man can never endure to be aided by any usual means.

The aid of the spirit is faith, by which a man is delivered from a second death

The grace and law of the Spirit furnished with the aid of God justifieth the wicked, reconcileth the sinfull, and giveth life to the dead.

Wise.

Wisedom and learning are the two chief aids to vertue and good conditions.

Law is the Queen of immortality, and aid the Lord which restores the oppressed.

Wise men are not aided by the Laws of men, but the rules of vertue *Solon.*

Evil aid and unconstant love is like the shadow of a cloud, which vanisheth as soon as it is seen.

Honest assistance is without hurt, without hate, and without penury.

The aid of a friend in law is half an end to the law.

He is rash witted that presumeth too much upon his own power.

God giveth his wrath by weight, and mercy without measure. *Erasmus.*

To try the aid of friends is to prove the hope of fortunes.

He is a monstrous fool that will presume to flie with the aid of waxen wings.

Homo homini, quicunque sit, ob eam ipsam causam quod sit, consulere debet.

Nihil habet alicujus fortuna melius, quàm ut possit, nec natura, quàm ut vellet servare plurimos. Cicero.

Of Mean.

Defin. *Mean is the mediocrity and best part of an action, and must be used in all things : it containeth the full effect of prudence touching government, and tranquillity concerning the Soul.*

T H E difference of good or bad consisteth in mediocrity, or a mean in all things

Curiosity and extremity banished man from the first modesty of his nature in all things.

Nothing too much, nothing too little, preserveth a mean in all things.

The mean estate is the best estate, indifferent equality is the easiest superiority. *Flo*   He

He that ſtarveth for drink by a fountain-ſide hath no means in his miſery.

The mean love is the ſureſt love to love extreme-ly procureth either death or anger.

Of two evils the leaſt is to be choſen, for that is the mean to well chuſing

The more men are threatned, the greater means they ſeek for their ſafety.

Firſt to become a Servant, is the beſt mean to be a Maſter. *Diogenes.*

As ſtorms wither flowers, ſo pride confounds mean callings.

The ſmalleſt hair hath its ſhadow, and the meaneſt eſtate his riſing and down-falling

Fire is never without ſmoke, nor extremity with-out croſſes.

Mountains having too much heat of the Sun, are burnt, Valleys, having too little heat thereof, are barren: but ſuch places as hold a mean are moſt fruitful.

Of all the parts in Muſick the mean is the ſweeteſt.

He that keepeth a mean in his diet ſhall never ſur-feit.

The increaſing of paſſion multiplieth complaints.

Extremity harbours where a mean is not kept.

Mean thoughts excel ambitious deeds

Wiſe men temper their actions to the time, and hold a mean in all matters.

The mean Cottage of a Swain ſtands in more ſafe-ty than the Palace of a Prince

Where there is no mean, there is no order: and where proportion is not kept, there is ſpeedy confu-ſion.

E'er miſchief come, the means to prevent it ought to be provided.

Eſt modus in rebus, ſunt certi denique fines,
Quos ultra citráque nequit conſiſtere rectum.

G 4 Suus

*Suus cuique modus est; tamen magìs offendit· nimium
quàm parum.*

Of Labour.

Defin. *Labour is (or ought to be) the honest recreation
of the mind, and that industrious work-master which
buildeth our knowledge, and makes men absolute by exercise of good letters, and continual travail in the Sciences.*

IT is not freedom to live licentiously, neither is it
liberty to live without labour.

Labour is a mortal enemy to love, and a deadly
foe to fancy.

Great labours require sometimes to be eased with
honest pastimes.

That which is done flowly is never done willingly.

Take good advisement e'er you begin, but the
thing once determined, dispatch it with all diligence.

Labour is a burthen, that man undergoeth with
pleasure. *Cicero.*

A man that doeth all he can do, doeth what he
should do.

By diligent and laborious examination of things
past, we may easily fore-see things to come.

He that endureth labour shall tast the fruit of his
travail.

As nothing mounteth swifter than fire, so nothing
atchieveth sooner than labour.

He that endeavoureth attaineth, he that neglect-
eth, repenteth.

All errours by labour are cured, huge mountains
levelled, and weak wits refined.

The hope of a good reward is a great incourage-
ment to labour.

Immoderate labours do weaken the body, but a
temperate kind of exercise conserveth the same in
health.

As

As the fmeeteft Rofe groweth upon the fharpeft prickles, fo the hardeft labours bring forth the fweeteft profits.

As brightnefs is to reftinefs, fo labour excelleth idlenefs. *Thales.*

No worthy act can be accomplifhed without pain and diligence.

No profit is denied to the painful perfon.

By ufe and labour a man may be brought to a new nature, *Demoft.*

Labour in youth waxeth ftrong with hope of reft in age.

Diligence is the Miftrefs of Learning, without which nothing can either be fpoken or done in this life with commendation, and without which it is altogether impoffible to prove learned, much lefs excellent in any Science.

Erudition gotten by induftry, though it be hard in conceiving, yet once obtained it is feldom forgotten.

Too much diligence breedeth fufpicion.

The God which is immortal doth as it were fell all things unto us for our labour and travel. *Cicero.*

Without care and diligence no eftate can profper.

Thofe ftudies which feem hard and troublefome in youthful years, are made right pleafant refts in old age

There is nothing fo hard but diligence and labour makes it feem eafie. *Virg.*

Nothing caufeth a man more diligently to do his duty, than to think what he would require of him that is a fervant.

As to every ftudious man diligence is the mother, fo negligence is a ftep-dame to all learning. *Boetius.*

There is nothing that fooner maketh a Horfe fat than the watchful eye of his Mafter, nor any thing maketh Land more fertile than the diligent labour of him that oweth the fame.

By

By Dangers, dread and doubtfulneſs, Diligence is greatly hindred ;

> *Qui ſtudet optatam curſu contingere metam,*
> *Multa tulit fecitque puer, ſudavit & alſit.*
>
> *Si quid feceris honeſtum cum labore, labor abit, hone-*
> *ſtum manet · ſi quid turpe cum voluptate, turpitudo ma-*
> *net, voluptas abit.* Cicero.

Of Gladneſs.

Defin. *Gladneſs or pleaſure is properly called that de-*
light which moveth and tickleth our ſenſes, which
quickly ſlideth and ſlippeth away, and for the moſt part
leaveth behind it occaſion rather of repentance, than
calling it again to remembrance!

OUR pleaſures are inductions to our griefs.

Oft hath a Tragick entrance a happy end.

Gladneſs is continually mixt with grief.

Sorrow foregoing gladneſs graceth it.

There is nothing more to be rejoyced at than a good and quiet conſcience, which at the latter day ſhall be a witneſs to juſtifie, and not to condemn us.

The gladneſs of the heart addeth length to our life, but ſorrow of life haſtens death.

Be glad of that day wherein thy tongue hath not miſ-ſaid, and thy heart hath repented of thy ſins

Diſordinate laughter cauſeth death, and violent pleaſures mighty dangers.

All men are glad to ſee their riches increaſe; but few men are diligent to amplifie their vertues. *Cra-tes.*

All worldly gladneſs rideth upon the wing of Time, and but in Heaven no perfect joy is found.

Be not glad of thy enemy's fall, for he that ſitteth fureſt may be overthrown.

It is better to enter the houſe of mourning than the habitation of gladneſs. *Orig*

Sith

Sith, joys are short, take gladness when it comes; for sorrows headlong follow one another.

Pleasures while they flatter a man, they sting him to death.

After the delectation and pleasures of the body, followeth the destruction of the flesh *Mar. Aurel.*

Pleasures unbridled carry a man headlong into all licentious living.

Pleasures bring loss and damage to the party that too much delighteth in them, they create in his mind sorrow, forgetfulness of wisdom and insolency.

The sweet and simple breath of heavenly gladness is the easier to be altered, because it hath not passed through worldly wickedness, nor feelingly found the mischief which evil carrieth with it.

He that is given to pleasure judgeth all things, not according to reason, but according to sense.

Pleasure is the root of all evils, quenching the light of the soul, hindring good counsel, and turning men aside from the way of vertue.

Pleasure is so much more odious, by how much more she hideth her venom under the garment of good liking.

Pleasure is a certain exultation, or an exceeding rejoycing, sprung from the events of things desired.

Pleasure amongst vertues is like a harlot amongst honest women, for by her flattery she destroys man. *Cic.*

Pleasure is of two sorts, the one is of honest and good things, the other of dishonest: in respect of honest things, it is called *voluntas*; in respect of dishonest, it is called *Voluptas.*

The companion of pleasure is pain.

A wise man ought not to be puft up with pleasure; for it is the food of filthiness, it killeth the body, weakeneth the judgment, and taketh away our understanding. *Arist.*

He

He is not worthy the name of a man that spendeth a whole day in pleasure.

Qui minus deliciarum novit in v ta, minùs timet mortem,

　Gaudia principium nostri sunt sæpe doloris
　Gaudia non remanent, sed fugitiva volant.

Of Liberty.

Defin　*Liberty is that freedom and happiness which bringeth the soul to its contentment and satisfaction after the troublous pilgrimages, travails and bondages of this world. Or otherwise, to live as a man lists.*

THrough too much liberty all things run to ruine and confusion　Liberty in the mind is a sign of goodness, in the tongue, of folishness, in the hands, of theft, in our life, of want of grace.

Nothing corrupteth more than liberty, for it maketh the son despise his father, the servant his master, and the citizen his magistrate

He is to be counted free　that serveth no loosness nor infirmity,

No man truly liveth at liberty, but he that liveth vertuously.

The wise man, that hath the reign of his own wit restrained in the hands of his discretion, is only free.

There is a natural discord between Tyranny and Liberty　*Demost.*

He enjoyeth the sweetest liberty that hath a quiet conscience　*Greg.*

Vertue only yieldeth men liberty, sin yieldeth shame and servitude.

If the liberty of the Commons be not restrained, the Common-wealth will be destroyed.

A man's mind may be at perfect liberty, though his body be fettered with irons.

Life

Life loft for liberty is a lofs full of piety.

It is better to live a miferable life being at liberty, than to live a magnificent flave in continual bondage.

Too much liberty is a little bondage, and too great bondage haftens fpeedy liberty.

A conftrained will feeketh every opportunity to flip his head out of the collar.

No man lives happily, if he want the freedom of liberty.

Death ought to be preferred before fervile flavery and bondage.

It is a hard thing to moderate a man much given to liberty, or to put a bridle to wanton affections

He that hath liberty to do more than is necef-fary, will oftentimes do more than is tending to ho-nefty.

Where liberty is given to offend, fin is fo fweet to the flefh, that there is no difference between men and beafts, but that men do exceed beafts in beaftli-nefs.

He is to be thought free that is not bond-flave to iniquity.

Ille mihi non videtur liber cui mulier imperat, cui lex imponit, prǽfcribit, jubet, vetat quod videtur, qui nihil imperanti negare poteft, nihil recufare audet. Si pofcit dandum eft: fi vocat veniendum, fi ejiciat, abeundum. fi minetur, extimefcendum.

Non poteft parvo conftare libertas; hanc fi magno ǽfti-mas, omnia alia parvo ǽftimanda funt.

Of Serving.

Defin. *Serving or fervitude is a certain flavifh bond of conftraint, by which either for commodity or love men bind themfelves to the will of others, making them-felves fubject to controlment.*

T O

TO ferve or to obey well is a great vertue, and proceedeth of Nature; which being good, is upholden by Education.

It is as necessary for him that serveth as for him that commandeth to be honestly-minded.

Servants must be obedient to their Masters, whether they be courteous or froward. *Plato.*

Nature, and the Laws which preserve Nature, bind men that will be servants to strict obedience.

The servants of Wisdom are the righteous of the Church, and their off spring is obedient.

Servants ought with patience to bear the corrections of their Masters *Chilo*

A crafty Servant ruleth his Master.

The bondage of a wise man is liberty. *Aug.*

The servant that dutifully honoureth his Master shall in time to come find love and obedience in his own houshold.

The only fruit of service is love and reward, and the pleasure thereof humility and obedience.

The first duty in a Servant is willingness to learn whatsoever is necessary; the second faithfulness, in performing truly whatsoever belongeth to his duty, the third carefulness, in seeking all honest means to profit his Master; the fourth silence in tongue, in not replying against his Master's speeches.

There ought to be in a servant double silence: the one in not replying, or contradicting, the other in not revealing abroad what his Master doth at home.

Servants ought not to obey with eye-service only, but also with singleness of heart.

It is a most commendable vertue in a Servant to know how to obey well.

A Servant once made malapert and sawcy will always after kick at his duty, and scorn the controlment of his Master. *Aug.*

Look

Look what kind of service a Servant doth unto his Master, the like shall surely be required when he keepeth Servants himself

Honest and gentle Masters have commonly proud and stubborn Servants, whereas a Master sturdy and fierce is able with a little wink to command more duty than the other shall with many words. *Aurel.*

Princes must be served both with life and goods, and that is the personal service of every natural subject.

All men must be subject to Principalities.

Men are bound to obey Magistrates, although they command things contrary to publick profit, except it be in such things as are contrary to the laws of God.

Serving justly is a seal of obedience, and a testimony of an upright conscience. *Chrys.*

Tyrants are termed the scourges of God.

It is treason against God and man for the Servant to offer violence to his Master, but most damnable for a Subject to touch the Lord's Anointed.

Nihil est fœdius servitute. ad decus & libertatem nati sumus. Cicero.

Si miserum est servire, multò miserius est servire iis quos non possis effugere.

Of Obedience.

Defin. *Obedience is the end whereunto vertue tendeth;*
namely, when in all our actions we observe honesty and
comeliness: it is that which bindeth, the soul, when
fully and willingly, without force and constraint, we
give to every one that which belongeth unto him; ho-
nour to whom honour, reverence to whom reverence,
tribute to whom tribute, and succour to whom succour
belongeth.

Obedience sheweth our nature, Rebellion our corrupt nature.

That

That Common-weal is always happy, where the Subjects are obedient, and the Magistrates merciful.

Wicked men obey for fear, but the good for love. *Aristotle.*

Servants in word and deed owe dutiful obedience unto their bodily masters.

Where reason ruleth, appetite obeyeth.

Nothing thriveth by strife and contention, but all things flourish through love and obedience.

Disobedience proceedeth from negligence: for he that governeth well shall be obeyed well, but he that giveth to his servants too much liberty shall be sure to have too much loss. *Theopompus.*

They commonly prove the best masters that have been the most obedient servants.

The obedience of the Law is the maintenance of the Law.

Treason hath no place where obedience holds principality. *Plato.*

Whosoever obeyeth his superiour instructeth his inferiour. *Cicero.*

It is a certain and infallible observation, that the son, who hath irreverently and disobediently dishonoured his father, is in his old age plagued by his own posterity *Aurel*

The humble and obedient gain honour, but the stubborn and obstinate, reproof.

The more obedient a man is, the more favour he purchaseth.

The blessedness of a Common-wealth is the obedience of Citizens. *Stobæus.*

Only obedience enjoyeth the merit of faith. *Bern.*

Obedience is the badge of devotion, the seal of contemplation, the safeguard of the penitent, and the School of the ignorant.

To obey the Law, is to fulfill the Law.

The will obedient to reason never strayeth; but

where men break all bonds of duty, there follow all
forts of plagues and punishments. *Justinian*

Obedience is a vertue due to God and Man ; to God
as our Creator, to man as our Superiour. *Bern.*

Where reason ruleth, appetite obeyeth

That Country is well kept, where the Prince knoweth how to govern, and the people how to obey.

The King himself is supreme head of all other authority, and obeyeth no man, but the Law only.

If thou vanquish thy parents with sufferance, thou
shalt surely be bleft for such obedience.

He obeyeth infinites that is a bond-flave to his lufts.
Crates.

Qui benè ducit, efficit ut rectè eum is quos ducit fe-
quantur.

Flectitur obsequio curvatus ab arbore ramus :
Franges, fi vires experiare tuas.

Of Opinion.

Defin. *Opinion is the rule of the mind, containing our*
woe, or pleafure : it is born of the mind, nurft with
unreft, and brought up only with imagination.

Opinion makes men arm themselves one against
another.

Opinion is one of the greatest pillars which uphold
Common-wealths, and the greatest mischief to overthrow them. *Pont.*

Opinion proceeding from a firm difcourse of reafon, purged from vanity, is perfect judgment.

Opinion never judgeth rightly of any thing as it is
indeed, but only as it feemeth to be

Opinion living in hope, pines in prefent, and lacketh whatever it hath.

Opinion is the torment of the mind, and the deftruction of the body, vainly promifing that reft
which could never be enjoyed.

Opinion draws on the ambitious with a vain conceit of immortality, making poffible impoffibility

The

The variety of opinions among the Learned begets both doubtfulnefs and fear in the ignorant. *Theophr*

The opinions of Judges have heapt fuits one upon another, and made them immortal.

By opinions chiefly is the majefty, and integrity of ancient Juftice loft. *Crates.*

All fedition fprings from opinion; and all fedition is evil, how honeft foever the ground be pretended.

Opinion is the original of difobedience, and difobedience is the beginning of fury.

The ground of the *Roman* civil wars was the diverfity of opinions betwixt the Nobility and the Senate.

The ftrength of falfe opinion is of fuch force, that it overthroweth the love betwixt man and wife, betwixt father and child, betwixt friend and friend, and betwixt mafter and fervant. *Demoft.*

To know the caufe of falfe opinions is the only mean to break the ftrength, and root out the force of falfe opinions.

Profit, Honour, Lofs and Difhonour are four caufes of disjoyned opinions.

Great opinions alter not at one inftant, but lofe their ftrength by degrees, by little and little, except they be violent.

Diffimilitude, being a diverfity of opinions in Religion is the caufe of Civil War.

The diverfity of opinions in Subjefts is very dangerous to Eftates and Sovereigns. *Phocion*

It is impoffible for any head to maintain an opinion contrary to the members.

Amongft men that are honeft and upright in life, and live contented with their calling, there never happeneth diverfity of opinions, nor Civil Wars for Religion.

Gravior & validior eft decem virorum fententia, quàm totius multitudinis imperitia Cicero.

Vereor de viris doctis judicare, nè quorum opinionem improbo, illos videar improbâffe. Of

Of Credulity.

Defin. Credulity is a certain ground and unfeigned trust which we repose in the object propounded to our imaginations: it is also the destruction of doubt, and an animater of us to those actions which we credit to be honest.

SO many men, so many minds, and so many minds, so many beliefs.

Credit is a constant trust in such things as are spoken or covenanted.

Credit is a figure of faith, or that which faith it self is, and is breathed by the Spirit of God into the godly. *Beza.*

Credit or faith consisteth above all things in prayer and meditation.

True belief breedeth constancy in prosperity, and patience in time of affliction.

A good life cannot be separated from a good belief. *August.*

Belief fails where God's truth stands uncertain.

The way to increase credit is first to have credit.

The fruit of belief is made manifest by the love we bear to our Neighbours, and by our patience in time of trial

True belief justifieth, and that justification is our Redemption.

Credulous belief knitteth together the joints of a Common-wealth.

The mean which constitutes Common-wealths preserves them. faith first constituted them, therefore faith upholds them.

No man believeth willingly more than he himself liketh. *Chrysost.*

No Gold is so precious as a faithful friend, whom a man may boldly credit.

Mens credit should be better than debts, for faith should exceed Oaths.   Slow

Slow belief is the handmaid of Wifdom. *S. P. S.*

Unexercifed credit is fickly, and unknown things are unadmitted.

Faith built upon any thing but divinity is dead faith, and like a frame that hath no fubftance or continuation.

From faith comes fear, from fear hate of fin, and from hate of fin everlafting falvation

In the greateft danger the greateft credit is beft deferved.

Truth is the daughter of time, and guide to all goodnefs.

He that through cuftom makes little account of his promife, may fwear often, but fhall feldom be believed

Cuftom without credit is no better to be accounted of than old Errour

Credulity is the only advantage of honeft hearts. *S. P S.*

It is as great a fault to believe every one, as to truft none. *Seneca.*

True faith in God maketh innumerable ftrong Champions, and invincible ftomachs, not only towards death, but alfo againft all the moft cruel devices that can be found to make death (if it were poffible) more painful than death. *Boetius.*

Credit is of greater worth than friendfhip, and friendfhip as worthy as may be.

Non patitur ludum fama. fides, oculus.
Non holocaufta Deus, fed corda fidelia quærit:
Hæc qui dona gerit, lege beatus erit.

Of Secrecy.

Defin. *Secrecy is a faithful humour, which ftrengthned by vertue concealeth in defpight of misfortune thofe things which one knoweth may either profit his enemy, or prejudice his friend or Country.*

H E

HE that knows not when to hold his peace, knows not when to speak

Gold boileth best when it is least bubbleth; and a flame preffed down inforceth the fire to fmother. *Pacuvius.*

Love that is kept in fecret confumes in forrows: and the flames of fancy raked up in filence will both fire the fenfes and fhrink the finews.

He beareth his mifery beft that hideth it moft *Arch.*

As filence is a gift without peril, and containeth in it many good things fo it were better our filence brought our fimplicity into fufpicion, than to fpeak either inconveniently, idlely, or unneceffarily.

Thofe things which are untold are undone: for there can be no greater comfort than to know much, nor any lefs labour than to fay nothing.

Venus's Temple is never fhut, *Cupid's* Regifter lies ever unfolded; and the fecrets of love, if they be concealed, breed either danger by filence, or death by fecrecy.

Better it is by fpeaking little to make a fmall fcar, than a deep wound by much babbling

Silence is a gift without peril, and a treafure with-out enemies. *Phocion.*

Women are fitter to conceive children than to con-ceal fecrets.

By mif-fpending treafures we lofe wealth; by dif-covering fecrets, honour and life.

That which thou wouldeft few fhould know, keep fecret to thy felf.

Silence is more fafe than fpeech when our enemies be the Auditours. *Saluft.*

In fome place, at fame time, and in fome company, it is better to be filent than talkative

Wine defcending into the body caufeth words to afcend.

In some cases silence is dangerous: and if any know of Conspiracies against their Country or King, or any thing that might greatly prejudice their Neighbour, they ought to discover it.

As we must render account for every idle word, so must we likewise for our idle silence.   *Ambrose.*

Quærit aquas in aquis, & poma fugacia captat
  Tantalus; hoc illi garrula lingua dedit.
Nonunquam tacuisse nocet, nocet esse loquutum.
Arcana scrutanda non sunt, nec commissa effutienda.

Of Oaths

Defin. *An Oath is a perswasion or calling God to witness that our assertions are just, true and honest. And of Oaths, some be lawful, some unlawful: The lawful Oath is that which is taken before Authority, the Oath unlawful is that which is vainly, and without occasion, uttered.*

THE Oath which is honest is a proof of fidelity, the violation whereof is impiety.

An Oath is the foundation of Justice, and the truth of incertainty.

It is better for a man never to take God to witness, than to forswear himself in mockery.   *Lact.*

Oaths do not credit men, but men their Oaths *Sophocles.*

It becometh a man to keep inviolate the Oath which he maketh to his adversaries, although mishap cause him to yield unto it.

Through neglect of keeping our Oaths, we stain our souls with lying

The greatest fault that can be in a Prince is Perjury

God's Oath is the confirmation of his promise. *Aug.*

The bare word of a Prince ought to stand as an Oath in Law, and his Faith as firm as an Oracle

To

To swear and forswear is a vice so hateful, that Slaves themselves judge it worthy of punishment. *Periander*

He is unwise that putteth any confidence in the promise of a common swearer.

He that accustometh his mouth to many oaths, procureth unto himself many plagues for a punishment. *Sigismundus.*

As it is not necessary to credit the oath of an infidel; so it is not lawful for a Christian to break his vow, although it be made to a Saracen.

Traitours bewitched with perjury fear not to betray themselves, so they may betray others.

He that layeth his faith in pawn bindeth his safety, his honour, and his soul also.

Where faith is taken from oath, justice is ruined, love wounded, and society confounded. *Niphus.*

God in his justice chastens perjury, even from the cradle to the grave.

Favour gotten by perjury is honour won by infamy.

Sin is punished with repentance, but perjury with damnation. *Quint.*

Vertue is never in that mouth where lavish oaths are resident.

Scarcity of oaths is a most blessed Scarcity.

The oaths uttered in fury, in calms are repented with tears

Wicked mens oaths are written in water *Stobæus.*

Faith gives no honour to any oath; yet oaths broken dishonour faith.

Faith is the devotion of the soul, and the redemption of the same. *Jerome*

Wise men think more than they speak: and to swear is the least part of their knowledge.

Solon tantam morum probitatem messe hominibus oportere dicebat, ut non opus esset ligare juramento.

Lycurgus

Lycurgus eatenus amicis & familiaribus auxiliandum
esse dicebat, ut interim perjurium non admitteretur.

Of Doubt.

Defin. *Doubts are any uncertain or irresolute opinions of*
things, whereby the mind is altogether unsatisfied and
perplexed.

DOubt being a frenzy of the soul, labouring to attain the truth, confounds it self in it self.

The hurts are boundless which come by doubts
and uncertainties.

To rest doubtful in Religion is worthy certainly of
high punishment.

There is nothing more troublesome than doubtful thoughts. *Archim.*

Ignorance is the mother of doubts, and doubt the
mother of irreligious opinions.

Doubt is contrary to faith, and whatsoever is contrary to faith is clean contrary to salvation.

Doubt proceeds from ignorance, and ignorance
comes from brutishness, and brutishness from want of
vertue or wisdom.

As doubts declare men to be base-minded, so courage and resolution erect a Prince.

The Scriptures are sufficient to dissolve all doubts
in Religion, and not to believe them, is to perish by
them.

By over-much trust in a man's own wit the greatest doubts are commonly conceived.

Doubtful presumptions prove certain confusions.

Love is careful, and misfortunes are subject to
doubtfulness. *S P. S*

Want of wit breeds doubt, and doubt leaves good
things unfinished.

Doubtful and melancholick minds are cheared with
musick, but wise men with resolution.

He

; He of neceſſity muſt err, that of force muſt be doubtful.

There is no greater ſhame than for a man to be reſolute in worldly actions, and yet wavering and doubtful in the chief points of his Religion.

He is worthy to live always in doubt, who doubts what no man elſe doubts, but he himſelf only.

To doubt or miſtruſt a man for his well-meaning, is the very next way to cauſe him to change his mind into falſe dealing. *Bias*

There is great doubt of that man's wiſdom which is too much ruled by the will of a woman. *Marc. Aurel.*

To live in doubt is to live in torment

He that doubteth every certainty, and admireth every trifle, ſhall ſooner be laughed at for his folly, than commended for his diſcretion *Bias.*

He that doubteth of that thing which he ſeeketh, ſhall never know when to find that which he lacketh.

Whatſoever is well done is adviſedly done, but whatſoever is ill, is doubtful.

Doubts chaſe away friends, ſtrengthen enemies, and ſlander all men

The beginning of errour is doubt, dreaming that our affects agree with the heavens.

Doubts are not overcome with violence, but with reaſon and underſtanding.

When doubts are known to be doubts, reſolution is better eſteemed.

Qui dutitat, neganti eſt proximus.

Dubitatio cogitationem ſignificat injuriæ.

Of Denial.

Defin. *Denial is a refuſal of any thing propounded, or an Apoſtate back-falling from a thing formerly affirmed, known, or taken.*

H   TO

TO deny principles is to deny truths ; and to deny truths is herefie.

To deny what we fear to defire, is to difprove our own beliefs.

It is hard to deny to mourn, when nature commands us to weep.

Vertue rather denies wealth, than to enjoy it by evil means.

Clouds cannot cover fecrecies, nor denials conceal truth. *Demoft.*

To deny the knot of marriage, is to break the bond of falvation.

The ftrength of thunder overthrows high Towers, and the back-fliding of Apoftates confounds fouls.

He that denies compaffion to the penitent, fhall find fmall favour, when he himfelf asketh forgivenefs.

Counfel confounds doubts, and diffolves falfe denials.

Denials make little faults great, and truth makes great faults indifferent

The denial of truth is a ficknefs of the foul, which can never be cured but by the fhame of reafon. *Herm.*

He which by denial hath falfified his oath fhall hardly after recover his credit.

There cannot be a greater folly, than to truft him that will deny the truth for advantage or promotion.

He getteth no profit that denieth the truth in hope of reward.

Wife men efteem many words and many lyes both alike.

He that will inftruct others in the truth, muft never deny the truth himfelf.

Common liars need more than common wits, elfe will their Tales be found double.

He that lyeth, bearing the countenance of an honeft man, by his outward fhew of honefty fooner deceiveth the ignorant, than many other which feem unhoneft.   He

He that dares presume to make a lye unto his Prince, will not spare to deny the truth before a meaner Magistrate. *Tho. Aquin.*

To boast the denial of truth is more worthy punishment, than to tell lyes.

Believe not him which to day telleth thee a lye of another body, for he will not stick to morrow to tell a lye of thee to another man.

There is no greater sign of wickedness than open heresie

He that obstinately denieth the truth before men upon earth, wilfully refuseth the soul's health in heaven.

He which denies the motions of the flesh, makes good the Divinity of the spirit.

To keep company with a notorious Lyar, is a means to make thy self suspected, when thou tellest the truth.

The man that through use and custom denieth truth, and doth as it were, make an occupation of lying, shutteth himself out from the company and presence of God, loseth his good name and credit amongst men, and most horribly joyns himself to the Devil, yielding all his endeavours to the furtherance of infernal service

Contra negantem principia non est disputandum.

Qui semel à veritate deflexit, hic non maiore religione ad perjurium quàm ad mendacium perduci consuevit.

Of Repetition.

Defin. *Repetition is a repeating or rehearsing again of things past, being either forgotten, or needful for present use or commodity : it is also an upbraiding of good turns, or a wearisome tediousness*

TO repeat offences is to make the committer ashamed of his faults.

Often to repeat one thing is wearisome to the hearer, and troublesome to the teller.

Though

Though the hearing of our fins repeated be bitter, yet the perfwafion of amendment is fweet.

Continually to upbraid men with their mifdoing is the next way to make them become defperate.

God himfelf ufeth to threaten us oftener than to fmite us. *Aug.*

Things oft repeated in memory make the memory more perfect

As it is neceffary to fmite the iron being hot; fo it is needful to repeat in private our own fins, before they prove odious

To repeat offences with penitence is a likelihood of amendment.

There can be nothing fo plainly repeated but it may be miftaken. *Terence.*

A wife man will not have one fin twice repeated unto him

Vain repetition is an accufation of dulnefs.

To repeat one thing often, being needlefs, is a fign of a flender capacity.

It is requifite to know men's natures before we repeat their difgraces.

Time is the repeater of all things.

He which maketh repetition of his deceit deferves to be intangled by deceits.

It is the property of fools and children often to repeat prophecies.

Though it be a fault general for all men to fin, yet very few can endure to hear their fins repeated.

The things that be moft fcant to be gotten are moft dear of price, and things feldom fpoken of are moft defired. *Plato.*

The beft garments grow old with often wearing, and ftrange reports wax ftale with too much telling.

Walls are faid to have ears, when needlefs repetition hath too much tongue.

The

The often repeating of our faults to our selves in private causeth more care in our actions publick.

We must be content to hear what we would not, when we forget our selves, and do that which we should not.

Good examples cannot too often be repeated, if we purpose to profit by them.

The often repeating of an injury received, makes manifest that the fact is not freely forgiven.

Write injuries in dust, but courtesies in marble.

It is more commendation for a man to be silent, than to make repetition of his good deeds performed. *Aur.*

Too much of any thing changeth the nature of every thing, *Terence.*

Fire were not to be counted fire, if it wanted heat; nor vertue to be known without repetition.

Qui vetera argumenta verbis nihil mutatis repetunt, auditores fastidio enecant.

Non unum hodie, cras aliud, semper idem.

Of Offence.

Defin. *Offence is an injury or indignity offered either in speech or act, whereby either life or reputation is called into hazard, making the world in doubt of their vertue.*

UNjust offences may escape for a time without danger, but never without revenge.

It were better for a man openly to be hurt with his enemy's sword, than secretly to be wounded with evil speeches. *Thal.*

Of little medling comes much rest, and of licentious talk oft-times ensueth much unquietness.

There is no sufficient recompence for an unjust slander.

A fault once excused is twice committed.

A false report is a wilful Lye.

Light heads and sharp wits are most apt to invent smooth Lyes.

When

When the tongue babbles fondly, it is a token that the heart abounds with foolishness.

As a Traitour that clippeth the coin of his Prince maketh it lighter to be weighed, but never the worse to be touched: so he that by sinister reports seemeth to impair the credit of his friend may make him lighter among the common sort, who by weight are oft-times deceived, but nothing impaireth his good name with the wise, who try all gold by the touch stone.

If thou speak what thou wilt, thou shalt hear what thou wouldst not. *Bias.*

The greatest barkers are not always the greatest biters as it is far easier with words to obtain the victory, than with deeds to attain the conquest.

To a vertuous mind an injurious word doth more hurt than the wound of a sword.

In the body of a man, the most necessary member is the heart, the goodliest instruments are the eyes, the parts most delicate are the ears, and the thing wherein most danger is, is the tongue. *Thales.*

Nature teacheth us to speak well, but wisdom teacheth us to speak in a fit time. *Epimenides* the Painter, after his return from *Asia*, being inquired of news, answered I stand here to sell pictures, not tell tidings.

There is no better Philosophy, than for a man to learn silence.

The *Lycaonians* had a Law, that if any stranger should enter into discourse with the Mistress of the house, he should for his offence have his tongue cut out.

The authors of offences and injuries are Liars. *Plot.*

Amongst the *Romans* it was held a great infamy for a man to praise the good wife of the house.

The eyes, hands and feet, ought not so soon to be subject to the penalty of the Law as the tongue, because they are members for common use, but the tongue is the instrument of vanity and villainy.

Where

Where there is any hope of amends to be looked for, there the first offence deserves pardon. *Portan.*

A small offence being renewed doth work some grievous displeasure in the end to the committer thereof.

The offender feareth the Law, but the innocent feareth fortune. *Boetius.*

Where offences of the best are never pardoned, the worst will amend for fear of extreme punishment.

Nihil est tam insigne, nec tam ad diuturnitatis memoriam stabile, quàm id in quo aliquem offenderis Cic

Nulla mala potentia est, in quam non irruat injuria Seneca.

Of Accusation.

Defin. *Accusation is the attainture or challenge of any party in a doubtful matter, and may be employed both in good and evil part, sometimes proceeding from an honest passionate zeal, and sometimes from the effects of farther malice.*

H E that accuseth another must look that he be not guilty of the same fault himself. *Salust.*

Spies and Accusers are necessary evils in a Common-wealth.

Perfect vertue terrifieth an accuser, indifferent vertue whets him on.

Whosoever presently gives credit to accusation, is either wicked himself, or very childish in discretion.

Things grown full grow out of frame; and accusation being at the highest either resteth or declineth.

Great accusations have hard beginnings, both through their own debates and their inventers.

If greatness could keep what it gets, it should never be accused of infortunes. *Olaus.*

We justly accuse him of prodigality, that spends in one day what should serve for two.

Other mens sins accuse our Consciences of frailty.

Ambi-

Ambitious men, raised once to dignity, accuse afterward all other estates of insufficiency. *Bod.*

Youthful counsel, private gain, and particular hate, accuse Kingdoms of short continuance.

Wars pretending publick good, done for spight, work most injustice, for they bend their accusations against the mightiest persons.

Flattery, the nurse of vice, is the mother of false accusations, but zeal, of just appeals.

Kings, because they can do most, are in accusation the worst, though they run into ills by compulsion.

Great men too much graced use rigour, and accuse humility of dulness.

He that accuseth himself is a just man. *Chrysost.*

Good must not be drawn from Kings by force, nor accusation by threats.

Fools weep when great men are accused, as pitying the fall of honour.

He that accuseth himself, and afterward answereth not, tempteth God. *August.*

General calamity accuseth Princes of general imbecillity.

When great men are accused and condemned, guilty Vassals are hopeless and desperate.

No man may be both the accuser and judge. *Plut.*

Princes endangered seek their peace by any means. and private persons injured seek revenge many times by false accusation.

The greatest wrongs that ever were effected were then performed, when Princes feared to fall by surmise or accusation.

The accused is not guilty until he be convicted. *Lactan.*

Ex defendendo, quàm ex accusando, uberior gloria comparatur. Cicero

Accusator nocere, monitor prodesse reprehendendo studet.

Of Slander.

Defin. *Slander is a part of envy, and every whit as vile*
and dangerous · it is the superfluity of a cankered heart,
which enraged with choler, after an injury received, or
after some report thereof, wanting other means of re-
venge, doth with slanderous and reproachful speeches
give testimony of his hate and malice.

F'Oul-mouthed Detraction is his neighbour's foe.
    The mouth of a slanderer calleth all things into
question, and approveth nothing.

We kill hurtful Vipers, if we spie them ; but we
nourish slanderers till they kill us.

As Rats and Mice eat and gnar upon other mens
meat, so the slanderer eateth and gnaweth upon the
life and flesh of other men.

A tale unaptly told may be depraved.

He that hurteth his neighbour by his tongue,
woundeth his own soul by his words.

They that speak evil and slander the dead are like
envious dogs, which bite and bark at stones *Zeno.*

The corrupt heart breaketh out by the leud tongue;
and such as speak evil of all men are monsters among
good men.

Whosoever useth to listen much to mis-reports, deserveth either to lose his hearing, or his ears *Pub.*

A common slanderer striving to bring other men
into hate, becomes odious himself

Believe not every report, neither be thou moved
by vain suggestions, lest through light trust thou lose
friends, or, which is more bad, be counted a fool.

There are three sorts of Man slayers; they which
kill, they which hate, and they which detract.

Itching ears do swallow many wrongs

He that trusteth to leud tongues is either swoln
with hate, plagued with envy, consumed with thought,
endangered by revenge, or lost in hope.

Nature

Nature hath given us two ears, two eyes, and but one tongue, to the end we should hear and see more than we speak. *Socrat.*

Though the tongue be but a small member, yet it many times doth more hurt than the whole body besides.

Keep thy tongue, and keep thy friend, for few words cover much folly, and a fool being silent is thought wise.

Diversity of meats hurt digestions, and changeableness of reports begetteth slander.

Long promises are figures of cruelty, and large slanders the signs of great envy.

Slander offends the living, and gnaws upon the dead.

The slanderer doth unjustly accuse, and ought to be punished in the same sort as the party accused should have been, if the accusation had been found true

Slanderers in ancient times have been marked in the forehead with a hot iron.

Apelles, after he had escaped a false slander, thus by his art described her in a Table painted, He pictured a Judge with the ears of an Ass, having on the one side two Ladies, Ignorance and Suspicion; before him false Accusation with a countenance full of fury, holding in the left hand a burning Torch, and with his right hand pulling a young man by the hair, who lifted up his eyes and hands to heaven, near unto him was a man looking pale, earthly, and asquint, which was Envy; two Damsels followed false Accusation, named Treason and Deceit, behind whom stood a Lady wailing and mourning, called Repentance, which fastened her eyes upon a very fair Lady called Truth declaring by this, that we ought not lightly to believe every accusation and slander that is brought unto us.

' *Aut in infamia, vulneribus aut morte, desinet calumnia.*

Detractor uno verbo tres simul jugulat homines : seip-sum, auscultantem, & eum cui detrahit.   Of

Of Scoffing.

Defin. Quips, or Scoffs, are depraving from the actions of other men, they are the overflowing of wit, and the superfluous scums of conceit.

TO play the scoffing fool well, is a sign of some wit, but no wisdom.

All kind of mockery ought to be shunned, which is a reproach covered with some fault, and which accustometh the mocker to rail and lye, and moveth more than an injury, when it proceedeth from a will to outrage and malice without necessity.

An Adder keeps his venome in his tail, but the poison of a scoffer is in his tongue.

What is sweet in the mouth is bitter in the stomach: and scoffs pleasant to the ear are harsh to the best understanding.

A fault wilfully committed by scoffing can scarce be amended by repentance.

He that mocks a wife man with flattery mocks him with insufficiency.

Scoffs have not reward, but disdain; nor praise, but ill employment.

Good and evil follow one another, so do scoffs and hateful estimation.

The least man can do some hurt, and the absurdest tongue can disparage.

He that most scoffs, shall be most scoffed at for his reward.

To jest is tolerable; but to do harm by jest is insufferable. *Bias.*

It is better to do well than to speak well, but easier to reprehend than to amend.

There are more mockers than well-meaners, and more foolish quips than good precepts.

Mocking is an artificial injury.

The

The faireſt beauty may prove faulty, and the wit-tieſt ſcoff ridiculous.

It is better to have an open enemy, than à private ſcoffing friend.

It is better to be born fooliſh, than to imploy wit unwiſely

The loſs that is ſuſtained with modeſty, is better than the gain that is gotten with impudence.

It is good to hold an Aſs by the bridle, and a ſcoffing fool at his wit's end

To be accounted a Nobleman's Jeſter, is to be a mercenary fool. *B as.*

He that makes an ordinary uſe of ſcoffing ſhall never be well thought of in his life, nor find happineſs at his death.

Qui pergit quæ vult dicere, quæ non vult audiet.
Prava necat morſu ſpatioſum vipera Taurum.
A cane non magno ſæpe tenetur aper.

Of Phyſick.

Defin. *Phyſick, is that natural Philoſophy which tendeth to the knowledge of man, and thoſe cauſes which concern the health and good eſtate of his body.*

PHyſick is a continual fountain or ſpring of knowledge, by which we maintain long life.

The ſick man deſireth not an eloquent Phyſician, but a skilful *Seneca.*

We begin to be ſick as ſoon as we be born. *Auguſt.*

The infirmity of the body is the ſobriety of the mind.

The ſtrength of the body is the weakneſs of the mind, and the weakneſs of the body the ſtrength of the ſoul.

Delicate fare is the mother of ſickneſs.

Phyſick rightly applied is the repairer of health, and the reſtitution of a weak or decayed nature.

Next

Next unto the glory of God, we ought to regard the profit of the Common-wealth, and then Philofophy, which is Phyſick, nothing being more commodious.

Phyſick, being rightly uſed, is an art to find out the truth both of divine and humane beginnings.

The ſcope of Phyſick is to glorifie God in the works of nature, teaching men to live well, and to help their neighbours.

A pratling Phyſician is another diſeaſe to a ſick man.

An Oratour doth not always perſwade, nor the Phyſician cure   *Ariſt.*

To know the uſe of Phyſick is ſweet, but to taſte it is unſavory.

It is requiſite that he be tormented with pain, which will not be eaſed by Phyſick.

Death holdeth a ſword againſt our throats, and Phyſick a preſervative of health to our hearts.

Death is moſt deſired of them that be miſerable, and Phyſick moſt eſteemed of them that be mighty.

They that be found themſelves are more ready in counſel than skilful in knowledge, to preſcribe rules of Phyſick to the ſick. *Bias.*

As a blind man cannot ſee the fault of another's eyes, ſo an unskilful Phyſician cannot perceive the defects of the body.

- To take Phyſick, when the diſeaſe is deſperate, is to deſire the Phyſician to help to conſume our ſubſtance.

Medicines be not meat to live by.

The Patient unruly maketh the Phyſician more cruel.

The thief is commonly executed that killeth but one man, and the Phyſician ſcapeth that killeth a thouſand.

Phyſicians oftentimes do uſe under the ſhew of honey to give their Patients gall, and by this means preſerve their health. whereas if they went plainly to work, the fick would never take that which were wholefome, if not toothfome.

The number of Phyficians is the increafing of difeafes.

Great variety of Medicines do no good at all to a weak ftomach.

Some have compared thofe which ufe often to take phyfick, to them which drive the Burgeffes out of the City, to place ftrangers in their room.

Hippocrates, above all other things, recommendeth to a Phyfician, that he fhould well advife himfelf, if in plagues and extraordinary difeafes be found nothing which was divine, that is to fay, whether the hand of God were not the proper caufe of the ficknefs of the party difeafed.

Phyficians are happy men, becaufe the Sun makes manifeft what good fuccefs foever happeneth in their cures, and the earth burieth what faults foever they commit. *Nicocles.*

Ægri quia non omnes convalefcunt, non idcirco nulla medicina eft. Cicero.

Dat Galenus opes, dat Juftinianus honores.

Ex aliis paleas, ex iftis collige grana.

Of Pain.

Defin. *Pain, adverfity, or perturbations, are but affections and inclinations which come from our will corrupted by the provocations and allurements of the flefh, and which wholly refift the divine nature of the reafonable part of the foul, faftning it to the body with the nail of difcontentment.*

PAin is always a companion of pleafure, and danger the handmaid attending on delight.

To trouble a troubled man, is to redouble his pain.

Where adverfities flow, there love ebbs, but friendfhip ftandeth ftedfaft in all ftorms.

Profperity getteth friends, but advefity trieth them. *Pacuv.*

In pain and judgment the quality with the quantity muft be confidered

It is lefs evil to fuffer one than to refift many.

The greateft mifery that may be is to fall into unknown mifery.

Mifery can never be fo bitter as eternal felicity is pleafant. *Erafmus.*

Danger always attendeth at the heels of pride and ambition.

Adverfity quickneth our fleepy fpirits: for by profperity we learn but ignorance, by adverfity we are taught knowledge.

Mifery and life are two twins, which increafe, are nourifhed, and live together.

He cannot rightly judge of pleafure that never tafted pain.

As no fortune can difmay him that is of a courageous mind: fo no man is more wretched than he that thinks himfelf to be unfortunate.

In the time of calamity moft men are more forry for that their enemies can fpeak of their diftrefs, than for the pain they endure.

Adverfities happening to good men may vex the mind, but never change their conftancy.

As the moft peftilent difeafes do gather unto themfelves all the infirmity wherewith the body is annoyed: fo doth the laft mifery embrace in the extremity of it felf all former mifchiefs, *S. P S.*

Patience breeds experience, experience hope, and hope cannot be confounded.

The pain of death is for fin, the Pain of confcience for fin, but the pain of hell is eternal.

The pain of the eye is luft, the pain of the tongue liberty, and the pain of both repentance.

Mifery is full of wretchednefs, fuller of difgrace, and fulleft of guiltinefs.
He

He fuffers double punifhment that hath his pain prolonged.

He finds helps in adverfity, that fought them in profperity.

The remembrance of pleafures paft aggravates the pains that are prefent.

A fawning friend in profperity will prove a bitter foe in adverfity.

It is hard in profperity to know whether our friends do love us for our own fakes, or for our goods. but adverfity proves the difpofition of mens minds

He that lendeth to another in time of profperity, fhall never want helps himfelf in the time of adverfity.

Ut fecunda moderatè tulimus; fic non folùm adverfam, fed funditus everfam fortunam fortiter ferre debemus.

Nullus dolor eft quem non longinquitas temporis minuat atque molliat. Cicero.

Ponamus nimios gemitus, flagrantior æquo

Non debet dolor effe viri, nec vulnere major. Juv.

Of Tears

Defin. *Tears, or Sorrow, is a grief or heavinefs for things which are done and paft : they are the only friends to folitarinefs, the enemies to company, and the heirs to defperation.*

Tears are no cures for diftrefs, neither do prefent plaints eafe a paffed harm.

There is no four but may be qualified with fweet potions ; nor any doleful malady but may be allayed with fome delightful mufick.

Tears crave compaffion, and fubmiffion deferveth forgivenefs. *Greg.*

The violence of forrow is not at the firft to be ftriven withal, becaufe it is like a mighty beaft, fooner tamed with following, than overthrown by withftanding.

Woe

Woe makes the shortest time seem long. *S P. S.*

Women are most prone to tears, and have them soonest at command   *Eurip.*

Sorrow bringeth forth tears as a tree bringeth forth fruit.

That grief is best digested that brings not open shame.

Bury the dead, but weep not above one day. *Homer.*

We shall sooner want tears than cause of mourning in this life. *Seneca*

Sorrows concealed are more four, and smothered griefs, if they burst not out, will break the heart

The heart that is greatly grieved takes his best comfort when he finds time to lament his loss.

Tears and sighs declare the heart to be greatly grieved.

A tear in the eye of a Strumpet is like heat-drops in a bright Sun-shine, and as much to be pitied as the weeping of a Crocodile.

Of sorrow and lamentation cometh watching and bleared eyes.

Tears are the badges of sorrow. *Archim*

Passion is a most cumbersome guest unto it self. *S. P. S.*

Deep-conceited sorrows are like to Sea-ivy, which, the older it is, the deeper root it hath.

Passions are like the arrows of *Cupid,* which if they touch lightly, prove but toys, but once piercing the skin, they prove deep wounds.

Where the smallest shew of tears is, there is oftentimes the greatest effect of sorrow

Tears in many ease the grieved heart, for grief is like to fire, the more it is covered, the more it rageth *Plutarch.*

Shedding of tears is the easing of grief.

Tears are the fruits of passion, the strength of women, the signs of dissimulation, the reconcilers of displeasures, and the tokens of a broken heart.

Tears

Tears are the food of the soul.

There are in the eyes three sorts of tears: the first of joy, which in old men shew their kindness; the second of sorrow, which in wretched men shew their misery, the third of diffimulation, which in women shew their nature.

Lay thy hand on thy heart when thy wife hath the tear in her eye, for then she intendeth either to sound thee or to sift thee.

When grief doth approach, if it be small, let us abide it, because it is easie to be born; but if it be grievous, let us bear with it, because our glory shall be the greater.

Care not for sorrow, it will either diffolve, or be diffolved.

How miserable is that grief which can utter nothing in torments! *Seneca.*

Men take a certain pleasure in weeping, when they lament the loss of friends.

Solon having buried his Son, did weep very bitterly: to whom when one said, his tears were all in vain; For that cause, quoth he, I do weep the more, because I cannot profit with weeping.

Too much sadness in a man is as much to be condemned, as over-much boldness in a woman is to be despised. *Bias.*

Lepidus by a long grief conceived of the misbehaviour of his wife shortned his own days.

To lament with tears the follies of our former life is profitable· but to grieve too much for worldly losses is a sign of foolishness.

Per lacrymas argumentum desiderii quærimus, & dolorem non sequimur, sed ostendimus; nemo enim sibi tristis est.

Curæ leves loquuntur, ingentes stupent. Senec.
Ratio dolorem vincat.

Of

Of Neighbours.

Defin. *Neighbours are those in whom we find towards us the greatest bonds of charity; and not, as is vulgarly taken, them that live near about us.*

THE greateſt love in us, next unto God, ought to be love towards our neighbours.

Whatſoever duties we perform in kindneſs towards our neighbours we perform unto God.

Love is the firſt foundation of marriage, and conjunction of neighbourhood.

The end of a man's being is the glory of his Creatour, and the love of his neighbour

The love of neighbours appertains mightily unto ſalvation.

Men are not born for themſelves, but for their Country, Parents, and Neighbours. *Cicero.*

All things on earth are created for men; and men are created to worſhip God, and aid one another.

Whoſoever will follow nature, muſt love his neighbour, and maintain ſociety.

Themiſtocles ſelling certain land, made it be proclaimed that it had a good neighbour. *Plutarch.*

No man may ſlander or lye for his profit, becauſe ſuch gain is his neighbour's indignity.

Duty and profit are two diſtinct things, and ſeparated, belonging to our neighbours and our ſelves.

We muſt eſteem our neighbour's love as dearly as the pureſt gold.

It is more praiſe worthy to relieve one neighbour, than to kill many enemies.

We muſt frame all our actions to the glory of God, to the love of our neighbours, and the profit of the Common-wealth.

The tiding of a bad man's burial comes never too ſoon to the ears of his neighbour.

The

The envy of a bad neighbour is worse than the sting of a Serpent.

He that lives alone lives in danger, society avoids many perils. *Marc. Aurel.*

The love of our neighbours binds us from unlawful actions against them.

Gold is proved in the furnace, and a neighbour's love tried in time of trouble.

That neighbour is to be well thought of which is ready in good will to help according to his power.

A rolling stone never gathers moss, nor a fickle-minded man love amongst honest neighbours.

The love of neighbours is the strongest pillar to support the Common wealth.

He is careless and uncharitable who will play at Cards whilst his neighbours house is burning.

Good turns done to unthankful neighbours are like water poured into open sieves.

Necessity ingendreth in a man war against himself, and malice to hurt his neighbour.

Ut in re rustica, non satis est teipsum bonum esse colonum, sed magni refert cujusmodi habeas & vicinum : sic in vita, non satis est si teipsum integrum virum præstes, sed refert cum quibus habeas consuetudinem.

Nunc ego illud verbum experior vetus, Aliquid mali esse propter vicinum malum. Plaut.

Of Proverbs.

Defin. *Proverbs are only sententious speeches of authentick authors, or the usual phrases begot by custom.*

A Little stream serveth to drive a light Mill.

A small sum will serve to pay a short reckoning.

A lean fee is a fit reward for a lazy Clerk.

A rolling stone gathers no moss.

All is not gold that glistereth.

Where is nought to be had, the King loseth his right

It

It is good to ſtrike the iron while it is hot.
The burned Child dreadeth the fire.
Soft pace goeth far.
Good wine needeth no buſh.
Hunger is the beſt ſauce.
Sweet meat muſt have four ſauce.
It is evil halting before a cripple.
Self doe, ſelf have.
Harm watch, harm catch.
Too much of one thing is good for nothing.
Hot ſup, hot ſwallow.
One ſcabbed ſheep will infect a whole flock.
Like maſter, like man.
Look not a given horſe in the mouth.
When the belly is full the bones would be at reſt.
He that reckoneth without his hoſt muſt reckon
twice.
A carrion Kite will never be a good Hawk.
He robbeth *Peter* to pay *Paul.*
Too much familiarity breeds contempt.
Rome was not built in one day.
Better late thrive than never
After death the Phyſician
After dinner Muſtard
No fire without ſome ſmoak.
A fool's bolt is ſoon ſhot.
All covet, all loſe.
After a ſtorm cometh a calm.
It is better to bow than to break.
Need makes the old wife to trot.
Death dealeth douotfully.
More coſt more worſhip.
It is an ill wind that blows good to none.
Much coin, much care.
Much meat, much malady.
Much learning, much ſorrow.
Look before you leap.

Time

Time and Tide tarry for no man.

Like lips like lettuce.

Many things chance between the cup and the lip

What is bred in the bone will never out of the flesh.

Every man for himself and God for us all.

Bare words are no lawful bargain.

It is good sleeping in a whole skin.

The end trieth all.

In little meddling lieth much rest.

Wake not a sleeping Lion.

The Vessel will savour of the first liquor.

One Swallow brings not a Summer.

White Silver dies black lines.

Fire is as hurtful as healthful.

Water is as dangerous as commodious.

Credit ought rather to be given to the eyes than to the ears.

Where many words are spoken, truth is held in suspicion. *Stobæus.*

He that goeth a borrowing goeth a sorrowing.

A friend in the Court is better than money in the purse.

He gives twice that gives quickly.

He that spareth to speak spareth to speed.

Service willingly offered is commonly refused and suspected.

A man's own manners do shape him either good or bad fortunes

A near friend is better than a far-dwelling kinsman.

> *Discipulus prioris posterior dies.*
> *Dulce bellum inexpertis.*
> *Grata brevitas. Festina lentè.*
> *Pauciloquus, sed eruditus.*

Of Sentences.

Defin. Sentences are the pithy and sweet flowers of wit, compiled in a ready and deliberate brain, and uttered in short and elegant phrases. H E.

HE that defireth to make a good market for his wares muft watch opportunity to open his fhop.

Where the foundation is weak the frame tottereth; and where the root is not deep, the tree falleth.

Where the knot is loofe, the ftring flippeth; and where the water is fhallow, no veffel will ride.

Where fundry flies bite, the gall is great; and where every hand fleeceth, the fheep goeth naked. *Demoft.*

He that talketh much and doth little, is like unto him that fails with a fide-wind, and is born with the tide to a wrong fhore.

Eagles fly alone, and they are but fheep that always flock together.

The mean man muft labour to ferve the mighty, and the mighty muft ftudy to defend the mean.

Standing pools gather filth, and flowing rivers are always fweet.

He that bites of every weed to fearch out the nature, may light upon poifon, and he that loves to be fifting of every cloud, may be fmitten with a thunder-ftroak.

A wanton eye is the dart of *Cephalus*, that where it levelleth there it lighteth, and where it hits woundeth deep.

Depth of wifdom, height of courage and largenefs of magnificence get admiration.

Truth of word, meeknefs, courtefie, mercy and liberality ftir up affeɗion.

There is no man fuddenly excellently good, or extremely evil, but grows either as he holds himfelf up in vertue, or lets himfelf flide to vice.

Cunning to keep is no lefs commendable than courage to command.

As life without learning is unpleafant, fo learning without wifdom is unprofitable.

He

He properly may be called a man, that in his behaviour governeth himself like a man, that is to say, conformable unto such things as reason willeth, and not as the motions of sensuality will.

Examples of the dead that were good do profit men more to live well than the counsel of the wicked that be living, which doth interr and bury those that are now alive.

Far better it is to be a tenant of liberty, than a landlord of thrall.

He that makes himself a sheep shall be eaten of the Wolf.

He that loseth favour on land to seek fortune at sea, is like him that stared so long at a star that he fell into a ditch.

Small helps joyned together wax stronger.

He is unworthy to be a Master over others that cannot master himself. *Pho.*

A master ought not to be known by the house, but the house by the master.

A busie tongue makes the mind repent at leisure.

By repentance we are drawn to mercy, without whose wings we cannot fly from vengeance.

Where the demand is a jest, the fittest answer is a scoff. *Archim*

When Dogs fall a snarling, Serpents a hissing, and Women a weeping, the first means to bite, the second to sting, and the third to deceive

A subtil Wolf will never hunt too near his own den.

Such as be born deaf or blind have commonly their inward powers the more perfect.

He that helpeth an evil man hurteth him that is good. *Crates.*

When that thing cannot be done that thou wouldest, then seek to compass that which thou knowest may be brought to pass

Con-

Contempt is a thing intolerable, forafmuch as no man can think himfelf fo vile that he ought to be defpifed.

Suddain motions and inforcements of the mind do often break out either for great good or great evil. *Hom.*

Many men labour to deliver themfelves from contempt, but more ftudy to be revenged thereof.

It is the corrupting of the good to keep company with the evil.

The eye can never offend, if the mind would rule the eye.

Where there is divifion there is confufion. *Solon*

That perfon is not worthy to live that taketh not care how to live well.

Negligence in private caufes is very dangerous.

Solitarinefs is a fly enemy, that doth moft feparate a man from doing well. *S P. S*

He that mindeth to conquer muft be careful.

Money borrowed upon ufury bringeth mifery, although for a time it feem pleafant.

Of a fhort pleafure long repentance is the heir. *Xenocrat.*

Private loffes may be holpen by publick pains.

Immoderate wealth caufeth pride, pride bringeth hatred, hatred worketh rebellion, rebellion maketh an alteration, and changeth Kingdoms.

That kind of contemplation that tends to folitarinefs is but a glorious title to idlenefs.

Liking is not always the child of beauty.

Jealoufie is the harbinger of difdain.

All is but lip-wifdom that wants experience.

Who will refift love, muft either have no wit, or put out his eyes.

Love is to a yielding heart a King, but to a refifting, a Tyrant. *S. P. S.*

L. W   Fear

Fear is the only knot that knitteth a Tyrant's people to him, which once being untied by a greater force, they all scatter from him, like so many birds whose cages are broken. *S. P. S.*

Ambition and love can abide no lingring.

No thraldom to the inward bondage.

The right conceit of young men is, that they think they then speak wisely when they cannot understand themselves.

He that will needs stir affections in others must first shew the same passion himself.

Things lost by negligence must be recoverd by diligence.

As rewards are necessary for well-doers, so chastisements are meet for offenders.

Vertue like the clear Heaven is without clouds. *S. P. S.*

He that will blame another must first be blameless himself, especially in the matter that he blameth another for.

Suspicion breedeth care, and the effects of cruelty stir up a new cause of suspicion.

It is best dealing with an enemy when he is at the weakest. *Agrel.*

The better sort eschew evil for shame, but the common people for fear of punishment.

Laws not executed are of no value, and as good not made as not practised.

Things that are wrongfully gotten have no certain assurance.

Not as men would, but as men may, and as the nature of things doth require, so should they deal.

Where flatterers bear rule, things come to ruine. *Pompeius.*

Such is the man and his manners as his delight and study is.

By diligence and pains-taking all may be amended that is amiss.   When

When things are in extremity, it is good to be of good chear, and rather endeavour to amend them than cowardly to faint and despair of all.

They that trust much to their friends know not how shortly tears be dried up.

God and nature do set all things to sale for labour.

Great is the value of order and foresight to govern things well.

Man can better suffer to be denied than to be deceived.

Lingring is most loathsome, when necessity requireth hast. *Quint.*

The carefulness of the wicked causeth the godly to look about them.

All passages are open to the stout and valiant minded man.

Flying tales and flattering news do never good to any State

It is better to fight with an enemy at his own home. than for him to fight with us in our Country.

Private welfare is not to be preferred before the Common-weal

Wise men being wronged are to be feared of the wrong-doers.

Careless men are ever most nigh unto their own harm.

Fair promises make fools feign; and flatterers seek by discrediting others, to benefit themselves.

Good men sometimes are in greater danger for saying the truth, than evil men for speaking falsly. *Plaut.*

Of one inconvenience oftentimes suffered many mischiefs commonly follow.

Forbearance of speech is most dangerous, when necessity requireth to speak.

A bold speech upon a good cause deserveth favour.

Sleep

Sleep and food are enemies to the mourning which paſſion perſwadeth to be reaſonable. *S. P. S.*

Often ſuſpecting of others cometh of ſecret condemning our ſelves.

Advancement is the moſt mortal offence to envy.

Through diligence and care things may be redreſſed, which were by ſloth and negligence ſo born *Aurel.*

He doth wrong that giveth cauſe of war, not he that ſeeketh the redreſs of wrong.

The leſs one feareth his enemy, the nigher he is to his own harm.

It is better to begin a war than to abide war.

Such as are careleſs in their own Cauſes hardly can be careful about other men's affairs. *Thales.*

Corrupt officers never want matter to ſatisfie their corrupt minds.

It is folly to refuſe the aid of a ſtranger when we may have it, and are in need thereof.

Theſe three chief points are neceſſarily belonging to a counſeller, to be bold, plain, and faithful.

That City is of no value which is not of ability enough to puniſh wrong doers: neither is that Common-weal any thing worth at all where pardon and interceſſion prevail againſt Laws.

The mind of man is his guide in all things, and the ſame is only to be inſtructed and trained up with knowledge and learning.

To know well, and to do well, are the two points belonging to vertue. *Origen.*

Vertue is praiſed of many men, but very few deſire to follow her effectually.

Honour got by vertue hath perpetual aſſurance *Cicero.*

That man cannot long endure labour which wanteth his natural kind of reſt.

The mind of man is man himſelf, and needeth continual teaching.

Though

Though that all new chances caufe prefently new thoughts; yet thereby we attain more ftedfaftnefs a-gainft mifhaps to come.

After the unlawful getting of a covetous father, followeth the riotous fpending of a prodigal fon.

Ità vivendum eft cum hominibus tanquam Deus vide-at, ita loquendum, tanquam Deus audiat.

Omnia præclara rara, nec quidquam difficilius quàm reperire quod fit omni ex parte in fuo genere perfectum.

Of Similitudes.

Defin. Similitudes, or Likenefs, are the Images or Pictures of the things to which they are compared, lively ex-plaining one thing in a far different object.

AS that member is nothing profitable, but rather hurtful to the body, which by corruption is lame and imperfect · fo that fubject whofe mind is drawn into fundry practices of difcord, working the difquiet of a common peace and tranquility, may be juftly cut off as an unprofitable part or canker in a Common-wealth.

As the vertue of a Prince is the chiefeft authority of the Magiftrate, fo are the good conditions of the Rulers the beft ftay and ftrongeft defence of inferi-ours. *Plut*

As he is not unfortunate which is poor and defor-med fo they are not to be accounted happy which are only rich and beautiful.

As plants meafurably watered grow the better, but being watered too much are drowned and die fo the mind with moderate labour is refrefhed, but with over-much is utterly dulled. *Erafmus.*

As any thing, be it never fo eafie, is hard to the idle, fo any thing be it never fo hard, is eafie to the wit well employed. *Ennius*

As

As as Ship having a fure Anchor may lie fafe in any place fo the mind that is ruled by perfect reafon is quiet every-where.

As that fire fmoaketh not much which flameth at the firft blowing . fo the glory that brightly fhineth at the firft is not greatly envied at; but that which is long in getting is always prevented by envy.

As the man that drinks poifon deftroyeth himfelf therewith. fo he that admitteth a friend e'er he per-fectly knows him may hurt himfelf by too much trufting him.

As the perfect Gold, which is of a pure fubftance, fooner receiveth any form than the fturdy Steel, which is grofs and maffic metal fo womens effemi-nate minds are more fubject to affection, and are fooner fettered with the fnares of fancy, than the hard hearts of men.

As golden Pillars do fhine upon the fockets of filver; fo doth a fair face with a vertuous mind. *Perian*

Like as a good Mufician, having any key or ftring of his inftrument out of tune, doth not immediately cut it off, and caft it away, but either with ftraining it higher, or flacking it down lower, by little and little caufeth it to agree fo fhould Rulers rather reform tranfgreffors by fmall corrections, than feek to caft them away for every trefpafs.

As *Apollodorus* was wont to fay of *Chryfippus*'s books, that if other men's fentences were left out, the pages would be void fo may we fpeak of Brokers, for if other men enjoyed their goods, their Ware houfes would be quickly empty.

As the ftrong bitternefs of the Aloe tree taketh a-way the fweetnefs of the fweeteft honey · fo evil works deftroy, and take away the praife of good deeds.

As a veffel is known by the found, whether it be whole or broken · fo are men proved by their fpeech, whether they be wife or foolifh *Demoft.*

As

As wine in *Plato*'s opinion is the mother of verity. so love in *Jamblichus*'s cenſure is the fruit of idleneſs.

As in feaſts hunger is the Left ſawce ſo of gueſts mirth is the beſt welcome.

As the occurrence of many things bringeth much trouble ſo the conſiderations thereof procure experience.

Like as a battered or crazed ſhip by drinking in of water, not only drowneth her ſelf, but all thoſe that are in her. ſo a Ruler, by uſing vicioulneſs, deſtroyeth not himſelf alone, but all others beſides that are under his government.

As ignorant governours bring their Country into many inconveniences ſo ſuch as are deviſhly politick utterly overthrow the State.

As truth is the centre of Religion ſo contrary opinions founded on evil examples are the corruptions of the world, and the bringers in of Atheiſm

As it becometh Subjects to be obedient to their Sovereign : ſo it behoveth that the king be careful for the commodity of his Common weal. *Sigiſ.*

As there is no deliberation good that hangeth on delay ſo no counſel is profitable that is followed unadviſedly.

As that Kingdom is moſt ſtrong where obedience is moſt nouriſhed. ſo that State is moſt dangerous where the ſoldier is moſt negligently regarded.

As no Phyſician is reputed good that healeth others, and cannot heal himſelf ſo he is no good Magiſtrate that commandeth others to avoid vices, and will not ſhun evil himſelf. *Marc. Aurel.*

As the green leaves outwardly ſhew that the tree is not dry inwardly ſo the good works openly teſtiſie the zeal of the heart inwardly. *Eraſ*

Like as a governour of a ſhip is not choſen for his riches, but for his knowledge ſo ſhould the chief Magiſtrate in every City be choſen rather for his wiſ-

dom.

dom and godly zeal, than for his wealth and great poffeffions.

As the goodnefs of wife men continually amendeth; fo the malice of fools evermore increafeth. *Pythag.*

As they which cannot fuffer the light of a candle, can much worfe abide the brightnefs of the Sun fo they that are troubled with fmall trifles would be more amazed in weighty matters.

As fire caft into the water is quickly quenched. fo a falfe accufation againft an honeft life is foon extinguifhed.

As the Canker eateth and deftroyeth iron: fo doth envy eat and confume the hearts of the envious.

As the favour of ftinking carrion is noifome to them that fmell it: fo is the fpeech of fools tedious to wife men that hear it. *Solon.*

As the wicked and malicious perfon is moft hardy to commit the greateft crimes: fo is he moft cruel and ready wickedly to give fentence againft another for the fame offence.

As men eat divers things by morfels, which if they fhould eat whole would choak them. fo by divers days we fuffer troubles, which, if they fhould all come together, would make an end of us in one day.

As fin is natural, and the chaftifement voluntary. fo ought the rigour of juftice to be temperate, fo that the minifters thereof fhould rather fhew compaffion than vengeance, whereby the trefpaffers fhould take occafion to amend their fins paft, and not to revenge the injury prefent, *Hermes*

As when the wood is taken from the fire, and the embers quenched, yet neverthelefs the ftones oft-times remain hot and burning fo though the flefh be chaftifed with hot and dry maladies, or confumed by many years in travel, yet concupifcence abideth ftill in the bones. *Antift.*

As

As after great ſtorms the a r is clear . ſo after the flouds of repentant tears the conſcience is at quiet.

As darnel ſpringeth up amongſt good wheat, and nettles among roſes. even ſo envy groweth up among vertues. *Theop.*

As the leaves of a book which is ſeldom uſed will cleave faſt together even ſo the memory waxeth dull, if it be not often quickned.

Like as an Adamant draweth by little and little the heavy Iron, until at laſt it be joyned with it ſo vertue and wiſdom draw men's minds to the practice thereof.

As a veſſel cannot be known whether it be whole or broken until it hath liquor in it· ſo can no man be known what he is before he be in authoiity.

As it is great fooliſhneſs to foiſake the clear foun-tains, and to drink puddle water. ſo it is great folly to leave the ſweet doctrine of the Evangeliſts, and to ſtudy the dreams of men's imaginations.

As ſight is in the eye, ſo is the mind in the ſoul. *Sophoc*

As deſire is glad to imbrace the firſt ſhew of comfoit. ſo is hope deſirous of peifect aſſurance. *S P. S.*

Ut ad curſum Equus, ad arandum Bos, ad indagandum Canis; ſic homo ad duas res, intelligendum & agendum natus eſt, quaſi immortalis Deus. Cicero.

Ut ager, quamvis fertilis, ſine cultura fructuoſus eſſe non poteſt, ſic ſine doctrina animus.

Of Bravery

Defin. *Bravery is riotous exceſs, either in apparel or other ornaments . it is alſo a part of pride, and contrary to decency and comelineſs.*

EXceſs of bravery brings a man of much wealth quickly to poverty.

Pride joyned with many vertues choaks them all.

They

They that rather delight to deck their bodies than their souls, seem men rather created for their bodies than their souls.

Excess in vanity hath never end.

Theft or violent death ever waiteth at the heels of excess.

They never can be careful to keep a mean in husbanding another man's wealth, which are careless in bestowing their own substance upon excess.

To spend much beyond power, and hope much upon promises, make many men beggars which were left wealthy.

He that employeth his substance in bravery shall quickly bring his estate to beggary

The cause why bravery is so much esteemed, is the respect the world taketh of the outward appearance, neglecting the inward excellence.

There are three things that cost dearly and consume quickly, a fair woman that is unchast, a rich garment that hath many cuts, and a wealthy stock on an ill husband.

A fool cloathed in a gay garment if he get any courtesie, may thank his weed, and not his wit. *Archim.*

As the weed cannot be esteemed precious for the fair flower which it beareth: so ought no man to be accounted vertuous for the gay garment which he weareth.

Building may be overthrown with wind, Apparel consumed with moths: what folly is it then for men to delight in that which the light wind can waste, and the small worm destroy?

He that wasteth his wealth to follow every fashion, and spendeth his substance to maintain his bravery, may be counted the Mercer's friend, the Taylor's fool, and his own foe. *Bias.*

Rich cloaths are beggars weeds to a discontented mind,

Bravery

Bravery of apparel is nothing worth, if the mind be miserable.

Desire of that we cannot get torments us, hope of that we may have comforts us, and the bravery of that we possess makes us become proud.

As oil being cast upon the fire quencheth not the flame · so bravery bestowed upon the body never humbleth the soul.

As it is no wisdom in admiring the scabbard to despise the blade : so it is mere folly to praise a man for his bravery, and discommend him for his decency.

Rain can never cause the Corn to bring forth any fruit which is sown upon hard stones, nor can speech perswade a proud man to become an enemy to brave apparel.

Gorgeous garments are marks of pride, and nets of righteousness

As a man would judge one to be ill at ease that weareth a plaister upon his face, or one that hath been scourged, to be punished by the Law, so doth painting betoken a diseased soul marked with adultery.

Woe to that beauty which sleepeth not with the face. *Horace.*

If by the Civil Law the Child may have an Action of the Case against him which shall deface the Pourtraicture of his Father; we may imagine how much it displeaseth God, if by artificial painting we seek to correct his workmanship.

Painting hastens wrinckles before old age comes. *Chrys.*

Those which are curious in decking of the body despise the care of the Soul.

All kind of painting, artificial garnishing, and colouring of hair, was forbidden among the *Spartans*.

Splendida fit nolo, sordida nolo cutis.

Sint procul à nobis juvenes ut fæmina compti.

Q 2

Of Boasting.

Defin. *Boasting is a part of pride, wherein a man seeketh to extol himself vain gloriously beyond his deserving, or the repute of the world for any action done.*

A Dog that barketh much will bite but little and the man that uses to make great promises will yield but small performance in the end.

Good wits are often hindred by shame-facedness, and perverse conceits are boldened by impudency

Many mens threatnings be more fearful in hearing than hurtful in effect.

He boasteth in vain of his great Lineage, that, having no goodness in himself, seeketh to be esteemed for the Nobility of his Ancestours.

Great offers are often promised in words, and seldom performed in deeds.

There be many who can boast of battles, that never fought in the fields.

Where the matter it self bringeth credit, a man for his glofs deserveth small commendation

Great boast giveth least courage, and many words are signs of small wit.

Arrogancy is always accompanied with Folly, Audacity, Rashness, Insolency and Solitariness. *Plato.*

A boasting tongue is a manifest sign of a cowardly heart. *Bias*

Crassus boasting of his mighty Army, was prettily answered, It is not their multitude which follow thee, but thy courage in leading them, which shall make thee famous.

No man may truly brag of what he hath, sith what he hath may be lost. *Eur.*

Tully gloried in that he had amplified the Latin Tongue.

The

The world can boaft of nothing but vanity, neither vanity brag of any thing more than the end.

He that boafteth himfelf to know every thing is moft ignorant and he that prefumeth to know nothing is wife. *Plato.*

Boaft is but the fcum of thought, vanifhing with fading pleafure, and entertained by foolifh objects.

Great threatnings are like big winds, they blufter fore, but they end foon .

It is a foolifh boaft whereby men make manifeft their own ignorance.

Where good Wine is, there needs no Garland. and where vertues are, there needs no commendation.

Of few words enfue many effects , of much boafting fmall belief.

Thofe that boaft moft fail moft , for deeds are filent.

To fill thy mouth with boafting, is to fill thy name with flander.

It is better to be filent, than to brag or to boaft vain-glorioufly any thing in our own commendation.

Vanam gloriam femper fequitur infamia , & qui infolenter utitur gloriâ incidit in ignominiam.

Phidias *fui fimilem fpeciem inclufit in clypeo* Minervæ, *cùm infcribere liceret.*

Of Nature.

Defin. *Nature is that fpirit or divine reafon which is the efficient caufe of natural works, and the preferving caufe of thofe things that have being thro' the only power of the heavenly Word, which is the workmafter of nature and of the whole world, and hath infufed into every thing a lively vertue and ftrength, whereby it increafeth and preferveth it felf by a natural faculty.*

NAture in defpight of time will frown at abufe. Nature hath a certain predominant power over the mind of man.

The

The man that lives obedient to nature can never hurt himself thereby.

As Art is a help to nature, so is experience the trial and perfection of Art.

As nature hath given beauty, and vertue given courage, so nature yieldeth death, and vertue yieldeth honour

Nature is above Art in the ignorant, and Vertue is esteemed all things of the wise.

It is hard to streighten that by art which is made crooked by nature. *Peri.*

Nature is placed in the Eye, Reason in the Mind, but Vertue in both.

Consider what Nature requires, and not how much Affection desires.

Nature guideth beasts, but Reason ruleth the hearts of men.

Such as live according to nature are never poor, and according to the opinion of Men, are never rich, because nature contenteth her self, and opinion doth infinitely covet

Philip, King *Alexander*'s Father, falling upon the sands, and seeing there the mark and print of his body, said, How little a plot of ground is nature content with, and yet we covet the whole World?

The God which is the God of nature doth never teach unnaturalness. *S P S*

Nature is higher prized than Wealth, and the love of Parents ought to be more precious than dignity.

Fire cannot be hid in straw, nor the nature of man so concealed but at last it will have its course.

In nature nothing is superfluous. *Arist*

Where nature is vicious, by learning it is amended, and where it is vertuous, by skill it is augmented.

There is no greater bond than duty, nor straiter law than nature and where nature enforceth obedience, there to resist is to strive against God. *LaTan.*

Liberal

Liberal Sciences are moſt meet for liberal men, and good Arts for good natures.

Nature without learning and good bringing up is a blind guide, Learning without nature wanteth much, and Uſe without the two former is unprofitable.

Nature being always in a perpetual motion deſireth to be driven to the better part, or elſe ſhe ſuffereth her ſelf to be weighed down as a balance to the worſer.

Nature is our beſt guide, whom if we follow, we ſhall never go aſtray *Ariſt.*

Nature friendly ſheweth us by many ſigns what ſhe would, what ſhe ſeeketh, and what ſhe deſireth, but man by ſome ſtrange mean waxeth deaf, and will not hear what ſhe gently counſelleth.

Nature is a certain ſtrength and power put into things created by God, who giveth to each thing that which belongeth unto it.

Quod ſatiare poteſt dives natura miniſtrat,
Quid docet infrænis gloria, fine caret.

Hoc generi hominum à natura datum, ut qua in familia laus aliqua fortè floruerit, hanc ferre qui ſunt ejus ſtirpis (quod ſermo hominum ad memoriam patrum virtute celebratur) cupidiſſimè perſequuntur.

Of Life:

Defin. *Life, which we commonly call the breath of this world, is a perpetual battel, and a ſharp skirmiſh, wherein we are one while hurt with envy, another while with ambition, and by and by with ſome other vice; beſides the ſuddain onſets given upon our bodies by a thouſand ſorts of diſeaſes, and floods of adverſities upon our ſpirits.*

Life is a Pilgrimage, a ſhadow of joy, a glaſs of infirmity, and the perfect path way to death.

All mortal men ſuffer corruption in their ſouls through vice, and in their bodies through worms.

It

It is a miserable Life where friends are feared, and enemies nothing mistrusted.

It is better not to live, than not to know how to live. *Salust.*

It is hard for a man to live well, but very easie to die ill

If a good man desire to live, it is for the great desire he hath to do good; but if the evil desire to live, it is for that they would abuse the world longer.

The Children of vanity call no time good, but that wherein they have according to their own desire, and do nothing but follow their own filthy lusts.

Man's life is like lightning, which is but a flash, and the longest date of years but a Bavin's blaze.

Men can neither enlarge their lives as they desire, nor shun that death which they abhor. *Menan*

A detestable life removeth all merit of honourable burial.

By life groweth continuance, and by death all things take end.

Life and death are in the power of the tongue. *Guevara.*

The man that desireth life and feareth death ought carefully to govern his tongue.

Life is short, yet sweet. *Eurip.*

Life to a wretched man is long, but to him that is happy, very short. *Menan.*

Man's life is a warfare. *Seneca.*

The mortal life which we enjoy is the hope of life immortal *Aug*

An undefiled life is the reward of age. *Aug*

No man is so old but he thinketh he may yet live another year. *Hieron.*

The breath that maintaineth life endeth ☙

A good life is the readiest way to a good name. *Aurel.*

Better

Better it is to be careful to live well, than defirous to live long.

A long life, hath commonly long cares annexed with it.

Moſt men in theſe days will have precepts to be ruled by their life, and not their life to be governed by precepts.

Fools, when they hate their life, will yet defire to live, for the fear which they have of death. *Crates.*

Man's life is lent him for a time, and he that gave it may juſtly demand it when he will

They live very ill who always think to live.

To a man in miſery life ſeemeth too long, but to a worldly-minded man living at pleaſure life ſeemeth too ſhort. *Chilo.*

What a ſhame is it for men to complain upon God for the ſhortneſs of their life, when as they themſelves as ſhort as it is, do through riot, malice, murthers, care and wars, make it much ſhorter, both in them-ſelves and others? *Theophraſtus.*

——————————*hoc eſt*

Vivere bis, vitâ poſſe priore frui.

Eſt noſtra vino vita quàm ſimillima;

Aceſcit, eſt quum re'iquo parva portio.

Of the Soul.

Defin. *The Soul is a created ſubſtance, inviſible, incor-poreal, immortal, reſembling the image of her Crea-tor, a ſpirit that giveth life to the body whereun-to it is joyned, a nature always moving it ſelf, ca-pable of Reaſon and the Knowledge of God, to love him, as being meet to be united to him through love to eternal felicity.*

THE greateſt thing that may be ſaid to be con-tained in a little room, is the Soul in a man's body *Plato.*

An

An holy and undefiled Soul is like Heaven, having for the Sun, Underſtanding, and the zeal of Juſtice and Charity, for the Moon, Faith, and vertue for the Stars.

Every Soul is either the Spouſe of Chriſt, or the Adultereſs of the Devil. *Chryſ.*

The mind is the eye of the Soul *Plat.*

The Soul is compounded of Underſtanding, Know-ledge, and Senſe, from which all Sciences and Arts proceed, and from theſe ſhe is called reaſonable.

The Soul is divided into two parts, the one ſpiritual or intelligible, where the diſcourſe of reaſon is; the other brutiſh, which is the ſenſual will, of it ſelf wandering where all motions contrary to Reaſon reſt, and delighting only to dwell where evil deſires do inhabit

The actions of the Soul are Will, Judgment, Senſe, Conceiving, Thought, Spirit, Imagination, Memory, and Underſtanding.

The imcompirable beauty of the Soul is Prudence, Temperance, Fortitude and Juſtice.

All the felicity of man, as well preſent as to come, dependeth on the Soul. *Clem.*

The Soul is the organ and inſtrument of God, whereby he worketh in us, and lifteth us up to the contemplation of his divine power and nature.

The ſweeteſt reſt and harbour for the Soul is a conſcience uncorrupted.

The Soul payeth well for hire in the body, conſidering what ſhe there ſuffereth.

The ſoul of the juſt Man is the ſeat of Wiſdom. *Aug.*

The body is the ſepulchre of a dead Soul.

The ſoul is the breathing of God. *Amb.*

'If thy ſoul be good, the ſtroak of death cannot hurt thee, for thy ſpirit ſhall live bleſſed in heaven. *Baſil.*

As they that have healthful bodies eafily endure both cold and heat · fo they that have a ftayed and fettled foul have the dominion over anger, grief, joy, and all other their affections. *Plato*

It is not death that deftroyeth the foul, but a bad life.

A found Soul correcteth the naughtinefs of the body

All mens fouls are immortal, but the Souls of the righteous are immortal and divine. *Socrates.*

It is good to have a regard to the health of the mind, that the body thereby may be preferved from danger.

The difeafes of the body are eafie to be cured, but for the malady of the mind no medicine can be found, fave in the Word of God.

The pleafure of the mind excelleth the pleafures of the body.

By what other name canft thou call the foul, than God dwelling in a man's body?

It is as great charity to edify the foul, as to fuftain the body. *Bern.*

The nobility of the foul is always to be thought upon.

The foul in the flefh is as amongft thorns. *Bern.*

The foul is the natural perfection of the body. *Aur.*

The body confidereth nothing but what is prefent, the mind conceiveth what is paft, and what is to come.

The foul of man is an incorruptible fubftance, apt to receive either joy or pain, both here and elfe-where *Solon.*

While the foul is in the Company of good people, it is in joy, but when it is amongft evil men, it is in forrow and heavinefs.

As the body is an inftrument of the foul, fo is the foul an inftrument of God.

The

The body was made for the foul, and not the foul for the body.

Look how much the foul is better than the body, fo much more grievous are the difeafes of the foul than the griefs of the body. *Diogenes.*

By the juftice of God the foul muft needs be immortal, and therefore no man ought to neglect it: for though the body die, yet the foul dieth not

The delights of the foul re to know her Maker, to confider the works of heaven, and to know her own ftate and being.

Tres vitales fpiritus creavit Omnipotens. unum; qui carne non tegitur, alium, qui carne tegitur, fed non cum carne moritur, alium, qui carne tegitur, & cum carne moritur primus Angelorum, Secundus hominum, tertius brutorum eft.

Of the Senfes.

Defin. *Senfes are the powers of foul and body, in number five; Seeing, Hearing, Smelling, Tafting, and Touching.*

Of Seeing.

TUlly would never leave until the Eye, the Ear, the Mouth, and every Senfe of his Auditors were full.

The eyes were given to men to be as it were their watch-towers and fentinels, the guiders and leaders of the body.

Of more validity is the fight of one eye than the attention of ten ears, for in that a man feeth is affurance, and that he heareth may be an errour.

The fight, the affections and the hands, are inftruments to gather bribes

What can faying make them believe whom feeing cannot perfwade? *S. P. S.*

A wanton eye is a meffenger of an unchaft heart. *Auguft.*

Marcus

Marcus Varro was furnamed *Strabo* for his quick fight, that from *Lilybæum*, a Promontory in *Sicilia*, he could tell the number of the fail of fhips which came out of the Haven of *Carthage*.

He that is born blind is wifer than the deaf or dumb. *Ariftotle*

Blindnefs it felt commends the excellency of fight. *Auguft*.

The eye is the moft precious part of the body, and therefore it is faid, *I will keep thee as the apple of mine eye*

The eyes are the windows of the body, or rather of the foul, which is lodged in it.

The fight is the chiefeft fenfe, and the firft miftrefs that provoketh men forward to the ftudy and fearching of knowledge and wifdom.

By hearing, not feeing, we come to the knowledge of truth.

Hearing is the preparation of the fight. *Bernard*.

That which the eye feeth the heart is often grieved at.

The fenfe of the eye anfwereth to the element of fire.

Man only of all creatures feeth and contemplateth at once.

Nihil eft difficilius quàm à confuetudine oculorum mentis aciem abducere.

Totius hominis debilitas eft oculos ſeididiſſe.

Of Hearing.

THE Ear trieth the words, as the Mouth tafteth meat

To whomfoever at the firft the fenfe of Hearing is denied, to them the ufe of the Tongue fhall never be granted.

As a ftone caft into the water maketh many rounds ſo a found that is begotten in the air hath his circles, which are multiplied until they come to the ear. *Ariftotle*   *Pliny*

Pliny writeth a wonderful-example of the fenfe of Hearing, that the battle which was fought at *Sybaris*, the fame was heard at *Olympia*, the places being above five hundred miles diftant.

The fenfe of Hearing is anfwerable to the element of the Air.

Qui audiunt, audita dicunt, qui vident, planè fciunt.
Auris, prima mortis janua, prima aperiatur & vitæ.
Bernardus.

Of Smelling.

THE fenfe of Smelling is nearly conjoyned with the fenfe of Tafting.

The fenfe of Smelling is not only for pleafure but profit.

Albeit every thing that fmelleth well hath not always a good tafte; yet whatfoever a man findeth good to his tafte, the fame hath alfo a good fmell; and that which is found to have an ill relifh, the fame hath alfo a bad fmell.

Sweet fmells are good to comfort the fpirits of the head, which are fubtil and pure, and ftinking favours are very hurtful for the fame.

The fenfe of Smelling agreeth with the air and fire, becaufe fmells are ftirred up by heat, as fmoak by fire, which afterwards by means of the air are carried to the fenfe of fmelling.

——*Non bene olet, qui bene femper olet.*

Odore morum fama dijudicat colorem confcientia. Bernardus

Of Tafting.

THE fenfe of tafte is that fenfe whereby the mouth judgeth of all kinds of tafte.

He that hath not tafted the things that are bitter is not worthy to tafte things which are fweet.

The

The judgment of taste is very neceffary for man's life, and efpecially for the nourifhment of all living creatures, becaufe all things which the earth bringeth forth are not good for them.

This fenfe of Tafting anfwereth to the element of Air.

Intellectus faporum cæteris eft in prima lingua, homini in palato.

Guftus mercatum invitat. Euripides.

Of Touching.

T H E fenfe of Touching anfwereth the Element of Earth, to the end it might agree better with thofe things that are to be felt thereby.

The vigour and fenfe thereof ought to be clofe together and throughout, and fuch as takes more faft and fure hold than any of the reft.

The fenfe of Touching, although it be the laft, yet is the ground of all the reft　*Ariftotle.*

One may live without Sight, Hearing, and Smelling ; but not without Feeling.

Senfuum ità clara judicia & certa funt, ut fi optio natuæ noftræ detur, & ab ea Deus aliquis requirat, Contentáne fit fuis integris incorruptifque fenfibus, an poftulat melius aliquid, non videam quid quærat amplius. Cicero.

Nos Aper auditu, Lynx vifu, Simia guftu,
Vultur odoratu, nos vincit Aranea tactu.

Of Children.

Defin. *Our Children are the natural and true iffues of our foul, of the fame mould and temperance, begot by the work of nature, and made by the power of the Almighty.*

CHildren are a bleffing of God, beftowed upon man for his comfort.

Children

Children, according to their bringing up, prove either great joy, or great grief to their Parents.

He is happy that is happy in his Children.

Where we behold our Children, we see a new light. *Theocritus.*

A good Son is a good Citizen. *Stob*

The Child is not bound in duty to those Parents of whom he never learned any vertuous instruction

Whatsoever good instructions Children learn in their youth, the same they retain in their age.

The wicked example of a Father is a great provocation of the Son to sin.

Nothing is better to be commended in a Father, than the teaching of his children by good example as much as by godly admonition.

Children by their lascivious and ungodly education grow in time to be persons very hurtful to the Common-wealth.

The fault is to be imputed to the Parents, if Children for want of good bringing up fall to any unhonest kind of life.

As those men which bring up Horses will first teach them to follow the bridle, so they that instruct Children ought first to cause them to give ear to that which is spoken

Men ought to teach their Children liberal Sciences; not because those Sciences may give any vertue, but because their minds by them are made apt to receive any vertue. *Seneca.*

Those Children which are suffered either to eat much or sleep much be commonly dull-witted and unapt to learn.

As wax is ready and pliant to receive any kind of figure or print so is a young Child apt to receive any kind of learning

That Child that hath his mind more constant than his years, yields much hopes of a stayed and toward age. He

He that letteth his Son run at his own liberty, shall find him more stubborn than any head-strong Colt. when he cometh to be broken. *Bias.*

The best way to make thy Children to love thee when thou art old, is to teach them obedience in their youth.

Nothing sinketh deeper nor cleaveth faster in the mind of man than those rules which he learned when he was a Child.

That Son cannot but prosper in all his affairs which honoureth his Parents with the reverence due unto them.

When thy Father waxeth old, remember the good deeds he did for thee when thou wast young.

Thou hast lived long enough, if thou hast lived to relieve the necessity of thy Father in his old age.

The law of nature teacheth us that we should in all kindness love our Parents.

Those Children that deny dutiful obedience unto their Parents are not worthy to live.

Solon made a Law, that those Parents should not be relieved in their old age by their Children, which cared not for their vertuous bringing up.

We ought to give good examples to our Children, because if they see no uncomeliness they shall be inforced to follow goodness and vertue. *Zenophon.*

The *Lacedemonians* answered *Antipater*, that they would rather die than give him their children, which he demanded for hostages. so great account made they of their education.

Such as leave great riches to their Children, without seeing them brought up honestly, are like unto them that give much provender to young Horses, but never break them at all, for so they wax fat, but unprofitable. *Socrates*

He which maketh his Son worthy to be had in estimation, hath done much for him, although he leave him but little wealth.   h   Chil-

Children ought to learn that which they should do when they are men. *Aug.*

No punishment can be thought great enough for that child which should offer violence to his Parents, whom (if there were an occasion offered) he should be ready to defend with the loss of his own life.

Strive not in words with thy Parents, although thou tell the truth.

Solon being asked why he made no laws for Parricides, answered, that he thought none would be so wicked.

Magnam vim, magnam necessitudinem, magnam possidet religionem paternus maternusque sanguis : ex quo si qua macula concepta est, non modo elui non potest, verùm eousque permanat ad animum, ut summus furor atque amentia consequatur eam.

Of Youth.

Defin. Youth is the fourth age of man　then do men grow in body, in strength and reason, in vice and vertue ; and at that age the nature of a man is known, and whereunto he bendeth his mind, which before could not be discerned, by reason of the ignorance of his age.

THE deeds that men commit in their youth were never yet found so upright and honest, but it was thought more praise-worthy to amend them than to declare them.

Youth, that heretofore delighted to try their vertues in hard Armours, take now their whole delight and content in delicate and effeminate Amours

Wantonness, liberty, youth and riches, are always enemies to honesty. *Solon.*

Youth going to wars ought to heed nothing but good and evil renown. *Eur.*

It is very requisite that youth be brought up in that part of learning which is called Humility. *Lactan.*

A man followeth all his life-long his firſt addreſſing in his youth : as if a tree bloſſoms not in the Spring, it will hardly bear fruit in Autumn.

As the Cypreſs tree, the more it is watered, the more it withereth, and the oftner it is lopped, the ſooner it dieth : ſo unbridled youth, the more it is by grave advice counſelled, or due correction controuled, the ſooner it falleth to confuſion.

Where vice is embraced in youth, there commonly vertue is neglected in age. *Cicero.*

Youth fireth his fancy with the flame of luſt, and old age fireth his affections with the heat of love.

Young years make their account only of the gliſtering ſhew of Beauty · but gray-hairs reſpect only the perfect ſubſtance of Vertue;

The mind of a young man is momentany, his fancy fading, his affections fickle, his love uncertain, and his liking as light as the wind , his fancy fired with every new face, and his mind moved with a thouſand ſundry motions, loathing that which of late he did love, and liking that for which his loving mind doth luſt · frying at the firſt, and freezing at the laſt.

The follies that men commit in their youth are cauſes of repentance in old age.

The prime of youth is as the flowers of the Pine-tree, which are glorious in ſight, and unſavoury in the ſmell.

Youth, if it bluſh not at beauty, and carry an antidote of wiſdom againſt flattery, folly will be the next Haven he ſhall harbour in.

He that in youth guideth his life by reaſon, ſhall in age find the ready foot path from ruin *Theopomp.*

There is nothing ſweeter than youth, nor ſwifter, decreaſing while it is increaſing.

Young willows bend eaſily, and green wits are intangled ſuddenly.

So tutour youth, that the fins of age be not imputed to thee. *Pythag.*

Impardonable are their offences, that for heaping up of riches forget to bring up their youth in honeſt manners.

Noble wits corrupted in their youth with vice are more ungracious than Peaſants born barbarous.

Youth well inſtructed maketh age well diſpoſed.

He is moſt perfect which adorneth youth with vertues. *Hermes.*

The better that a child is by birth, the better ought he in his youth to be inſtructed.

The impreſſion of good doctrine ſtampt in youth, no age nor fortune can out wear

Examples are the beſt leſſons for youth.

The humour of youth is, never to think that good whoſe goodneſs he ſeeth not *S. P. S.*

The death of youth is a ſhipwreck.

Youth ought to uſe pleaſure and recreation, but as natural eaſe and reſt.

The inſtructions which are given to youth ought not to be tedious for being pithy and ſhort, they will the ſooner hear them, and the better keep them.

Young men are no leſs bound to their Tutours for the vertues they teach them, than to their Parents for the life they give them.

Semper magni ingenii adoleſcentes refranandi, potius à gloria quàm invitandi ſunt . amputanda ſunt plura illi ætati, ſi quidnam effloreſcit ingenii laudibus

Vicina eſt lapſibus juventus, quia vernarum æſtus cupiditatum fervore calentis ætatis inflammatur.

Of Muſick.

Defin. *Muſick is an unſearchable and excellent Art, in which by the true concordance in ſounds a ſound of harmony is made, which rejyceth the ſpirits, and unloadeth grief from the heart, and conſiſteth in time and number.* THE

THE moſt commendable end of Muſick is the praiſe of God.

Diſagreeing Muſick and vain paſtimes are the hinderance of delight.

The brutiſh part of the ſoul, depending of the feeding beaſt without reaſon, is that which is pleaſed and ordered by ſounds and Muſick.

Muſick is fitter for funerals than feaſts, and rather meet for paſſions of anger than dalliance and delight. *Euripides.*

Muſick uſed moderately, like ſleep, is the body's beſt recreation

Love teacheth Muſick, though a man be unskilful. *Plat*

Muſick is the gift of God

The better the Muſick, the more delighted in.

To ſing well and live ill, is abominable before God.

Nothing raviſheth the mind ſooner, than Muſick, and no Muſick is more ſweet than Man's voice

There is no Law to be compared with Love, nor any Art to the Art of Muſick.

The ignorance of Muſick hindreth the underſtanding of the Scriptures.

One day takes from us the credit of another, and one Muſick extinguiſheth the pleaſure of another.

Muſick overcometh the heart; and the heart ruleth all the other members

Beauty is no beauty without Vertue, and Muſick no muſick without Art.

Muſick is a comfort to the mind oppreſſed with melancholy.

That Muſick loſeth moſt his ſound and grace which is beſtowed upon a deaf man.

It is impoſſible with great ſhoaks to make ſweet muſick

The

The loud found of Drums and Trumpets is counted a Captain's warfaring Mufick. *Bias.*

Hope is grief's beft mufick, and overcomes the defire of the foul.

Mufick over our Souls is both Queen and Miftrefs.

All things in this World are but the Mufick of in-
confancy.

Mufick, which comforts the mind, hath power to
renew Melancholy.

All things love their likes, and the moft curious
ear the delicateft mufick.

Too much fpeaking hurts, too much galling fmarts,
and too much mufick glutteth and diftempereth.

Youth ought to exercife themfelves in Mufick, and
to imploy their time in thofe harmonies which ftir up
to commendable operations and moral vertues tempe-
ring defire, greedinefs and forrows, forafmuch as mufick confifteth in certain proportions and concord of
the voice.

Mufick is the Load ftone of fellowfhip, the chear-
ful reviver of dulled fpirits, and fole delight of Dancing.

Sylveftres homines facer interprefque Deorum
Cædibus & fœdo v ctu deterruit Orpheus,
Dictus ob id lenire Tigres rabidófque Leones.

Ut quidam magnetes ferrum attrahunt, & Theame-
des, qui in Æthiopia nafcitur, ferrum abigit refpuit-
que: ità eft muficæ genus quod fedet affectus, eft quod
incitet.

Of Dancing.

Defin. *Dancing is an active motion of the body, which*
proceedeth from the lightnefs of the heart, judicially
obferving the true time and meafure of Mufick.

Time and Dancing are twins, begot together ·
Time the firft-born, being the meafure of all
moving, and Dancing the moving of all in meafure.

Dancing is Love's proper exercise.

Dancing is the child of Musick and Love

Love brought forth the three Graces with hand in hand dancing an endless round, and with regarding eyes, that still beware that there be no disgrace found among them

Dancing is, The fair character of the world's consent, The heaven's great figure, and earth's ornament.

The Virgins of *Basil* on the Festival days use to dance publickly, without the company and leading of men, and to sing chast Songs. and by this means Effeminacy, Idleness and Lasciviousness being avoided, they become the mothers of well-knit and manly Children.

Pyrrhus's play was invented in *Crete*, for the Soldiers to exercise themselves in Arms, wherein he taught divers gestures, and sundry shifts in movings, whence it proceedeth that the first use of Wars was a kind of dancing in Arms, as *Dionysius Halicarnasseus*, in his seventh Book, testifieth.

When the Mermaids dance and sing they mean certain death to the Mariner.

When the Dolphins dance, some dangerous storm approacheth.

The soberer and wiser sort among the Heathen, have utterly disliked dancing; and among the old *Romans* it was counted a shame to dance

Dancing is the chiefest instrument of Riot and Excess.

Sempronia, a *Roman* Lady, although fortunate in husband and children, and famous for her knowledge in Learning, yet was blemished with the note of Lasciviousness, for more than necessary expertness in footing a Dance.

Plato and *Aristippus* being invited to a banquet by *Dionysius*, and being both by him commanded to ar-

ray

ray themfelves in Purple, and to dance, *Plato* refufed, with this anfwer, I am born a man, and know
not how to demean my felf in fuch a womanifh effeminacy   *Arift ppus* arrayed himfelf in Purple, and
prepared himfelf to dance, with this anfwer, At the
Solemnities of our Father *Liber* a chaft mind knoweth not how to be corrupted.

Callifthenes, King of *Sicyon,* having a daughter mar-
riageable, commanded that it fhould be proclaimed
at the Games of *Olympus,* that he that would be
accounted *Callifthenes's* Son in Law fhould within
fixty days repair to *Sicyon.*   When many wooers had
met together, *Hippoc'ides* the *Athenan,* fon of *Tifander,* feemed the fitteft   but when he had trod the
Laconick and Antick meafures, and had perfon-ted
them with his legs and arms, *Callifthenes* ftomaching
it, faid, O thou fon of *Tifander,* thou haft dan-
ced away thy marriage

Albertus the Emperour, father of *Ladiflaus,* was
wont to fay, that Hunting was the exercife of a man,
but Dancing of a woman.

Frederick the third, Emperour of *Rome,* would often ufe to fay, that he had rather be fick of a burning Fever than give himfelf to Dancing.

Alphonfus, that moft puiffant King of *Arragon,* and
Sicily, was wont to tax the French-men of great
lightnefs, who the more ancient in years they waxed,
the more they delighted themfelves with vain and
frantick dancing.

The fame *Alphonfus,* when he had beheld a woman dance very lafcivioufly and impudently, Behold,
quoth he, by and by *Sibylla* will deliver an Oracle .
he reputing dancing to be a kind of francticknefs . *Sibylla* the Prophetefs never yielding any Oracle, except
poffeffed firft with a fury.

The

The fame noble King hearing that *Scipio* was wont to recreate himfelf with dancing, faid, that a Dancer did differ nothing from a Mad-man, but only in the length of time, the one being mad fo long as he liveth, the other whilft he danceth. *Alphon.*

The *Romans*, *Lacedæ nonians*, and other well ordered Common-wealths, banifhed out of their Countries all vain pleafure, and above all Dancing, as ferving for none other ufe, but to effeminate young men, and to allure them to vice

No man danceth except he be drunk or mad *Tully*

The vertuous Matrons by dancing have oftentimes loft their Honours, which before they had long nourifhed . and Virgins by it learn that which they had been better never to have known. *Plutarch.*

Tully finding fault with an enemy of his, called him in derifion a brave Dancer.

They which love dancing too much feem to have more brains in their feet than their head, and think to play the fool with reafon. *Terence.*

A lamentable tune is the fweeteft mufick to a woful mind   *S. P S.*

Mufick is the fweet-meat of forrow.

In the fea of Hiftories mention is made of an Archbifhop of *Magdeburg*, who broke his neck dancing with a Danfel

He danceth well to whom Fortune pipeth.

Socrates, which was now pronounced by the Oracle of *Apollo* to be the wifeft man in all *Greece*, was not afhamed in his old age to learn to dance, extolling dancing with wonderful praifes.

It is neceffary that our foot-fteps be as well ruled as our words ought to be.

God threatned the daughters of *Sion*, for that they went winding and prancing, making their fteps to be heard again.

Apud antiquos tanto in pretio habita est saltatio, ut populi Præsides & Antesignani Præsultorum nomine honorarentur

Saltatio non ad pudicos, sed adulteros, pertinet.

Of Man

Defin. Man is a creature made by God after his own Image, just, holy, good and right by nature, and compounded of soul and body: of soul, which was inspired of God with spirit and life, and of a perfect natural body, framed by the same power of God.

A Man may be without fault, but not without sin. *Aug*

Man was created to set forth the glory of his Creatour, and to speak and do those things which are agreeable unto him, through the knowledge of his benefits.

Man is nothing but calamity it self. *Hero.*

Mans nature is desirous of change.

Man was wonderfully created, more wonderfully redeemed. *August.*

Man is the example of Imbecillity, the prey of Time, the sport of Fortune and Envy, the Image of Unconstancy, and the very seat of Phlegm, Choler and Rheums *Plut.*

A good man always draweth good things out of the treasury of his heart, and a wicked man that which is wicked. *Chrys.*

Man is so excellent a creature, that all other creatures are ordained for his use.

The duty of man consisteth in knowing of his own nature, in contemplating the Divine nature, and in labour to profit others.

Man is only a breath and a shadow, and all men are naturally more inclined to evil than goodness, and in their actions are frail and unconstant as the shadow of smoak.   The

The end of men's knowledge is Humiliation and Glory. *Bonaven.*

Man wilfully-minded depriveth himself of all happiness.

Miseries have power over Man, not Man over Miseries

To the greateft men the greateft mischiefs are incident

Whatfoever chanceft to one man may happen likewise to all men.

Man by nature keepeth no measure in his Actions, but is carried away through the violence of his sundry paffions.

No creature but Man hath any knowledge of God.

Man hath no power over his life, but lives ignorant of the certain time of his death, even as a beaft, only comforting himself with confidence

To every man belong two powers, a defire, and an opinion the firft body-bred, leading to pleafure, the other foul bred, leading to good things.

Opinion and defire hold in man great controverfies for when opinion is victor, then he is fober, difcreet and chaft, but when defire overcometh, he is riotous, wild and unfatiate

All men naturally have fome love and liking of the truth.

All things are refolved into thofe things whereof they are compounded the body of man, being earth, fhall return to earth, and the foul, being immortal, fhall enter into immortality.

A man that paffeth his life without profit (as one unworthy to live) ought to have the reft of his life taken from him. *Plato*

As much as a man is from head to foot, fo much is he between his two longeft fingers ends, his arms being ftretched out. *Pliny.*

All

All men are by nature equal, made all of the earth by one workman, and, howſoever we deceive our ſelves, as dear unto God is the poor Peaſant as the mighty Prince. *Plato.*

Miſery then ſeemeth to be ripe for man when he hath age to know miſery

The Philoſophers knew man's imperfections, but could never attain to know the true cauſe of them.

Nonne vides hom n m ut c lſos ad ſidera vultus
Suſtu'erit Deus, ac ſublimia finxerit ora,
Deum pecudes, volucrumque genus, formaſque ferarum,
Segnem atque obſcænam paſſin ſtraviſſet in alvum ?

Of Choice.

Defin   *Choice doth belong unto the mind, and is either of the power of knowing, or of appetite it is the will of man, and the more noble part of his mind, always joyned with Reaſon.*

HE that makes his choice without diſcretion doth ſow his Corn he wots not when, and reaps he knows not what.

It is better to brook an inconvenience than a miſchief, and to be counted a little fond than altogether fooliſh.

In chaſing a Wife, chuſe her not for the ſhape of her body, but for the good qualities of her mind, not for her outward perſon, but her inward perfection.

He that chuſeth an apple by the skin, and a man by his face, may be deceived in the one, and over-ſhot in the other

He that is free, and willingly runneth into Fetters, is a fool, and whoſoever becometh Captive without conſtraint, may be thought either wilful or witleſs.

If the eye be the chuſer, the delight is ſhort, if the will, the end is want, if reaſon, the effect is wiſdom. *Theopomp.*   If

If thou chufe beauty, it fadeth, if riches, they waft, if friends, they wax falfe, if wifdom, fhe continues.

Chufe thy friend, not by his many vows, but by his vertuous actions for who doeth well without boaft, is worthy to be counted a good man, but he that vows much, and performs nothing, is a right worldling. *Chilo.*

In chufing a Magiftrate, refpect not the riches he hath, but the Vertues he enjoyeth for the rich man in honour feareth not to covet, the vertuous man in all fortunes is made for his Country *Solon.*

It is a prefage of good fortune to young Maidens, when flowers fall from their Hats, falfhood from their hearts, and inconftancy from their choice.

Choice is fooneft deceived in thefe three things: in Broakers wares, Courtiers promifes, and Womens conftancy.

Jealoufie if the fruit of rafh election *S P S*

We chufe a fair day by the gray morning, the ftout moil by his fturdy limbs, but in the choice of pleafures we have not election, fith they yield no ufe *Bodinus.*

Zeno of all vertues made his choice of Silence, for by it, faith he, I hear other mens imperfections, and conceal mine own.

All fweet choice is four, being compared with the four choice of fweet love

Who chufeth Love chufeth fear and tears

After the choice of a momentany pleafure enfueth an endlefs calamity

Artemifia the Queen being demanded what choice fhould be ufed in love, quot' fhe, imitate the good Lapidaries, who meafure not the nature of the ftone by the outward hue, but by the inward virtue.

So many Countries, fo many Laws fo many choices, fo many feveral opinions.

He

He that chufeth either Love or Loyalty will never chufe companion.

A little Pack becomes a fmall Pedlar, and a mean choice an humble conceit.

Electio non eſt de præterito, ſed de futuro. Plut.

Liber eſſe non poteſt, cui affeEtus imperant, & cupiditates dominantur.

Of Marriage.

Defin. *Marriage, being the chief ground and preſervation of ſocieties, is nothing elſe but a communion of life between the Husband and the Wife, extending it ſelf to all the parts that belong to their houſe.*

NUptial faith violated ſeldom or never ſcapes without revenge. *Crat.*

There is no greater plague to a married woman, than when her husband diſchargeth on her back all his jars, quarrels and paſſions, and reſerveth his pleaſures, joys and company for another.

Let men obey the Laws, and women their Husband's will. *Socrat.*

Barren marriages have many brawls. *Baſil.*

Humble Wedlock is better than proud Virginity. *Aug.*

It is not meet that young men ſhould marry yet, or old men ever *Diog.*

Marriage is an evil to be wiſhed.

A Woman without dowry hath no liberty to ſpeak. *Eurip.*

Unhappy is that man that marrieth being in poverty.

A woman bringeth a man two joyful days, the firſt of her marriage, the ſecond her death. *Stobæus.*

A man in making himſelf faſt undoes himſelf.

Old age and marriage are alike: for we deſire them both, and once poſſeſſed, then we repent. *Theod*

Give

Give thy wife no power over thee. for if thou suffer her to day to tread upon thy foot, she will not stick to morrow to tread upon thy head.

Amongst the *Rhodians*, the fathers were commanded in marrying their sons to travel but one day, to marry one vertuous daughter, to travel ten years. *Aurel.*

No man suffereth his wife much, but he is bound to suffer more. *Aurel.*

The *Grecian* Ladies counted their years from their marriage, not their birth.

The *Caspians* made a Law, that he which married after he had passed fifty years, should at the common assemblies and feasts sit in the lowest and vilest place, as one that committed a fact repugnant to nature, terming him nought else but a filthy and doting old Lecher.

He that marrieth one fair and dishonest, weddeth himself to a world of miseries. and if to one beautifull, and never so vertuous, yet let him think this, he shall have a woman, and therefore a necessary evil.

Such as are desirous to marry in haste have oftentimes sufficient time to repent at leasure

If thou marry in age, thy wife's fresh colours will breed in thee dead thoughts and suspicion, and thy white hairs her loathsomeness and sorrow.

Cleobulus meeting with his Son *Ireon*, solemnizing the ceremony of Marriage, gave him in his hand a branch of Henbane meaning by this, that the vertuous disposition of a Wife is never so perfect, but it is interlaced with some froward fancies.

Inequality in marriage is often an enemy to love. *Bias.*

The roundest Circle hath his Diameter, the favourablest Aspects their incident oppositions, and Marriage is qualified with many trifling griefs and troubles.

He

He that marries himfelf to a fair face, ties himfelf oftentimes to a foul bargain. *Bias*

A good husband muft be wife in words, mild in converfation, faithful in promife, circumfpect in giving counfel, careful in provifion for his houfe, diligent in ordering his goods, patient in importunity, jealous in bringing up his youth.

A good wife muft be grave abroad, wife at home, patient to fuffer, conftant to love, friendly to her neighbours, provident for her houfhold. *Theophraftus.*

Marriage with peace, is this world's Paradife , with ftrife, this life's Purgatory

Silence and patience caufe concord between married couples.

It is better to marry a quiet Fool, than a witty Scold.

In marriage rather inquire after thy Wife's good conditions than her great Dowry.

Spiritual marriage beginneth in baptifm, is ratified in good life, and confummated in a happy death.

Thales, feeing *So on* lamenting the death of his Son, faid, That for the prevention of fuch like troubles he refufed to be married

He which would fain find fome means to trouble himfelf, needs but to take upon him either the government of a Ship, or a Wife *Plaut.*

A chaft Matron, by obeying her husband's will, hath rule over him.

The firft conjunction of man's fociety is Man and Wife.

Qui cogitat de nuptiis, non cogitat bene,
Cogitat enim, contrah t dehinc nuptias,
Malorum origo quum fit hec mortalibus.
Dotatam enim fi fortè pauper duxerit,
Non jam ille conjugem, fed habet heram fibi,
Cui fervit : at fi pauper aliquam duxerit

Nil

Nil afferentem, servus ille rursum erit;
Dum victum utrique, non sib. tantùm, parat.
Duxitne fœdam? vita dehinc acerba erit.
Et jam pigebit ingredi limen domûs
Duxitne formosam? n h o erit hæc magis
Sui mariti quàm sui v cini
Ità in aliquod necesse est ut incidit malum.
Matrimonii encomium
Felices ter & amplius,
Quos irrupta tenet copula, nec malis
Divulsus querimoniis
Supremâ citiùs solvet amor die. Hor.

Of Chastity.

Defin *Chastity is the beauty of the soul, and purity of life, which refuseth the corrupt pleasures of the flesh, and is onely possessed of those who keep their bodies clean and undefiled · and it consisteth either in sincere Virginity, or in faithful Matrimony,*

Chastity is of small force to resist, where wealth and dignity joyned in league are armed to assault.

Pure Chastity is beauty to our souls, grace to our bodies, and peace to our desires. *Solon.*

Frugality is the sign of Chastity.

Chastity in Wedlock is good, but more commendable it is in Virginity and Widowhood.

Chastity is a vertue of the soul, whose companion is Fortitude. *Amb.*

Chastity is of no account without Humility, nor Humility without Chastity *Greg.*

Chastity is the seal of Grace, the staff of Devotion, the mark of the Just, the crown of Virginity, the glory of Life, and a comfort in Martyrdom.

Chastity groweth cheap, where God is not thought dear.

The

The firſt degree of Chaſtity is pure Virginity, the ſecond, faithful Matrimony.

Idleneſs is the enemy to Chaſtity.

As Humility is neceſſary, ſo chaſtity is honourable.

Chaſtity, Humility and Charity, are the united vertues of the ſoul.

Chaſtity without Charity is a lamp without oil.

Chaſtity and Modeſty are ſufficient to enrich the poor

Rather make choice of honeſty and manners, than looſeneſs of behaviour with great lands and rich poſſeſſions.

Chaſtity is known in extremity, and crowned in the end with eternity.

If Chaſtity be once loſt, there is nothing left praiſeworthy in a woman. *Nymph.*

The firſt ſtep to Chaſtity is to know the fault, the next to avoid it.

Though the body be never ſo fair, without Chaſtity it cannot be beautiful.

Beauty by Chaſtity purchaſeth praiſe and immortality.

Beauty without Chaſtity is like a Mandrake apple, comely in ſhew, but poiſonous in taſte

Feaſts, Dances and Plays, are provocations to unchaſtity. *Quint*

Beauty is like flowers in the Spring, and Chaſtity like the ſtars of Heaven.

Where neceſſity is joyned to unchaſtity, there authority is given to uncleanneſs   for neither is ſhe chaſt which by fear is compelled, neither is ſhe honeſt which with need is obtained. *Aug.*

A wandring eye is a manifeſt token of an unchaſt heart.

Gracious is the face which promiſeth nothing but love, and moſt celeſtial the reſolution that lives upon Chaſtity.

The

The true modefty of an honeft man ftriketh more fhame with his prefence, than the fight of many wicked and immodeft perfons can ftir to filthinefs with their talkings.

Chaftity with the reins of reafon bridleth the rage of luft.

Do not fay thou haft a chaft mind, if thine eye be wanton, for a lafcivious look, is a fign of an inconftant heart. *Bern.*

Amongft all the conflicts of a Chriftian foul, none is more hard than the wars of a chaft mind. for the fight is continual, and the victory rare. *Cyprian.*

A chaft ear cannot abide to hear that which is dishoneft.

———*Nullâ reparabilis arte*
Læfa pudicitia eft : deperit illa femel,
Lis eft cum forma magna pudicitiæ.

Of Content.

Defin. *Content is a quiet and fettled refolution in the mind, free from ambition and envy, aiming no farther than at thofe things already poffeffed.*

Ontent is great riches, and patient poverty is the enemy of Fortune.

Better it is for a time with content to prevent danger, than to buy feigned pleafures with Repentance.

He that cannot have what he would, muft be content with what he can get.

Content is fweet fauce to every difh, and pleafantnefs a fingular portion to prevent a mifchief.

Content is more worth than a Kingdom, and love no lefs worth than life.

A wife man preferreth content before riches, and a clear mind before great promotion.

Mifery teacheth happy content. *Solon.*

What

What can be fweeter than content, where man's life is affured in nothing more than in wretchednefs?

Content makes men happy, but Pride ruins them.

Many men lofe by defire, but are crowned by content. *Plato*

To covet much is mifery, to live content with fufficient is earthly felicity.

To will much is folly, where ability wanteth, to defire nothing is content, that defpifeth all things

The riches that men gather, in time may fail, friends may wax falfe, hope may deceive, vain-glory may tempt; but content can never be conquered.

Content is the bleffing of nature, the falve of poverty, the mafter of forrow, and the end of mifery.

To live, nature affordeth, to live content, wifdom teacheth.

Content, though it lofe much of the world, it partakes much of God.

To live to God, to defpife the world, to fear no mifery, and to flie flattery are the enfigns of content.

What we have by the world is mifery, what we have by content is wifdom. *Aurel.*

The eye's quiet, the thought's medicine, and the defire's mithridate, is content.

To be content kills adverfity if it affault, dries tears if they flow, ftays wrath if it urge, wins heaven if it continue.

He is perfectly content which in extremes can fubdue his own affections

No riches are comparable to a contented mind. *Plut.*

He that is patient and content in his troubles, preventeth the poifon of evil tongues in their lavifh talkings.

Content and Patience are the two vertues which conquer and overthrow all anger, malice, wrath and backbiting.

To

To live in content in our eftate is the beft means to prevent ambitious defires.

——*Nemo, quam fibi fortem*
Seu ratio dederit, feu fors objecerit, illâ
Contentus vivit. Horace. *Vivitur parvo bene.*

Of Conftancy.

Defin. *Conftancy is the true and unmovable ftrength of the mind, not puffed up in profperity, nor depreffed in adverfity: it is fometimes called Stability, and Perfeverance, fometimes Pertinacy, the laft part of Fortitude.*

Onftancy, except it be in truth and in a good caufe, is impudency.

It is the part of conftancy to refift the dolours of the mind, and to perfevere in a well deliberated action. *Arift.*

Conftancy is the health of the mind, by which is underftood the whole force and efficacy of wifdom. *Cicero.*

He that hath an inconftant mind is either blind or deaf

Conftancy is the daughter of Patience and Humility. *Niphus.*

Conftancy is the mean between elation and dejection of the mind, guided by reafon. *Plato.*

Conftancy is the only *Nepenthes,* which whofo drinketh of, forgetteth all care and grief.

Nothing in the world fooner remedieth forrows than conftancy and patience, which endureth adverfity and violence without making any fhew or femblance *Agrippa.*

It is the lightnefs of the wit rafhly to promife what a man will not, or is not able to perform. *Caffiodorus.*

The bleffed life is in Heaven, but it is to be attained unto by perfeverance.

It

It is a' great shame to be weary of seeking that which is most precious *Plato.*

Many begin well, but few continue to the end.

Perseverance is the only daughter of the great King, the end and confirmation of all vertues, and the vertue without which no man shall see God. *Bern.*

Perseverance is the sister of Patience, the daughter of Constancy, the friend of Peace, and the bond of Friendship.

Not to go forward in the way of God, is to go backward.

The constant man in adversity mourneth not, in prosperity insulteth not, and in trouble pineth not away: He is always an even tempered man.

In vain he runneth that fainteth before he comes to the Goal. *Greg.*

The unconstant man is like *Alcibiades*'s Tables, fair without, and foul within.

The only way to constancy is by wisdom.

A constant minded man is free from care and grief, despising death: and is so resolved to endure it, that he remembreth all sorrows to be ended by it. *Cicero.*

Constancy is the ornament of all vertues.

He is not to be reputed constant, whose mind taketh no fresh courage in the midst of extremities. *Bern.*

Raræ felicitatis est celeritas & magnitudo, rarioris diuturnitas & constantia. Demost.

Tardè aggredere, & quod aggressurus sis perseveranter prosequere

Constans est, qui adversa æq' è ac prospera æquanimiter suffert.

Sperat infestis, metuit secundis
Alteram fortem bene præparatum pectus. Hor.

Of Religion

Defin. *Religion is a justice of men towards God, or a divine honouring of him in the perfect and true knowledge*
of

*of his word, peculiar only to man. it is the ground of
all other vertues, and the only means to unite and re-
concile man unto God for his salvation.*

NO errour is so dangerous as that which is committed in Religion; forasmuch as our salvation,
quiet and happiness consisteth therein.

Man was created for the service of God, and ought
above all things to make account of Religion.

If it be a lewd part to turn the traveller out of his
way, and so to hinder him in his journey, then are
such as teach false doctrine much more to be detested,
because through such a mischief they lead men to
destruction *Aug.*

Saint *Augustine* reproveth *Varro* and *Pontifex Scæ-
vola,* who were of opinion, that it was very expedient
men should be deceived in Religion, because that
there is no felicity or certain rest but in the full assurance thereof, and in an infallible truth: without
Divinity and the Doctrine of God, none can make
any principle at all in the discipline of manners.

The Word is a medicine to a troubled spirit, but
being falsly taught it proveth a poison *Bern.*

Religion is like a square or balance, it is the canon
and rule to live well by, and the very touch-stone
which discerneth the truth from falshood.

The ancient Fathers have given three principal
marks by which the true Religion is known first,
that it serveth the true God, secondly, that it serveth
him according to his Word, thirdly, that it reconcileth that man unto him which followeth it.

Vices border upon Vertues, Superstition upon Religion, Prodigality upon Bounty.

The true worship of God consisteth in spirit and
truth *Chrysost.*

Where Religion is, Arms may easily be brought,
but where Arms are without Religion, Religion may
hardly be brought in. There

There can be no furer fign of the ruine of a Kingdom than contempt of Religion.

There can be no true Religon, where the Word of God is wanting.

Thofe men are truly religious who refufe the vain and tranfitory pleafures of the world, and wholly fet their minds on divine meditations.

He which is negligent and ignorant in the fervice of the Creator, can never be careful in any good caufe.

Religion doth link and unite us together, to ferve with willingnefs one God Almighty. It is the guide of all other vertues, and they who do not exercife themfelves therein to withftand all falfe opinions, are like thofe Souldiers which go to war without weapons.

True Religion is the well tempered mortar that buildeth up all Eftates.

The principal fervice of God confifteth in true obedience, which the Prophets call a Spiritual Chaftity, not to fwerve therefrom, not to think that whatfoever we find good in our own eyes pleafeth him

The knowledge of true Religion, Humility and Patience entertaineth Concord.

If men did know the truth, and the happinefs which followeth true Religion, the voluptuous man would there feek his pleafure the covetous man his wealth, the ambitious man his glory, fith it is the only mean which can fill the heart, and fatisfie the defire it ferveth alfo for a guide to lead us unto God, whereas the contrary doth clean withhold us from him.

No creature is capable of Religion but only man. *Bafil.*

The firft Law that fhould be given to men fhould be the increafe of Religion and Piety.

It is a very hard matter to change Religion.

Where no Religion refteth, there can be no vertue abiding. True

True Religion is to be learned by faith, not by reason.

Religion is the stay of the weak, the master of the ignorant, the Philosophy of the simple, the oratory of the devout, the remedy of sin, the counsel of the just, and the comfort of the troubled.

Pure Religion and undefiled before God the Father is this, to visit the fatherless and widows in their adversity, and for a man to keep himself unspotted of the world.

Philosophia pernosci non potest sine Christiana veráque religione: quam præcellentem si tollis, fateo, ecce & clamo, ludibrium alla, vanitas, delirium.

Oportet Principem ante omnia esse Deteplam.

Of our Country, or Common-wealth

Defin. Our Country is the Region or Climate under which we are born, the Common mother of us all, which we ought to hold so dear, that in the defence thereof we should not fear to hazard our lives.

THere can be no affinity nearer than our Country. *Plato.*

Men are not born for themselves, but for their Country, Parents, Kindred, and Friends. *Cicero.*

There is nothing more to be desired, nor any thing ought to be more dear to us, than the love of our Country.

Children, Parents, Friends are near to us, but our Country challengeth a greater love, for whose preservation we ought to oppose our lives to the greatest dangers.

It is not enough once to have loved thy Country, but continue it to the end.

Wheresoever we may live well, there is our Country.

The resemblance of our Country is most sweet. *Livius.*

I   To

To fome men their Country is their fhame, and fome are the fhame of their Country.

Let no man boaft that he is the Citizen of a great City, but that he is worthy of an honourable Coun-try. *Arift.*

We ought to behave our felves towards our Coun-try thankfully as to a mother.

The profit of the Country extendeth it felf to every City of the fame. *Stob.*

Our Country, faith *Cicero*, affordeth large fields, for every one to run to honour.

Our Country firft challengeth us by nature.

The whole world is a wife man's Country.

Neceffity compelleth every man to love his Coun-try. *Eurip.*

The love which we bear to our Country is not piety, as fome fuppofe, but charity : for there is no piety but that which we bear to God and our Pa-rents.

Many love their Country, not for it felf, but for that which they poffefs in it.

Sweet is that death and honourable which we fuf-fer for our Country. *Horace.*

If it be asked to whom we are moft engaged, and owe moft duty; our Country and Parents are they that may juftly challenge it.

The life which we owe to death is made everlaft-ing, being loft in defence of our Country.

Happy is that death which, being due to nature, is beftowed upon our Country.

Happy is that Common-wealth where the people do fear the Law as a Tyrant *Plato*

A Common-wealth confifteth of two things, Re-ward, and Punifhment.

As the body is without members, fo is the Com-mon-wealth without Laws.

Peace in a Common-wealth is like harmony in Mu-fick. *Auguft.*　　　　　　　　　　　　　　　Men

Men of defert are leaft efteemed of in their own
Country. *Eraf.*

Nefcio quâ natale folum dulcedine cunctos
Dicit, & immemores non finit effe fui. *Ovid.*

Omnibus qui patriam conferuaverint, adjuverint, aux-
erint, certus eft in cælo & definitus locus, ubi beati aui
fempiterno fruentur. *Cicero.*

Of Hope.

Defin. *Hope is that vertue whereby the mind of man put-*
teth great truft in honeft and weighty matters, having
a certain and fure confidence in himfelf; and this hope
muft be ftrong'y grounded upon a fure expectation of the
help and grace of God, without which it is vain and
imperfect.

TO be clean without hope is a hap incident to the
unhappy man.

He that will lofe a favour for a hope hath fome wit,
but fmall ftore of wifdom. *Bias.*

Fortune may take away our goods, but death cannot deprive us of hope.

Hopes above Fortune are the fore-pointers of deep
falls.

If thou chance to love, hope well whatfoever thy
hap be.

That which is moft common is Hope.

Hope is a waking man's dream. *Plin.*

To put our confidence in the creature, is to defpair
of the Creatour *Greg.*

Vain is the hope that doth not fear God.

This mortal life is the hope of the immortal. *Aug.*

They only hope well who have a good confcience.

Hope is the companion of Love.

Hope cannot be without Faith.

Hope is the God of the wretched. *Ber.*

Hope

'Hope grounded on God never faileth, but built on the world it never thriveth.

Hope apprehendeth things unseen, and attaineth things by continuance. *Plato.*

The evening's hope may comfort the morning's misery.

Hope is the Merchant-man's comfort, and the Souldier's companion, but vain hope is the fool's Paradise, and the ambitious man's overthrow.

'Hope of life is vanity, hope in death is life, and the life of hope is vertue.

'Hope waiteth on great men's tongues, and beguileth believing followers,

Sweet words beget hope, large protestations nourish it, and contempt kills it.

He that supposeth to thrive by hope may happen to beg in misery. *Bion.*

The apprehension of hope derideth grief, and the fulness of hope consumeth it.

As each one part laboureth for the conservation of the whole body, so hope for the accomplishment of all desires.

Sadness is the punishment of the heart, hope the medicine of distress. *Crates.*

Hope is a pleasant passion of the mind, which doth not only promise us those things that we most desire, but those things also which we utterly despair of.

Our high hopes have oftentimes hard fortunes; and such as reach at the tree commonly stumble at the root.

To hope for requital of benefits bestowed may rather be counted usury than vertue.

A cowardly Lover without hope shall never gain fair love without good fortune.

To hope against all hope is the excellency of a mighty resolution.

In

In a little place is hid a great treasure, and in a small hope a boundless expectation.

Confidence, except it be guided by modesty, and proceed from judgment, may rather be called arrogancy than hope

Hope of all passions is the sweetest and most pleasant, and hereof it is said, that hope only comforteth the miserable.

Hope is the governour of men.

Perdiccas seeing *Alexander* largely bestow many benefits upon his friends, asked him what he would leave for himself? he answered, Hope.

A good and vertuous man ought always to hope well, and to fear nothing

Hope is the beginning of victory to come, and doth presage the same. *Pind.*

Sola spes hominem in miseriis consolari solet.
Miserum est timere, cùm speres nihil.
Sperare qui nihil potest, desperet nihil.

Of Charity.

Defin. *Charity is the indissoluble band of God w th us, whereby we are inflamed with the love of him for that which we owe unto him, and thereby are induced to love our neighbour's for the love of God.*

Charity is the scope of all God's Commandments. *Chrys.*

Charity delayed is half lost.

Charity ransometh us from sin, and delivereth us from death.

Charity increaseth Faith, begetteth Hope, and maketh us at one with God.

As the Body without the Soul enjoyeth no life, so all other vertues without Charity are cold and fruitless.

Charity

Charity is a good and gracious effect of the Soul, whereby man's heart hath no fancy to esteem any thing in this world before the study to know God.

The charitable man is the true lover of God. *Severus*

As the Sun is to the world, and life to the body, so is Charity to the heart.

Charity resembleth fire, which inflameth all things it toucheth. *Eraf.*

Charity in adversity is patient, in prosperity temperate, in passions strong, in good works quick, in temptations secure, in hospitality bountiful, amongst her true children joyful, amongst her false friends patient.

Charity in the midst of injuries is secure, in heart bountiful, in pleasures meek, in concealing evils innocent, in truth quiet, at others misfortunes sad, in vertues joyful.

Charity in adversity fainteth not, because it is patient, and revengeth not injuries, because it is bountiful.

He that truly loveth, believeth and hopeth. *Aug.*

By Charity one seeth the glorious light of God *Aug.*

He always hath to give that is full of Charity. *Bernard.*

To love with all the soul, is to love wisely; to love with all the strength, is manfully to suffer for truth; to love with all our heart, is to prefer the love of God before all things that flatter us. *Aug.*

The measure in loving God is to love him without measure. *Bernard.*

Charity is the way of man to God, and the way of God to man. *Aug.*

If any man abound with the love of God, he is streightways apt and ready to all good, he laboureth, and is not weary; he is weary, and feeleth it not, the malicious mock him, and he perceiveth it not. *Ber.*

The

The love of God hath power to transform man into God.

Charity maketh a man absolute and perfect in all other vertues.

Neither the multitude of travels, nor the antiquity of service, but the greatnefs of Charity increaseth the reward.

The nature of charity is to draw all things to it self, and to make them participate of it self. *Lactan.*

God is charity; what thing is more precious? and he that dwelleth in charity dwelleth in God, what thing is more secure? and God in him; what thing is more delectable?

There is no vertue perfect without love, nor love without charity.

Charity is never idle, but worketh for him it loveth.

The greatest argument of godly love is to love what God loveth.

Charitable love is under no rule, but is lord of all laws, and a boundlefs Emperour.

There is true charity where two several bodies have one united heart.

Charity is the child of Faith, and guide to everlasting felicity

All charity is love, but not all love charity. *Aug.*

The filthy effects of bribery hinder exceedingly the works of charity. *Plato.*

Charity causeth men to forsake sin, and embrace vertue.

Charity is a word used of many, but understood of few.

By charity with God we learn what is our duty towards man.

By charity all men, especially Christians, are linked and bound in conscience to relieve one another.

It

It is the true property of a charitable minded man, lovingly to invite the poor, courteously to intreat them, and quickly to suffer them to depart.

A poor man being in charity is rich, but a rich man without charity is poor. *August.*

Charity and Pride do both feed the poor; the one to the praise and glory of God, the other to get glory and praise amongst men.

Tyrannorum vita est in qua nulla est charitas, nulla fides, nulla stabilis benevolentia, aut fiducia, omnia semper suspecta & sollicita sunt, nullus locus amicitia.

Ad prata &c. atra pecudum greges ligantur isto modo, quod fructus ex iis capiuntur, hominis charitas & amicitia gratuita.

Of Humility.

Defin. Humility is a voluntary inclination of the mind, grounded upon a perfect knowledge of own condition. a vertue by the which a man in the most true consideration of his inward qualities, maketh least account of himself.

HE that gathereth vertues without Humility, casteth dust against the wind. *Greg.*

As *Demosthenes*, being demanded what was the first precept of eloquence, answered, To pronounce well; being asked what was the second, answered the like, and so the third. to the precepts of Religion, the first, second, and third, are Humility.

It is no commendation to be humble in adversity. but in the midst of prosperity to bear lowly sail, deserveth great praise.

Pride, perceiving Humility to be honourable, desires oft-times to be covered with the cloak thereof; for fear lest, appearing always in his own likeness, he should be little regarded. *Demost.*

The

The chief point of man's humility confifteth in this, to fubject his will unto the will of God.

Happy is that man whofe calling is great, and fpirit humble.

The beft armour of the mind is humility

Humility for her excelling fhould be the fifter of true Nobility. *Pontanus.*

Humility is more neceffary than Virginity. *Bern.*

There are three degrees of Humility the firft of Repentance ; the fecond, Defire of Righteoufnefs, the third, Works of Mercy

Pride wageth war in the Kingdom of Humility. *Greg.*

Humility only is the repairer of decayed Chaftity

The eafieft way to Dignity is true Humility.

True difcretion is never purchafed but by true Humility.

When all vices in a manner decay in age, only Covetoufnefs increafeth. *Aug*

Sith the Country which we defire to dwell in is high and heavenly, and the way thither Lowlinefs and Humility, why then, defiring this Country, do we refufe the way ? *Aug.*

Of all vertuous works the hardeft is to be humble.

Humility hath many times brought that to pafs which no other vertue nor reafon could effect

To the humble minded man God revealeth the knowledge of his truth

If thou defire to afcend where God the Father fitteth, thou muft put on the Humility which Chrift the Son teacheth.

The vertue of Humility is the only repairer and reftorer of decayed Charity.

Humility teacheth a man how to rule his affections, and in all his actions to keep a mean.

The Spirit of God delighteth to dwell in the heart of the humble man. *Eraf.*

If thou intend to build any stately thing, think first upon the foundation of Humility.

As lowliness of heart maketh a man highly in favour with God, so meekness of words maketh him to sink into the hearts of men.

Humbleness of mind stirs up affection, augments, benevolence, supports good equity, and preserveth in safety the whole estate of a Country.

Men are not in any thing more like unto their Maker, than in Gentleness and Humility.

Charity and Humility purchase immortality.

God dwelleth in Heaven· if thou arrogantly lift up thy self unto him, he will flie from thee; but if thou humble thy self before him, he will come down to thee. *August.*

Hum les deus extollit, superbos vero deprimit humiliatque.

Humilitas animi sublimitas Christiani.

Tria sunt quæ radicata nutriant humilitatem; assiduitas subjectionis, consideratio propriæ fragilitatis, & consideratio rei melioris.

Of Old age.

Defin. *Old age is the gift of heaven, is the long expence of many years, the exchange of sundry fortunes, and the school of experience.*

Sickness and Old age are the two crutches whereon life walketh to death, which arresteth every one to pay the debt which they owe unto nature. *Theopomp.*

It is a vain thing for him that is old to wish that he were young again.

It is a lamentable thing to be old with fear, before a man comes to be old by age.

A gray beard is a certain sign of old age, but not an assured token of a good wit

Age ought to keep a streight diet, or else will ensue a sickly life. Hoary

Hoary hairs are Embaſſadours of great experience. *Chilo.*

As old folk are very ſuſpicious to miſtruſt every thing, ſo are they likewiſe very credulous to believe any thing.

Youth never rideth well, but when age holdeth the bridle.

Age rather ſeeketh food for ſuſtenance, than followeth feaſts for ſurfeits.

The benefit of old age is liberty. *Soph.*

When all things by time decay, knowledge by age increaſeth. *Ariſt.*

Old age enjoyeth all things, and wanteth all things, *Democ.*

In age we ought to make more readineſs to die than proviſion to live: for the ſteel being ſpent, the knife cannot cut; the Sun being ſet, the day cannot tarry; the flower being fallen, there is no hope of fruit; and old age being once come, life cannot long endure. *Aurel*

Thoſe that ſpend their youth without reſtraint, would lead their age without comroulment

Beware of old age, for it cometh not alone *Eurip.*

Every age of man hath end, but old age hath none. *Cicero.*

In youth ſtudy to live well, in age to die well; for to die well is to die willingly. *Seneca.*

Old men are young mens precedents.

An old man hath more experience to make a perfect choice, than a young man skill in a happy chance.

Age directeth all his doings by wiſdom, but youth doateth upon his own will.

Age, having bought wit with pain and peril, foreſeeth dangers and eſcheweth them.

The difference between an old man and a young man is this, the one is followed as a friend to others, the other is eſchewed as an enemy to himſelf.

The

The *Brachmans* and *Gymnosophists* made a Law, that none under the age of forty should marry without consent of their Seniors, lest in their choice without skill, the man in progress of time should begin to loath, or the woman not to love.

Old men are often envied for their virtue, but young men pitied for their vice.

Old men by reason of their age, and weakness of their strength, are subject to sundry imperfections, and molested with many diseases. *Pacuvius*.

Gray hairs oft times are intangled with love, but heedless youth is intrapped with lust

Age is more to be honoured for his wisdom, than youth commended for his beauty

The mind of an old man is not mutable, his fancies are fixed, and his affections not flitting, he chuseth without intention to change, and never forsakes his choice till death makes challenge of his life.

The old Cedar-tree is less shaken with the wind than the young bramble, and age far more stayed in his affairs than youth.

Old men are more meet to give counsel, than fit to follow wars.

Though young men excel in strength, yet old men exceed in stedfastness

Though all men are subject to the sudden stroke of death, yet old men in nature seem nearest to the grave.

Age is a Crown of Glory, when it is adorned with righteousness, but the dregs of dishonour, when it is mingled with mischief

Honourable age consisteth not in the term of years, neither is it measured by the date of many days, but by godly wisdom, and an undefiled life

Age is forgetful, and gray hairs are declining steps of strength.

Age

Age is given to melancholy, and many years are acquainted with many dumps

Age speaketh by experience, and liketh by trial but youth leaneth unto wit which is void of wisdom.

He that will not be advised by age, shall be deceived by youth

Old age is the fore-runner of death

Age and Time are two things which men may fore-think of, but never prevent.

Men of age fear and fore-fee that which youth never regardeth

Old folks oft times are more greedy of coin, than careful to keep a good conscience.

Age may be allowed to gaze at beauty's blossom, but youth must climb the tree and enjoy the fruit

Nature lendeth age authority, but gentleness of heart is the glory of all years

Children are compared to Spring time, striplings to Summer-season, youth to Autumn, and old men to Winter.

An old man ought to remember his age past, and to bethink himself how he hath spent his time if he find himself faulty in neglecting such good deeds as he might have none, he ought forthwith to be careful to spend the remainder of his life in liberality towards the poor

Old men are commonly covetous, because their getting days are past

It is a great shame for an old man to be ignorant in the principles of Religion.

An old man ought to be reverenced for his gravity sooner than for his grey hairs.

If young men had knowledge, and old men strength, the world would become a new Paradise.

A man aged and wise is worthy of a double reverence.

Infancy

Infancy is but a foolish simplicity, full of lamenta-
tions and harms, as it were laid open to a main sea
without a stern

Youth is an indiscreet heat, outrageous, blind,
heady, violent and vain

> *Non est senectus (ut tu opinaris, pater)*
> *Onus gravissimum , sed impat intius*
> *Qui fert, sibi ipse est author illius mali.*
> *Patienter atqui sibi quietem comparat,*
> *Dum dexterè ejus moribus se accommodat,*
> *Non ulli solùm detrahit molestiam,*
> *Accersit aliquam sed voluptatem sibi.*
> *Si navigandum sit quatuor per dies,*
> *De commeatu cura nobis maxima ·*
> *At si in senectam qui licet comparare,*
> *Non instruemus nos eo viatico ?*

Of Death.

Defin. Death is taken three manner of ways. The first
is the separation of the Soul from the body, with the
dissolution of the body until the Resurrection · the second
is death of sin, sith he is said to be dead which lieth
sleeping in sin . the third is eternal death, into which
the wicked shall be condemned in the day of the general judgment.

DEath is the Law of Nature, the tribute of the
flesh, the remedy of evils, and the path either
to heavenly felicity, or eternal misery. *Heraclit.*

Destiny may be deferred, but can never be prevented

An honourable death is to be preferred before an
infamous life.

That man is very simple that dreadeth death, because he feareth thereby to be cut off from the pleasures of this life.

Death hath his root from sin. *Aug*

Death is the end of fear, and beginning of felicity

There is nothing more certain than death, nor any thing more uncertain than the hour of death

No man dieth more willingly then he that hath lived moſt honeſtly.

It is better to die well, than to live wantonly. *Socr.*

Death it ſelf is not ſo painful as the fear of death is unpleaſant.

Death is the end of all miſeries, but infamy is the beginning of all ſorrow. *Plut.*

While men ſeek to prolong their life, they are prevented by ſome ſudden death.

While we think to flie death, we moſt earneſtly follow death.

Who is he that being luſty and young in the morning, can promiſe himſelf life until the evening?

Many men deſire death in their miſery, that cannot abide his preſence in the time of their proſperity.

An evil death putteth great doubt of a good life, and a good death partly excuſeth an evil life.

The death of evil men is the ſafety of good men living. *Cicero*

He that every hour feareth death, can never be poſſeſſed of a quiet conſcience.

Nothing is more like to death than ſleep, who is death's eldeſt brother. *Cic.*

There is nothing more common than ſuddain death, which being conſidered by the great Philoſopher *Demorat*, he therefore warned the Empeiour *Adrian*, and ſuch others as lived at their pleaſure and eaſe, in no wiſe to forget how in a very ſhort moment they ſhould be no more.

Death woundeth deeply, without either dread or dalliance

Sith death is a thing, that cannot be avoided, it ought of all men the leſs to be feared.

By

By the same way that life goeth death cometh. *Aurel*

Nature hath given no better thing than Death. *Pliny*

The most profitable thing for the world is the Death of covetous and evil people.

Death is common to all persons, though to some one way, and to some another

If we live to die, then we die to live.

All things have an end by death, save only death, whose end is unknown.

Death is metaphorically called the end of all flesh. *Arist.*

The last cure of diseases is death.

Death despiseth all riches and glory, and ruleth over all estates alike *Boetius*

None need to fear death, save those that have committed so much injury as after death deserves damnation *Socrat.*

Wisdom maketh men to despise death, it ought therefore of all men to be imbraced as the best remedy against the fear of death *Hermes.*

So live and hope as thou wouldst die immediately. *Plin.*

Non deterret sapientem mors, quæ propter incertos casus quotidie imminet, & propter brevitatem vitæ nunquam longe potest abesse

Tria sunt genera mortis una mors est peccati, ut, anima quæ peccat, morte morietur, altera mystica, quando quis peccato moritur, & Deo vivit, tertia, quâ cursum vitæ hujus explemus. *Aug.*

Of Time.

Defin. *Time is a secret and speedy consumer of hours and seasons, older than any thing but the first, and both the bringer forth and master of whatsoever is in this world.*

THERE

Here is no fore which in time may not be folved, nor care which cannot be cured, no fire fo great which may not be quenched, no love, liking, fancy, or affection, which in time may not either be repreffed or redreffed.

Time is the perfect Herald of Truth. *Cic.*

Time is the beft Oratour to a refolute mind

Daily actions are meafured by prefent behaviour

Time is the Herald that beft emblazoneth the conceits of the mind

Time is the fweet Phyfician that alloweth a remedy for every mifhap

Time is the Father of mutability. *Solon*

Time fpent without profit bringeth repentance, and occafion let flip when it might be taken is counted prodigality,

There is nothing among men fo entirely beloved, but it may in time be difliked, nothing fo healthful, but it may be difeafed, nothing fo ftrong, but it may be broken, neither any thing fo well kept, but it may be corrupted

Truth is the daughter of Time, and there is nothing fo fecret but the date of many days will reveal it.

In time the ignorant may become learned, the foolifh may be made wife, and the wildeft wanton may be brought to a modeft matron *Bias.*

The happier our time is, the fhorter while it lafteth *Plin.*

Say not that the time that our fore fathers lived in was better than this prefent Age.

Vertue and good life make good days, but abundance of vice corrupteth the time *Jerome*

As Oil, though it be moift, quencheth not the fire fo Time, though never fo long, is no fure covert for fin.

Nothing is more precious than Time, yet nothing lefs efteemed of *Bern*

As

As a sparkle raked up in cinders will at last begin to glow and manifestly flame so treachery hid in silence, and obscured by time, will at length break forth and cry for revenge.

Whatsoever villainy the heart doth think, and the hand effect, in process of time the worm of conscience will bewray.

Time draweth wrinkles in a fair face, but addeth fresh colours to a fresh friend

Things past may be repented, but not recalled *Liv.*

A certain Philosopher being demanded what was the first thing needful to win the love of a Woman, answered, Opportunity being asked what was the second, he answered, Opportunity and being demanded what was the third, he still answered, Opportunity

Procrastination in peril is the mother of ensuing misery

Time and Patience teach all men to live content.

Take time in thy choice, and be circumspect in making thy match: for nothing so soon gluts the stomach as sweet meat, nor sooner fills the eye than beauty

Opportunities neglected are manifest tokens of folly.

Time limiteth an end to the greatest sorrows

Actions measured by time, seldom prove bitter by repentance.

Reason oftentimes desireth execution of a thing which time will not suffer to be done, not for that it is not just but because it is not followed

Many matters are brought to a good end in time, that cannot presently be remedied with reason

Time is life's best Counsellour   *Arist*

Time is the best Governour of Counsels

Time trieth what a man is for no man is so deep a dissembler, but that at one time or other he shall be easily perceived.   Time

Time is the inventer of novelties, and a certain register of things ancient. *Marc An.*

Time maketh some to be men, which have no childish conditions.

Times daily alter, and men's minds do often change.

A little benefit is great profit, if it be bestowed in due time. *Curtius.*

Time is so swift of foot, that being once past he can never be overtaken.

The fore-locks of time are the deciders of many doubts.

Time in his swift pace mocketh men for their slowness.

Non est, crede mihi, sapientis dicere, Vivam:
  Sera nimis vitæ est crastina, vive hodie.
Omnia tempus edax depascitur, omnia carpit,
  Omnia sede movet, nec sinit esse diu.

Of the World.

Defin. *This word* World, *called in Greek* Cosmos, *signifieth as much as Ornament, or a well disposed order of things.*

HE that cleaveth to the customs of the World, forsaketh God.

Cicero and the *Stoicks* were of opinion, that the world was wisely governed by the gods, who have care of mortal things.

The World is vain, and worldly joys do fade,
But heaven alone for godly minds is made.

He that trusteth to the World is sure to be deceived. *A chün.*

The disordinate desire of the goods of the World begetteth self-love.

Our honours and our bodily delights are worldly poisons to infect our souls.

The

The World seduceth the eye with variety of objects, the scent with sweet confections, the taft with delicious dainties, the touch with soft flesh, precious cloathings, and all the inventions of vanity

He that mortifieth his natural paffions, is feldom overcome with worldly impreffions.

No man that loveth the World can keep a good confcience long uncorrupted.

The worldly man burning in heat of fire, is ravifhed with the thoughts of revenge, inraged with the defire of dignity, briefly, never his own, till he leave the world.

This World, though never fo well beloved, cannot laft always

This World is deceitful, and tempteth men to wickednefs, but repentance is the hand which lifteth men up to God.

This World is but the pleafure of an hour, and the forrow of many days *Plato.*

The World is an enemy to thofe whom it hath made happy. *Aug.*

The World is our prifon, and to live to the world is the life of death.

The delights of this World are like bubbles in the water, which are foon raifed, and fuddainly laid.

The World hateth contemplation, becaufe contemplation difcovereth the treafons and deceits of the World. *Eraf*

We may ufe the World but if we delight in it, we break the love we fhould bear to him that created it.

Man hath neither perfect reft nor joy in this World, neither poffeffeth he always his own defire.

He that loveth the World, hath inceffant travail, but he that hateth it, hath reft.

The World hath fo many fundry changes in her vanity, that fhe leadeth all men wandring in unftedfaftnefs.

He

He that feeketh pleafures from the world, followeth a fhadow, which when he thinketh he is fureft of, it vanifheth away and turneth to nothing. *Socrat.*

The World, the Flefh, and the Devil, are three e-nemies that continually fight againft us, and we have great need to defend us from them.

The vanities of this world bewitch the minds of many men.

God created this world a place of pleafure and re-ward wherefore fuch as fuffer in adverfity fhall in another world be recompenced with joy. *Hermes.*

He which delighteth in this world muft either lack what he defireth, or elfe lofe what he hath won with great pain.

He that is enamoured of this world is like one that entreth into the Sea : for if he efcape perils, men will fay he is fortunate, but if he perifh, they will fay he is wilfully deceived.

He that fixeth his mind wholly upon the world, lo-feth his foul · but he that defireth the fafety of his foul, little or nothing regardeth the world.

After the old Chaos was brought into form, the Poets feign that the World was divided into four A-ges, the firft was the Golden Age, the fecond was the Silver Age, the third the Brazen Age, and the fourth the Iion Age · All which may be more largely read of in the firft Book of *Ovid's Metamorphofis*

The World in the four Ages thereof may be com-pared to the four feafons of the year, the firft refem-bling the Spring-time, the fecond Summer, the third Autumn, and the fouth Winter, *Perdiccas.*

He that yieldeth himfelf to the world ought to dif-pofe himfelf to three thing which he cannot avoid : Firft to poverty, for he fhall never attain to the riches that he defireth, Secondly, to fuffer great pain and trouble, Thirdly, to much bufinefs without expediti-on. *Solon.*

Mundus regitur numine deorum, éstque quasi communis
vrbs, & civitas omnium. Cicero.
Mundus magnus homo, homo parvus mundus esse di-
citur.

Of Beginning.

Defin. *Beginning is the first appearance of any thing;*
And there can be nothing without beginning, but only
that Almighty power which first created all things of
nothing.

Evil beginnings have most commonly wretched
endings.

In every thing the greatest beauty is to make the
beginning plausible and good.

It is better in the beginning to prevent, than in the
exigent to work revenge.

That thing never seemeth false that doth begin
with truth.

The Preface in the beginning makes the whole
book the better to be conceived.

Nature is counted the beginning of all things,
Death the end. *Quintil.*

To begin in truth, and continue in goodness, is
to get praise on earth, and glory in heaven.

The beginning of Superstition was the subtility of
Satan; the beginning of true Religion, the service
of God.

There is nothing wisely begun, if the end be not
providently thought upon.

Infants begin life with tears, continue it with travels, and end it with impatience.

A foolish man beginneth many things, and endeth
nothing.

The beginning of things is in our own power; but
the end thereof resteth at God's disposing. *Stobæus.*

Never

Never attempt any wicked beginning in hope of a good ending

The most glorious and mighty beginner is God, who in the beginning created the world of nothing.

Small faults not hindred in the beginning, amount to mighty errours e'er they be ended.

A work well begun is half ended. *Plato.*

In all works the beginning is the chiefest, and the end most hard to attain.

The beginning, the mean and the end, is a legacy which every one enjoyeth.

Suddain changes have no beginning.

Nothing is more ancient than the first beginning.

That which is between the beginning and the end is short, *Greg*

The fear of God is the beginning of Wisdom. *Sirac.*

The beginnings of all things are small, but gather strength in continuance

The beginning once known, with more ease the event is understood.

Begin nothing before thou first call for help of God : for God, whose power is in all things, giveth most prosperous furtherance and happy success unto all such acts as we do begin in his Name.

Take good advisement e'er thou begin any thing ; but having once begun, be careful speedily to dispatch it.

He that preventeth an evil before it begin, hath more cause to rejoyce than to repent.

Take good heed at the beginning to what thou grantest, for after one inconvenience another will follow.

Begin to end, and ending so begin,
As entrance to good life be end of sin.

Principiis obsta: serò medicina paratur,
　Cùm mala per longas invaluere moras.
Principii nulla est origo, nam ex principiis oriuntur
omnia, ipsum autem nulla ex re alia nasci potest

Of Ending.

Defin. *The end is that whereto all things are created by*
God, which is the glory of his Name and Salvation
of his elect albeit the order which he observeth, the
cause, reason and necessity of them are hid in his
secret counsel, and cannot be comprehended by the sense
of man.

THE End of the World is a good man's meditation, for by thinking thereon he preventeth sin
Basil.

The end of trouble bringeth joy, and the end of a
good life everlasting felicity.

What thing soever in this world hath a beginning,
must certainly in this world have also an ending

The last day hath not the least distress

Felicity is the end and aim of our worldly actions,
which may in this life be described in shadows, but
never truly attained but in heaven only

Nothing is done but it is done for some end *Arist.*

The end of labour is rest, and the end of foolish
love repentance.

The end is not only the last, but the best of every
thing *Arist*

The end of every thing is doubtful. *Ovid*

The end of war is a just Judge *Livie*

As there is no end of the joys of the blessed, so
there is no end of the torments of the wicked *Greg.*

The end we hope for is ever as then our hopes

What was doubtful in the beginning is made certain by the end thereof,

　　　　　　　　　　　　　　　　Seeing

Seeing the event of things does not answer to our wills, we ought to apply our wills to the events of them *Ar st.*

The end of a dissolute life is most commonly a desperate death, *Bion*

Our life is given to use and possess, but the end is most uncertain and doubtful.

The end of sorrow is the beginning of joy.

At the end of the work the cunning of the workman is made manifest.

Good respect to the end preserveth both body and soul in safety

Before any fact be by man committed, the end thereof is first in cogitation.

Many things seem good in the beginning which prove bad in the end

Ex tus acta probat caveat successibus cepto,

   Quisquis ab eventu facta notanda putat

Multa laudantur in principio, sed qui ad finem perse-
verat beatus est.

Of Day or Light.

Defin *The word Dies, which signifieth a Day, is so cal-*
led, quod sit divini operis. *It is God's first crea-*
ture, and the chiefest comfort of man, who by his word
made the Light thereof to beautifie it to the world's
end.

THose children which are born between the four and twenty hours of midnight, and midnight, with the *Romans* are said to be born in one day.

Numa Pompilius, as he divided the year into months, so he divided the month into days, and called them *Festos, Profestos & Intercisos,* the first dedicated to the gods, the next to men for the dispatching of their business the last as common for their gods as men

A day natural hath twenty four hours, a day artificial hath twelve hours.

The day beginneth with the *Ægyptians* at Sun-setting, and with the *Persians* at Sun-rising.

The *Athenians* count all the time from the setting of the Sun, to the setting of the Sun again, but one day.

The *Babylonians* count their day from the Sun-rising in the morning, till the Sun-rising the next.

The *Umbrians* an ancient people in *Italy*, account their day from Noon-tide till Noon-tide the next day following.

The wicked and evil-living man loveth darkness, and hateth the light.

One day taketh from us the credit that another hath given us, and the last must make reckoning of all the rest past.

By daily experience we wax wiser and wiser.

He that refuseth to amend his life to day, may happen to be dead e'er to morrow

Let no day be spent without some remembrance how thou hast bestowed thy time.

Vespasian thought that day lost wherein he had not gotten a friend.

Of all numbers we cannot skill to number our days. we can number our sheep, our oxen, and our coin; but we think our days are infinite, and therefore we cannot number them.

> One day the valiant brood
> Of *Fabius* sent to fight.
> Thus sent, one day did see
> Them nobly dead e'er night.

The *Romans* called *Jupiter Diespiter*, which signifieth the Father of the Day, or Light.

Light is sometimes taken for Day, and Darkness for Night.

No

No day cometh to man wherein he hath not fome caufe of forrow *Quintil.*

The entrance of adolefcency is the end of infancy, man's eftate the death of youth, and the morrow-day's birth the overthrow of this day's pride.

Light is the Queen of the eyes. *Aug.*

God in the beginning made two great lights, one for the day, another for the night.

Day is the Image of life, night of death.

The pleafure of the day is the Sun, called of the Philofophers the golden eye, and heart of heaven.

The light of learning is the day of the mind. *Aug.*

Every day that paffeth is not to be thought as the laft, but that it may be the laft. *Senec.*

The Sun melteth wax, and hardneth clay.

Abbreviare dies poteris, producere nunquam :
Abbreviare tuum eft, fed prolongare Tonantis.
Optima quæque dies miferis mortalibus ævi
Prima fugit, fubeunt morbi triftifque-feneftus,
Et labor, & duræ rapit inclementia mortis.

Of Night.

Defin. *Night or Darknefs is the time of reft and peace after labours, being commonly that part of the day natural in which the Sun is hidden from us, fhining to the Antipodes.*

THE longer the night is in coming, the more it is defired of the oppreffed, yet no fooner feen than wifht to be departed.

Night is the benefit of nature, and made for man's reft *Livius.*

Sufpicion and fear are Night's companions.

Darknefs is not evil but in comparifon of the light. *Auguft.*

Every light hath his fhadow, and every fhadow of

night

night a fucceeding morning.

The darknefs of our vertues, and not of our eyes, is to be feared. *Aug*

It is not darknefs, but abfence of the light, that maketh night

Darknefs cannot be feen. *Aug*

The breath we breath in the morning is often ftopt and vanifhed before night.

Night followeth day, as a fhadow followeth a body. *Arift.*

This our life is as it were night.

Night is more comfortable to the miferable than the day.

Night, which is the nurfe of eafe, is the mother of unquiet thoughts.

Night, which is all filence, hears all the complaints of the afflicted.

The deeds of the night are loathfome to the day, neither hath light to do with darknefs.

Night is war's enemy, yet it is the only finder out of martial ftratagems.

A dark night and a dead refolution beget caufe of the day's lamentation.

Night is the cloak to cover fin, and the armour of the unjuft man. *Theophr.*

Night begets reft, and reft is the refrefhing of tired fpirits

Whatever is over-wearied by the days exercife, is as it were new born by the night's reft and quiet. *Tully.*

Night and Sin hold affinity, and joyntly aid each other

It is impoffible to wear out the day in travel, if fm nor of the night be not fpent in reft.

*homines furgunt de nofte latrones ,
non expergifceris?* Horat.

Infe-

Interiores tenebræ cæcitas mentis, exteriores infernus.

Of Wickedneſs.

Defin. *Wickedneſs is any ſin, vice or evil committed or imagined in the whole courſe of our lives, and the mean by which we loſe God's favour, and expoſe our ſelves to the danger of hell-fire.*

THE proſperity of evil men is the calamity of the good.

When wicked men rejoyce, it is a ſign of ſome tempeſt approaching.

It is the corruption of the good, to keep company with the evil.

Rejoyce as often as thou art deſpiſed of evil men, and perſwade thy ſelf that their Opinion of thee is moſt perfect praiſe.

Ill men are more haſty than good men are forward in proſecuting their purpoſe.

He that worketh wickedneſs by another, is guilty himſelf of the fact committed. *Bias.*

It is better to deſtroy the wickedneſs it ſelf than the wicked man.

Unexperienced evils do hurt moſt.

Philip King of *Macedon* aſſembled together the moſt wicked perſons, and fartheſt from correction of all his ſubjects, and put them into a Town which he built of purpoſe, calling in *Poneropolis*, the City of wicked perſons.

Continuance in evil doth in it ſelf increaſe evil. *S. P. S.*

A wicked life is the death of the ſoul. *Chryſ.*

Who can be more unfortunate than he which of neceſſity will needs be evil.

Whoſoever he be that ſpareth to puniſh the wicked, doth thereby much harm to the good. *Anachar:*

It

It is a praife to the godly to be difpraifed of the wicked, and it is likewife a difpraife to be praifed of them.

Sin blindeth the eyes of the wicked, but punifhment opens them. *Greg*

The wicked man is duly drawn to punifhment, and is ignorant thereof.

The mind of an ill-difpofed perfon is more unftable than the fuperficies of the water

When wicked men be in the midft of all their jollity, then fome misfortune comes knocking at the door.

When the evil man would feem to be good, then he is worft of all

He is evil that doth willingly affociate himfelf with wicked men.

Wicked men ought, as much as may be, to be avoided.

Vertue is health, but vice is ficknefs. *Plato.*

The wicked man attempteth things impoffible. *Arift.*

The wicked man is ever in fear *Plato.*

He wrongeth the good that fpareth the wicked.

A good fentence proceeding from a wicked man's mouth lofeth its grace.

The progeny of the wicked, although it be not wholly infected, yet it will favour fomething of the father's filthinefs

As vertue is a garment of honour, fo wickednefs is a robe of fhame.

Curfed is that man that knoweth not to be a man, but by his wickednefs is far otherwife than he fhould be

He that intendeth not to do good fhould refrain from doing evil. but it is counted evil if we refrain to do good.

Purifie thine own wickednefs, then prate of others fins.

The wicked man, in a monftrous kind of pride rever heard of before, glorieth and boafteth of his evil deeds

When a man doth fubject himfelf to the wicked affections of his own mind, he doth weaken and cut in funder the ftrings of underftanding. *Cicero.*

Wicked counfel is moft hurtful to the giver.

In good things nothing is either wanting or fuperfluous, which made the *Pythagoreans* fay, that wickednefs could not be comprehended, but godlinefs might.

The ways to wickednefs are many, plain and common, but to goodnefs are not many, but one, and that fame is hard to find, becaufe it is but little troden.

Non ob ea folum incommoda quæ eveniunt improbis, fugienda eft improbitas fed multo etiam magis, quod cujus in animo verfatur, nunquam finet eum refpirare, nunquam requiefcere

Si impietas improbè molita quippiam eft, quamvis occultè fecerit, nunquam tamen confidat id fore femper occultum. plerumque enim improborum facta primo fufpicio infequitur, deinde fermo atque fama, tum accufatorum judex; multi etiam fe judicant. Cicero.

Of Infamy.

Defin. *Infamy is the livery of bad deferts in this world, and that which for our malignities and evil doing ftameth our names and our fucceffions with a perpetual difgrace, through the report of our mifdeeds and unjuft attempts.*

SHame and Difhonour are the two greateft preventers of mifhap.

Infamy galleth unto death, and liveth after death.

Infamy and Shame are inseparable sequels of Adultery.

That man is very wicked and unhappy whose life the people lament, and at whose death they rejoyce. *Solon.*

There is no greater infamy than to be lavish in promise, and slack in performance.

Begging is a shameful course, and to steal is a great blot of dishonour.

He that hath born sail in the tempest of shame, may ever after make a sport of the shipwreck of his good name

Infamy is so deep a colour, that it will hardly be washed off with oblivion.

Such as seek to climb by private sin shall fall with open shame

They that covet to swim in vice shall sink in vanity. *Crates*

Greater is the shame to be accounted an Harlot, than the praise to be esteemed amiable.

The infamy of man is immortal. *Plato.*

It were great infamy to the person, and no small offence to the Common-wealth, to behold a man basely toiling that deserveth to govern, and to see him govern that deserveth to go to plough

Shame is the end of treachery, and dishonour ever fore-runs repentance.

What it once spotted with infamy, can hardly be worn out with time. *Aurel.*

When the bow-string is broken, it is hard to hit the white and when a man's credit is called in question, perswasions can little prevail

An honourable man shall never die, and an infamous man deserveth not to live.

The infamous man is wholly miserable · for good men will not believe him, bad will not obey him, no man accompany him, and few befriend him.

As

As beauty adorneth wealth, maintaineth honour and countenance so infamy woundeth all.

The occasions and greatness of infamy are better untried than known.

The tongue is the readiest instrument of detraction and slander.

Every inferior doth account that thing infamous wherein he seeth his superior offend

It is infamy to seek praise by counterfeit vertue.

It is infamy to dispraise him that deserveth well, because he is poor, and to commend the unworthy, because he is rich.

He that by infamy slandereth his friend is most monstrous.

To be praised of wicked men is as great infamy, as to be praised for wicked doings.

Pride is the cause of hatred, and sloth of infamy.

The life of a noted infamous man is death.

Cicero inveighing against *Cataline*, saith, Thy naughty and infamous life hath so obscured the glory of thy predecessours, that although they have been famous, yet by thee they will come to oblivion.

If a man's good name be not polluted, although he have nothing else, yet it stands him in more stead than the possession of very great riches

Emori præstat per virtutem, quàm per dedecus vivere. Cicero.

Quis honorem, quis gloriam, quis laudem, quis ullum decus tam unquam expetit, quam ignominiam, infamiam, contumilias, dedecus fugit ? Cicero.

Of Dishonesty.

Defin. *Dishonesty is an an act which engendereth its own torment. for from the very instant wherein it is committed, and with the continual remembrance thereof, it filleth the soul of the malefactor with shame and confusion.*

HE that is difpofed to mifchiefs will never want occafions.

Difhonefty ruinates both fame and fortune.

Shame is the hand maid to difhoneft attempts. *Crates*

The infatiate appetite of gluttony doth obfcure the inferiour vertues of the mind.

He that fears not the halter will hardly become true, and they that care not for fufpects are feldom honeft.

It is difhoneft victory that is gotten by the fpoil of a man's own Country. *Cicero*.

There never rifeth contention in a Common-wealth, but by fuch men as would live without all honeft order

The evil inclination of men may for a time be diffembled; but being once at liberty, they cannot cloak it.

Many times the wicked bear envy unto the good, not becaufe the vertuous fuffer them to do well, but for that they will not confent with them to do evil.

Many be fo malicious and perverfe, that they take more delight to do evil to others than to receive a benefit unto themfelves.

If he be evil that giveth evil counfel, more evil is he that executeth the fame.

Nothing is profitable which is difhoneft. *Tully*.

Then mifchief is at the full ripenefs, whenas difhoneft things be not only delightful in hearing, but alfo moft pleafant in practice. and there is no remedy to be hoped for, where common vices are accounted vertues.

A man given to difhonefty can neither be friend to himfelf, nor trufty to another.

The overthrow of a Common-wealth is the difhonefty of the Rulers.

Difho-

Dishonesty is the pillager of the soul, which spoileth men of their ornaments and heavenly apparel.

All things are tolerable save those things which are dishonest.

Califte the harlot said she excelled *Socrates*, because when she was disposed she could draw his Auditours from him. No marvel, saith he, for thou allurest them to dishonesty, to which the way is ready; but I exhort them to vertue, whose way is hard to find.

Honesty is joyned with misery, dishonesty with all kind of worldly felicity but the misery which we suffer for honesty shall be turned to everlasting comfort, and the felicity gotten by dishonesty shall be changed into perpetual torment.

——*sæpe* Diespiter
Neglectus incesto addidit integrum,
Raro antecedentem sceleftum
Deferuit pede pœna claudo. Horace.
Difce bonas artes, moneo, Romana juventus.
Sit procul omne nefas · ut ameris, amabilis efto.

Of vices in general

Defin. *Vice is an inequality and jarring of manners, proceeding from man's natural inclination to pleasures and naughty defires.*

A Man seldom repenteth his silence, but he is often sorrowful for his hasty speeches

He that is rooted in sin will hardly be by good counsel reformed.

He that doubts of God, with *Protagoras*, and he that denieth God, with *Diagoras*, are both to be had in Abomination for their infidelity.

Consent and sin are both of one kind.

Vice is the habitude of sin, but sin is the act of that habitude.

He that pampers his flesh doth nourish many worms. *Demonax.*

Ex-

Excessive sleep is found the body's foe

Lust bringeth short life, prodigality wretched life, and perseverance in sin eternal damnation.

As by nature some men are more inclined to sickness than other some ; so one man's mind is more prone than another's to unrighteousness.

The sickness of old age is avarice, the errour of youth inconstancy *Theop.*

A most horrible and damnable offence that is to be judged, whose revenge belongeth unto God. *Aug.*

Craft putteth on it the habit of policy, malice the shape of courage, rashness the title of valour, lewdness the image of pleasure. thus dissembled Vices seem great Vertues.

Where Elders are dissolute and past gravity, there the younger sort are shameless and past grace

Every vice fighteth against nature.

Vice ruleth where Gold reigneth *Greg.*

We ought not to hate the man, but his vices. *Aug.*

There are more vices than vertues. *Greg.*

Riches gotten with craft are commonly lost with shame.

Folly in youth, and negligence in age, breed at length woe; to both. the one ending in sorrowful grief, the other in lamentable misery.

Where youth is void of exercise, there age is void of honesty.

Flattery, and soothing great men, in their humours, getteth more coin than true speeches can get credit. *Bias*

Fair faces have gotten foul vices, straight personages crooked manners, and good complexions bad conditions.

A merry mind doth commonly shew a gentle nature, where a sour countenance is a manifest sign of a froward disposition.

Sobriety

Sobriety without fullenneſs is commendable, and mirth without modeſty delectable.

Every vice hath a cloak, and creepeth in under the name of vertue.

We ought to have an eſpecial care leſt thoſe vices deceive us which bear a ſhew of vertue.

Craft oft-times accompanieth Policy, too much Auſterity Temperance, Pride a reſolute mind, Prodigality Liberality, Temerity Fortitude, and Superſtition Religion.

What nation doth not love gentleneſs, thankfulneſs, and other commendable parts in a man? Contrarily, who doth not hate a proud, diſdainful, unhoneſt and unthankful perſon?

Cùm fateamur ſatis magnam vim eſſe in vitiis ad miſeram vitam, fatendum eſt etiam eandem vim in virtute eſſe ad beatam vitam, contrariorum enim contraria ſunt conſequentia

Qui voluptatibus ducuntur, & vitiorum illecebris & cupiditatum lenociniis ſe dedeunt, miſſos faciant honores, nec attingant rempublicam, patiantur viros fortes labore, ſe otio ſuo perfrui.

Of Ingratitude.

Defin. Ingratitude is that which maketh men impudent, ſo that they dare join together to hurt thoſe which have been their beſt friend, and them to whom they are bound both by bloud, nature, and benefits

Ngratitude challengeth revenge by cuſtom, and is a vice moſt hateful before God and man

Ingratitude for great benefits maketh men to deſpair of recompence, and of faithful friends cauſeth them to become mortal foes

Impudency is the companion of that monſter Ingratitude. *Stobæus.*

He is unthankful that being pardoned ſinneth again. There

There can be no greater injury offered to a free mind and a bashful face, than to be called unthankfull, sith such reproaches sink most deeply into the reputation of Honour.

Ingratitude springeth either from covetousness or suspect. *The phrase.*

It is a shameful and unthankful part always to crave, and never to give. *Mac.*

Princes rewarding nothing, purchase nothing, and desert being neglected, courage will be unwilling to attempt.

'Benefits well bestowed establish a Kingdom, but service unrewarded weakneth it. *Archim.*

The nature of man is ambitious, unthankful, suspectful, not knowing rightly how to use his friends, or with what regard to recompence his well-willers for their benefits bestowed.

It is better to be born foolish, than to understand how to be unthankful.

Ingratitude loseth all things in himself, in forgetting all duties to his friend.

To do good to an unthankful body is to sow corn on the sand.

Two contraries give light one to the other, and ingratitude and thankfulness are best discerned one by the other.

There is no affection among men so firmly placed, but through unthankful dealing it may be changed to hatred. *Bias.*

There cannot be a greater occasion of hatred, than to repay good turns with unthankful dealing.

An ungrateful Commonwealth, which hath banished men of true desert, finding its hinderance by their absence, too late repenteth. *Lactantius.*

Nothing waxeth sooner old than a good turn or benefit. *Diog.*

An

An unthankful man is compared to a veſſel bored full of holes. *Lucianus.*

Old kindneſs ſleepeth, and all men are unthankful. *Pindarus.*

The ungrateful man through his impudency is driven to all villainy and miſchief, and maketh himſelf a ſlave *Xenophon.*

Plato called *Ariſtotle* a Mule, for his ingratitude. *Ælianus.*

The unthankful man hath ever been accounted a more dangerous buyer than the debtor. *Cognat.*

The ungrateful man is of worſe condition than the Serpent, which hath venom to annoy others, but not it ſelf

It is better never to receive a benefit, than to be unthankful for it

Thankfulneſs doth conſiſt in Truth and Juſtice: Truth doth acknowledge what is received, and Juſtice doth render one good turn for another. *Stobæus.*

He is unthankful with whom a benefit periſheth; he is more ungrateful which will forget the ſame; but he is moſt ungrateful that rendreth evil for the good he hath received, *Bias.*

He which receiveth a benefit ſhould not only remember, but require the ſame liberally and fruitfully, according to the nature of the earth, which rendreth more fruit than it receiveth ſeed. *Quint.*

The *Egyptians* of all vices moſt abhorred Ingratitude, in which (as *Tully* ſaith) all wickedneſs is contained.

If we be naturally inclined to do good to them of whom we conceive good hope, how much more are we bound to thoſe at whoſe hands we have already received a good turn? *Seneca.*

Thou canſt not call a man by a worſe name, than to ſay he is an unthankful perſon.

Plutarch

Plutarch interpreteth *Pythagoras*'s Symbol, of not receiving of swallows, thus, that a man ought to shun unthankful people.

Xenophon, among the praises which he gave unto *Agesilaus*, reputeth it a part of injustice, not only not to acknowledge a good turn, but also if more be not rendred than hath been received.

Whofoever receiveth a benefit felleth his own liberty, as who would say that he made himself subject to render the like.

The laws of *Athens*, *Perfia* and *Macedonia*, condemned the unthankful person to death.

Lycurgus esteemed it a most monstrous ingratitude, not to acknowledge a benefit.

In the old time Liberties and Franchises for ingratitude were revoked.

An ungrateful person cannot be of a noble mind, nor yet just. *Socrat.*

A man ought to remember himself how often he hath received courtesie and pleasure.

Every gentle nature quickly pardoneth all injuries, except ingratitude, which it hardly forgetteth.

Ingratitude was the cause of the sin and death of man.

No man's life is void of ingratitude.

The life of the ignorant is unthankful, wavering and unstayed in things present, through the desire of things to come. *Seneca.*

Impudence and ingratitude are companions.

All humane things grow old and come to the end of their time, except ingratitude: for the greater the increafe of mortal men is, the more doth ingratitude augment. *Plat.*

We shall avoid this shameful vice of ingratitude, if we esteem the benefit which we receive of another greater than it is, and contrarywife repute that less than it is which we give.

The.

The unworthier he is that receiveth the benefit, the more he is to be commended from whom it cometh.

Est aliqua ingrato meritum exprobrare voluptas.
Ingratus, qui beneficium accepisse se negat quod accepit, ingratus, qui id dissimulat, rursum ingratus, qui non reddit: at omnium ingratissimus est qui oblitus est.

Of Pride.

Defin. *Pride is an unreasonable desire to enjoy Honours, Estates and great Places; it is a vice of excess, and contrary to all Modesty, which is a part of Temperance.*

HE that bruiseth the Olive-tree with hard iron, fretteth out no oil, but water and he that pricketh a proud heart with perswasion, draweth out only hate and envy.

It is impossible that to a man of much pride fortune should be long friendly.

It chanceth oftentimes to proud men, that in their greatest jollity, and when they think their honour spun and woven, then their estate with the web of their life in one moment is suddenly broken.

Ambitious men can never be good Counsellers to Princes.

The desire of having more is a vice common to Princes and great Lords, by reason of ambition and desire to rule, bringing forth in them oftentimes an unsatiable cruelty and beastly nature. *Plut.*

Pride is the cause of the corruption and transgression of man's nature

Pride causeth that work to become wicked, which of it self is good so that humble submission is better than the proud boasting of our needs; which causeth

a proud

a proud man oftentimes to fall into more deteſtable vices than he was in before.   *Plut.*

It is natural to proud men to delight themſelves in, and to ſet their whole minds upon vain deſires.

Men that have their thoughts high, and their eſtates low, live always a penſive and diſcontented life.

Pride ſhould of young men be carefully avoided, of old men utterly diſdained, and of all men ſuſpected and feared.   *Soc.*

Pride hath two ſteps, the loweſt bloud, and the higheſt envy.

Pride eateth gold, and drinketh bloud, and climbeth ſo high by other mens heads that ſhe breaketh her own neck.

It is better to live in low content, than in high infamy, and more precious is want with honeſty than wealth with diſcredit.

Aſpiring Pride is like a vapour, which aſcendeth high, and preſently vaniſheth away in ſmoak.   *Plut.*

A proud heart in a beggar is like a great fire in a ſmall cottage, which not only warmeth the houſe, but burneth all that is in it.

The ſpring of pride is lying, as truth is of humility.   *Phil.*

Men that bear great ſhapes and large ſhadows, and have not good nor honeſt minds, are like the pourtraiture of *Hercules* drawn upon the ſands.

The more beauty the more pride, and the more pride the more preciſeneſs

Ambition is the ground of all evils.

Pride is a Serpent which ſlily inſinuateth her ſelf into the minds of men.

Exalt one of baſe ſtock to high degree, and no man living will ſooner prove proud than he.

An ambitious body will go far out of the right way, to attain to the height which his heart deſireth, *S. P. S.*

Pride is the mother of Superstition

The proud man, seeking to repress another man, in stead of superiority attaineth indignity

The proud man is forsaken of God, being forsaken, he groweth resolute in impiety, and after purchaseth a just punishment for his presuming sin. *Plato.*

A proud man is compared to a ship without a Pilot, tossed up and down upon the Seas by Winds and Tempest. *Aug.*

The Son of *Agesilaus* wrote unto King *Philip*, who much gloried in some of his victories, that if he measured his shadow, he should find it no greater after his victories than it was before.

King *Lewis* the eleventh was wont to say, when Pride was in the Saddle, Mischief and shame was on the Crupper.

Pride, Envy, and Impatience, are the three capital enemies of man's constancy *Aug*

Pride is always accompanied with Folly, Audacity, Rashnefs, and Impudency, and with Solitariness, as if one would say, that the proud man is abandoned of all the world, ever attributing to himself that which is not, having much more bragging than matter of worth. *Plato*

Pride did first spring from too much abundance of wealth *Antist.*

Chrysippus, to raise an opinion of knowledge to himself, would set forth those books in his own name, (a fault common in our age) which were wholly written by other men

The proud boasting man doth feign things to be which indeed are not, or maketh them appear greater than they are *Ar.*

Pride is the mother of Envy, which if one be once able to supprefs, the daughter will be soon suppressed. *Aug.*

Husband.

Husbandmen think better of thofe ears of corn which bow down and wax crooked, than thofe which grow ftraight; becaufe they fuppofe to find more ftore of grain in them than in the other.

Socrates, when he faw that *Alcibiades* waxed proud, becaufe of his great poffeffions, fhewed him the Map of all the World, and asked him whether he knew which were his Lands in the Territory of *Athens :* who anfwering, They were not defcribed there : How is it then (quoth he) that thou braggeft of that which is no part of the World ?

It is the property of proud men to delight in their own foolifh inventions.

He that knoweth himfelf beft efteemeth himfelf leaft. *Plato.*

The glory of the proud man is foon turned to infamy. *Saluft.*

The beft way to be even with a proud man, is to take no notice of him.

The proud man thinketh no man can be humble. *Chryfoft.*

Antiochus had that admiration of himfelf, that he thought he was able to fail on the Earth, and go on the Seas

Pompey could abide no equal, and *Cæfar* could fuffer no fuperiour.

It is a hard matter for a rich man not to be proud.

If a proud rich man may fcarcely be endured, who can away with a poor man that is proud ?

The proud man refembleth the Fifherman in *Theocritus,* who fatisfied his hunger with dreams of Gold.

The Pride of unquiet and moving fpirits never content themfelves in their vocations. *Perdic.*

Themiftocles told the *Athenians,* that unlefs they banifhed him and *Ariftides,* they could never be quiet.

Perdita tunc urbi nocuerunt fecula, poftquam
Ambitus & luxus & opum metuenda facultas

Tranf-

Tranſverſo mentem dubiam torrente tulerunt.

In rebus proſperis, & ad voluntatem noſtram fluenti-
bus, ſuperbia magnopere eſt fugienda: nam ut adverſas
res, ſic ſecundas, immoderatè ferre, levitatis eſt. Cicero.

Of Prodigality.

Defin. *Prodigality is the exceſs of Liberality, which com-*
ing to extremity proves moſt vicious, waſting vertues
faſter than ſubſtance, and ſubſtance faſter than any ver-
tue can get it.

PRodigality without care waſteth that which diligent labour hath purchaſed.

Prodigality is called the fire of the mind, which
is ſo impatient in heat, that it ceaſeth not, while any
matter combuſtible is preſent, to burn neceſſary things
into duſt and cinders. *Pliny.*

Where Prodigality and Covetouſneſs are, there
all kind of vices reign with all licence in that ſoul.
Theop

Prodigality ſtirreth up evil wars and ſeditious injuries, to the end that her humour may be fed ; fiſhing
in all troubled water, that ſhe may have wherewith
to maintain her prodigal expences.

Exceſs of apparel is an argument of the inconſtancy
of the ſoul, and rather whetteth the eyes of the behol-
ders to wicked deſires, than to any honeſt thoughts.
Eraſmus.

Deck not thy ſelf with curious wrought Tapeſtry,
and fair painted Pictures, but with Temperance and
Honeſty. *Epict.*

Poverty followeth ſuperfluous expence.

Prodigality maketh youth a tyrant in his own eſtate,
a deſtroyer of his own wealth, and a corroſive to his
own friends.

To

To spend much without getting, to lay out all without reckoning, and to give all without considering, are the chiefest effects of a prodigal mind

He that giveth beyond his power is prodigal, he that giveth in measure is liberal, he that giveth nothing at all is a niggard

Prodigality is a special sign of incontinency *Mac. Aurel.*

He that is superstitious in his diet, sumptuous in apparel, and lavish of his tongue, is a Cook's hope, a Tailour's thrift, and the Son of repentance.

The end of much expence is great grief

Straton Sidonius could in no wise abide that any one should go beyond him in prodigal expences, whereupon arose a great contention betwixt *Nicocles Cyprius*, and him, whilst the one did what he could to exceed the other *Theo.*

Who spends before he thrives, will beg before he thinks.

Riches lavishly spent breed grief to our heart, sorrow to our friends, and misery to our heirs.

A proud Eye, an open Purse, a light Wife, breed mischief to the first, misery to the second, and horns to the third

What is gotten with care, ought to be kept with wisdom

Prodigality is a dissolution, or too much loosing of vertue *Zeno.*

An unthrift is known by four things, by the Company he keepeth, by the Taverns he haunteth, by the Harlots he cherisheth and the expence he useth

An excess in meats breeds surfet, in drink drunkenness, in discourse ignorance so in gifts excess produceth prodigality.

It is better to be hated for having much, than to be pitied for spending all. *Bias.*

Prodi

Prodigality confisteth not in the quantity of what is given, but in the habit and fashion of the giver.

He is truly prodigal which giveth beyond his ability, and where his gifts are needless.

It is not possible for a prodigal mind to be without envy. *Cato.*

Prodigal lavishing and prodigal sensuality brought Pericles, Callias the son of *Hipponicus*, and *Nicias*, not only to necessity, but to extreme poverty, and when all their money was spent, they drinking a poisoned potion one to another, died all three.

Prodigality is born a Wonder, and dies a Beggar. *Menas.*

No kind admonition of friends, nor fear of poverty, can make a prodigal man become thrifty.

Prodigality in youth is like the rust in Iron, which never leaveth fretting it till it be wholly consumed.

Fire consumeth fuel without maintenance, and prodigality soon emptieth a weak purse, without it be supplied.

The prodigal minded man neither observeth time, nor maketh end of riot, until both himself and his patrimony be consumed.

A prodigal humour is hardly purged, because the nourishments are many and sweet.

The prodigal minded man, to spend lustily, and to fare daintily, so he have it, he cares not how he gets it, and so he spends it, he cares neither on whom nor in what sort he consumes it.

> ———— *O prodigorum*
> *Inemnie, numq' are vos contenta paratu,*
> *De quesitum ter à relinque ciborum*
> *Ambitioja fures, & lute gloria miself*
> *Ducitie quà puvo licet producere vitam,*
> *Et quantum natura jetat————*

Of Gaming.

Defin. Gaming is a stealing away of time, abusing our understanding in vain things without any profit.

CHilo being sent from *Lacedæmon* to *Corinth* in Embassage, to intreat a peace between them, and finding the Noblemen playing at Dice, returned back again without delivering his Message, saying, He would not stain the glory of the *Spartans* with so great ignominy, as to joyn them in society with Dice-players.

Players at Dice, by the council of *Constantinople* under *Justinian*, were punished with excommunications.

Alphonsus son of *Ferdinando* King of *Spain*, streightly commanded that no Knight should presume to play at Dice or Cards for any money, or give his consent to any such play in his house, upon pain of forfeiting his wages for one whole month, and himself to be forbidden another month and an half from entring into the King's Palace.

It is a very hard matter, to follow ordinarily the deceitful practices of cozening skill, or skilful cozenage, without the discredit of a man's good name, by the mark of reproach, or badge of open infamy.

The fame or good name of a man is no sooner in question than, when he is known to be a common Gamester.

It is no freedom to be licentious, nor liberty to live idlely.

Such game is to be abhorred herein wit sleepeth, and idleness with covetousness is only learned.

The gain which ariseth to any party in play should be bestowed upon the poor, to the end that both the Gamesters, as well the winner as the loser might be equally punished. *Aug.*

Aurelius

Aurelius Alexander, Emperour of *Rome*, made a Law, that if any man was found playing at the Dice, he should be taken for frantick, or as a fool natural, which wanteth wit and discretion to govern himself.

The same Emperour likewise, after the promulgation of the foresaid Law, counted Dice players no better than Thieves and Extortioners

Gaming at Cards and Dice is a certain kind of smooth, deceitful and slight theft, whereby many are spoiled of all they have.

Who would not think him a light man, of small credit, that is a Dice-player or a Gamester?

How much cunninger a man is in Gaming and Dice playing, so much the more is he corrupted in life and manners.

Justinian made a Law, that none privately or publickly should play at Dice or Cards

Old men's Gaming is a privilege for young men.

The Devil was the first inventer of Dice and Gaming

Dicing Comedians bring often Tragical ends.

Plato seeming to commend Table-play, compareth it to the life of man. as an evil chance may be holpen by cunning play, so may a bad nature be made better by good education.

Cicero in the Senate-house put *Antonius* to silence, by saying he was a Dicer.

Dicing neither beseemeth the gravity of a Magistrate, nor the honour of a Gentleman, for that the gain is loaded with dishonest practices, and the loss with unquiet passions

As a dead Carcass in an open field is a prey for many kinds of Vermine, so a plain-minded man is an assured prey for all sorts of shifters.

In *Turkey* he is noted of great infamy, that is found playing for money; and grievous pains are appointed for punishment, if he return to it again.

The

The *Lydians* were the first inventers of Gaming, when their Country was brought into great necessity for want of victuals, to the end that by playing they might find some means to resist and sustain hunger the better.

Horace avoucheth in his time, that Dice-playing, was forbidden by their Law.

Lewis the Eighth, King of *France*, made a Law that all Sports should be banished his Realm except shooting.

Cyrus, to punish them of *Sardis*, commanded them to pass away their time in Playing and Banqueting; thereby to render them less men, and keep them from Rebellion.

Ars aleatoria, dum aliena concupiscentiâ suâ profundit, patrimonii nullam reverentiam tenet.

Est ars mendaciorum, perjuriorum, furtorum, litium, injuriarum, homicidiorúmque mater; est verè malorum dæmonum inventum, quæ, exciso Asiæ regno, inter everse urbis manubias varia sub specie migravit ad Græcos.

Of Covetousness.

'**Defin.** *Covetousness is a vice of the soul, whereby a man desireth to have from all parts without reason, and unjustly with-holdeth that which rightly belongeth unto another body: it is also a sparing and niggardlness in giving, but open handedress to receive whatsoever is brought, without conscience, or any regard whether it be well or ill attained.*

THE property of a covetous man is, to live like a beggar all the days of his life, and to be found rich in money at the hour of his death. *Archim.*

Gain gotten with an ill name is great loss.

Covetous men little regard to shorten their lives, so they may augment their riches.

Trea-

Treafures hoarded up by the covetous are moft commonly wafted by the prodigal perfon.

He that coveteth riches is hardly capable of good inftruction. *Plotin.*

It is a hard matter for a man to bridle his defire; but he that addeth riches thereunto is mad.

Covetoufnefs is a vice of the foul, whereby a man defireth to have from all parties without reafon, and unjuftly with-holdeth that which belongeth to another. *Arift.*

Covetoufnefs is fparing in giving, but exceffive in receiving

Covetoufnefs is a blind defire of good. *Luc.*

Unto a covetous man the obtaining of that he would have, is always the beginning of the defire of having more.

Covetous men fcrape together like mighty men, and fpend like bafe, mechanical, and handy crafts men.

Covetous men are compared to Rats and Mice that are in golden Mines, which eat the golden Oar, and yet nothing can be gotten from them but after their death.

Gold is called the bate of fin, the fnare of fouls, and the hook of death, which being aptly applied may be compared to a fire, whereof a little is good to warm one, but too much will burn one altogether.

It is better to be the fheep than the fon of a covetous man. *Diog.*

Pertinax being advanced to the degree of Emperour, did not forget his niggardlinefs, but parted Lettice and Artichoakes into two, that the one half might be for his Dinner, and the other for his Supper

Dionyfius the elder, being advertifed of one that had hidden great ftore of money, commanded him upon pain of death to bring it to him which he did, al-

N 2 thoug!

though not all, but with the remainder dwelt in another place, and beſtowed it upon an Inheritance When *Dionyſius* heard thereof, he ſent him that which he took from him, ſaying, Now thou knoweſt how to uſe riches, take that I had from thee.

The Chariot of Covetouſneſs is carried upon four wheels of Vices, Churliſhneſs, Faint courage, Contempt of God, and Forgetfulneſs of death, drawn by two Horſes, called Greedy to catch, and hold faſt the Carter that driveth it is Deſire to have, having a Whip called Loath to forgo.

A covetous man is good to no man, and worſt friend to himſelf

A covetous man wanteth as well that which he hath, as that which he hath not.

He that covereth much wanteth much

There is a greater ſorrow in loſing-riches, than pleaſure in getting them. *Pub.*

Covetouſneſs is the root of all evil, from whence do proceed, as from a fountain of miſ-hap, the ruine of Common-weals, the ſubverſion of Eſtates, the wreck of Societies, the ſtain of Conſcience, the breach of Amity, the confuſion of the Mind, Injuſtice, Bribery, Slaughter, Treaſons, and a million of other miſchievous enormities. *Arel*

All vices have their taſt, ſave only Covetouſneſs.

The gain of gold maketh many a man to loſe his ſoul.

A covetous man paſſeth great travails in gathering riches, more danger in keeping them, much law in defending them, and great torment in departing from them.

Covetouſneſs is the mother of poverty.

The excuſe of the covetous man is, that he gathereth for his children. *Apollonius.*

Th

The covetous minded man in seeking after riches, purchaseth carefulness for himself, envy from his neighbours, a prey for thieves, peril for his person, damnation for his soul, curses for his children, and law for his heirs.

A covetous rich man, in making his Testament, hath more trouble to please all, than himself took pleasure to get and possess all.

A covetous man's purse is never full.

We fear all things like mortal men, but we desire all things as if we were immortal. *Sen*

Covetousness in an old man is most monstrous. for what can be more foolish, than to provide more money and victuals when he is at his journey's end?

Covetousness is a disease which spreadeth through all the veins, is rooted in the bowels, and being inveterate cannot be moved. *Tully.*

To fly from Covetousness, is to gain a Kingdom.

Gold guides the Globe of the Earth, and Covetousness runs round about the World.

Most covetous is he which is careful to get, desirous to keep, and unwilling to forgo.

By liberality men's vices are covered, by covetousness laid open to the world. *Aug.*

A covetous man's eye is never satisfied, nor his desire of gain at any time sufficed.

The Glutton's mind is of his belly, the Lecher's of his lust, and the covetous man's of his gold. *Ber.*

The covetous man is always poor. *Ariel.*

Ardua res hæc est, opibus non tradere morem,
Et cùm tot Crœsos viceris, esse Numam.
Usque adeo solus ferrum mortemque timere
Ausit nescit an si . pereant discrimine illo
Amissæ leges, sed pars vilissima rerum,
Certamen movistis, opes——

Of Usury.

Defin. *Usury of the* Hebrews *is called* Biting *and an unlawful gain got by an unlawful mean. It is that cruelty which doth not only gnaw the Debtor to the bones, but also sucketh out all the bloud and marrow from him, ingendring money of money, contrary to nature, and to the intent for which money was first made.*

USury is compared to Fire, which is an active and unsatiable Element, for it burneth and consumeth all the wood that is laid upon it. So the Usurer, the more he hath, the more he desireth, and he is never satisfied.

An Usurer is a filching and corrupt Citizen, that both stealeth from his neighbour, and defraudeth himself.

The intent of Usury bewrays the crime.

Usury is the nurse of Idleness, and Idleness the mother of Evils.

Amasis King of Ægypt made a Law, that the Pretor should call every one to account how they lived, and if by Usury, they should be punished as Malefactours.

There was a Law amongst the ancient *Grecians* and *Romans,* which forbad all Usury surmounting one peny in the hundred by the year, and they called it *Unciary* Usury.

This Law was since that brought to a half-peny a year among the *Romans*, and not long after Usury was clean taken away by the Law *Genuntia,* because of usual seditions which rose through the contempt of Laws concerning Usury.

Usury makes the Nobleman sell his Land, the Lawyer his *Justinian*, the Physician his *Galen*, the Souldier his Sword, the Merchant his Wares, and the World its Peace.

Money engendreth Money, contrary to nature.

Ufury is an ancient mifchief, and caufe of much civil difcord.

A little lewdly come by is the lofs of a great deal well gotten

Ufury is like a Whirl-pool, that fwalloweth whatfoever it catcheth. *Crates*

He that with his Gold begets Gold, becomes a flave to his Gold

Inordinate defire of wealth is the fpring of Ufury, and Ufury fubverteth credit, good name, and all other vertues.

Covetoufnefs feeketh out Ufury, and Ufury nourifheth Covetoufnefs.

An Ufurer can learn no truth, becaufe he loatheth the truth.

Ufury taketh away the title of Gentry, becaufe it delighteth in ignobility.

Ufury oftentimes deceives the belly, and altogether lives carelefs of the foul's fafety

As the greedy Ravens feek after carrion for their food, fo doth the covetous Ufurer hunt after Coin to fill his Coffer. *Philo*

No kind of people in the world are fo notorious livers, nor ufe fo much to falfifie their faith in all practices, as Ufurers.

Appian, in his firft Book of Civil Wars, writeth, that by the ancient Law at *Rome*, Ufury was forbidden upon very great pain

As he which is ftung with an Afp dieth fleeping, fo fweetly doth he confume himfelf which hath borrowed upon Ufury.

An Ufurer is more dangerous than a Thief *Cato*

Ufury is moft hated of thofe whom fhe doth moft pleafure

Ufury maketh thofe that are free-born, bondflaves *Publius.*

Ufury is the manifeſt ſign of extreme impudency *Chryſ.*

To be an Uſurer is to be a man-ſlayer. *Cato.*

Uſurers were not ſuffered to enter the Temple of ſparing and well ordering Expence.

The *Egyptians* and *Athenians*, ſeeing the errour of covetous Uſury to take footing in their Provinces, by approved judgment concluded, that by no Inſtrument, Plea, Execution, or other means in Law, a body might be detained, the original being for corrupt gain.

In *Thebes* it was by ſtreight order forbidden that any man ſhould be put in office, which in ten years before the election had practiſed any unlawful chaffering

Uſury is the daughter of Avarice and Ambition.

The more wealth that an Uſurer winneth by his extortion, the more doth the ſin of covetouſneſs daily corrupt his conſcience.

The ill gotten gain, that cometh by Uſury, brings with it contempt, many curſes, and infamy

He that liveth by the loſs of the poor, meriteth the plague of God for his puniſhment,

> ———*Turpia lucra*
> *Fænoris, & velox inopes uſura trucidat*
> *Non ſunt ficienda mala, ut indè eveniant bona*
> *Uſura & fœnus una cum infidelitate & bello ex hominum cupiditate manarunt.*

Of Deceit.

Defin. *Deceit or Craft is the exceſs of prudence: it is that which leadeth a man through wilful ignorance, to oppoſe himſelf againſt that which he knoweth to be dutiful and honeſt, cauſing him, under the counterfeit name of prudence, to ſeek to deceive thoſe that will believe him. This vice is the chiefeſt cauſe of ambi-*

tion and covetoufnefs, wh ch moft men ferve in thefe days : b t above all th ngs it is an enemy to juftice, and feeketh by all means to overthrow the true effect thereof

CRaft moft commonly is repayed with craft, and he that thinketh to deceive another is fome-times deceived himfelf

The craftier and fübtiler a man is, the more he is to be fufpected and hated, as one that hath loft all credit or goodnefs. *Cic*

All knowledge deviating from Juftice, ought ra-ther to be called craft than fcience

It is more wifdom fometimes to diffemble wrongs, than to revenge them.

The difference between craft and wilynefs is, the one is in dexterity wit natural, the other is gotten by experience.

A man's look is the gate of his mind, declaring outwardly the inward deceit which the heart contain-eth. *Livius*

He that never trufteth, is never deceived.

Our negligence maketh fubtil fhift prefume, where diligence prevents falfe deceit.

The Serpent hidden in the grafs ftingeth the foot, and a deceitful man under the fhew of honefty oft-times deceiveth the fimple.

There is nothing that fooner deceiveth the mind than vain hope, for whilft our thoughts feed on it, we fuddenly and affuredly lofe it.

The man moft deceitful is moft fufpectful.

It many times falls out, that what the heart craftily thinketh, the looks deceitfully betray *Leo*

The deceitful are like the Cameleon, apt to all objects, capable of all colours, they cloak Hate with Holinefs, Ambition with good Government, Flattery

N 5 with

with Florence but whatsoever they pretend is dishonesty

Deceits are transcrib'd the foolish in

When there is a shew of some likelyhood of truth in a lye, they are rather seduced by fables,

High ... .. and faint ... are most apt to deceive others by false tales

... apt not dangerously in a man to speak that one ... and do another ...

The ... call this Cove, when, to deceive another, a man ... semblance of one thing, and yet notwithstanding doth the clean contrary

Frederick the Emperour desired, that his Counsellours would at the entring in of his Country aside all deceit and dissembling.

Speech is but a shadow of deeds, and there ought to be such an unity, that there be so little difference at all ... great deceit to speak other ... the ... ... than ... mean without ...

The Emperour *Pertinax* was sur-named *Chrest* his ... that is to say, well speaking, but ill doing.

Fortune's gifts are mere deceits *See*

No der a ... thou art deceived by a wicked man, but consider that they are not deceived. *De...*

It is a deceit to deceive the deceiver

... ... much wit to devile the truth ...

He is not ... to find the truth that directly seeketh her

It is more ... to be deceitful, than to ... the truth ...

Deceit is dangerous ... other ...

Always so to ... ... that we understand, ... write great, but it ... ... purple

The deceitful man's proceedings may be likened to the

                                                              An...

Apothecaries painted pots, which carry a description of excellent drugs, but within them there is either nought available, or else some poison contained in

Alexander being counselled by *Parmenio*, to seek the subversion of his enemies by craft and subtlety answer'd, that his estate would not suffer him so to do, but if he were *Parmenio*, he would do it

All deceits are proper to a base and bad mind, but to be detested of an honest man

The answers of the Oracles were always doubtful and full of deceit.

He is worthy to be abhorred which beareth his brains to work wickedness, and seeketh by subtlety to bring other men to misery

A deceitful man chuseth hypocrisie and dissimulation for his companions

Sic ovibus falla... and ... hamus
Callidus ... it is decepit e'ca fellis
Cr ... ce ... natam ... ... fub ... ... tet

Of Lying.

Defin. *Lying* is a false signification of speech, with a will to deceive, a sickness of the soul, which cannot be cured but by abstinence, it is a monstrous and wicked evil, that faithfully informeth and defileth the tongue of man, which if God otherwise consecrated, even to the truth, and to the utterance of his praise

Take heed of a Liar, for it is time lost to be led by him, and of the other, for it is mere deceit to believe him

Lying is a member of injustice turning topsey tur- vy all humane society, and the amity due unto our neighbour. As

A3

As certain it is to find no goodnefs in him that uſeth to lye, as it is ſure to find no evil in him, that telleth truth

The liar is double of heart and tongue, for he ſpeaketh one thing, and doth another

From truth depraved do ariſe an infinite number of Abſurdities, Hereſies, Schiſms, and Contentions. *Socrat*

The Thief is better than a man accuſtomed to lye

In *Alman* a lye hath been always extremely hated, and ſhunned as it were a plague; and Baſtards could never obtain the price of any Occupation whatſoever, nor take degree in Art or Science   *Xen.*

Thou canſt not better reward a Liar, than in not believing what he ſpeaketh   *Ariſt.*

Within thy ſelf behold well thy ſelf, and to know what thou art, give no credit to other men.

Pope *Alexander* the ſixth never did what he ſaid, and his ſon *Borgia* never ſaid what he meant to do, pleaſing themſelves in counterfeiting and diffembling, to deceive and falſifie their faith   *Guic*

It is the property of a Liar to put on the countenance of an honeſt man, that ſo by his outward habit he may the more ſubtilly deceive. *Bias.*

Lying is contrary to nature, aided by reaſon, and ſervant or hand maid to truth

As the worms do breed moſt gladly in ſoft and ſweet Woods ſo the moſt gentle and noble Wits inclined to honour are ſooneſt deceived by Liars, and Flatterers

Through a Lye *Joſeph* was caſt into Priſon, and Saint *Chryſoſtome* ſent into Baniſhment

All kind of wickedneſs proceedeth from Lying, as all goodneſs doth proceed from truth.   *Chilo.*

The *Ægyptians* made a Law, that every Liar ſhould be put to death

The ſhame of a Liar is ever with him.

A lye

A Lye is not capable of pardon. *Xen*

Liars only gain this, that albeit they speak the truth, yet shall they never be believed.

The *Scythians* and *Garamantes* followed the same Law, and condemned them to death that prognosticated any falſe thing to come.

The *Perſians* and *Indians* deprived him of all honour and farther ſpeech that lyed.

Cyrus told the King of *Armen a*, that a Lye deſerved no pardon

The *Parthians* for lying became odious to all the world

There is no difference between a Liar and a Forſwearer for whomſoever (ſaith *Cicero*) I can get to tell a Lye, I may eaſily intreat to forſwear himſelf.

An honeſt man will not lye, although it be for his proſt

Lying or falſhood in doctrine is moſt pernicious

He that dares make a Lye to his Father, ſeeking means to deceive him, ſuch an one much more dareth to be bold to do the like to another body.

Liars are the cauſe of all the ſins and crimes in the world. *Epictetus*

A Liar ought to have a good memory, leſt he be quickly found falſe in his tale. *Pliny*

It is a double Lye for a man to belye himſelf. *Stob.*

A Lye is the more hateful, becauſe it hath a ſimilitude of truth *Quintil*

All Idolatry, Hypocriſie, Superſtition, falſe Weights, falſe Meaſures, and ill Cozenages, are called Lying, to the end that by ſo deformed a name we ſhould the rather eſchew them

Alexander would conſent to nothing but truth, and *Philip* his father to all kind of falſhood.

Old men and Travellers lye by authority

It is wickedneſs to conceal the fauſt of that which a man ſelleth. *Lactan.*

Lying

Lying in a Prince is moſt odious. *Hier.*

Si qui ob emolumentum ſuum cupidiùs aliquid dicere videntur, iis credere non convenit Falſum maledictum eſt malum mendacium.

Of Drunkenneſs.

Defin. *Drunkenneſs is that vice which ſtirreth up luſt, grief, anger, and extremity of love, and extinguiſheth the memory, opinion and underſtanding, making a man twice a child : and all exceſs of drink is drunkenneſs.*

THE ancient *Romans* would not ſuffer their wives to drink any wine.

The crafty wreſtler (Wine) diſtempereth the wit, weakeneth the feet, and overcometh the vital ſpirits. *Ariſt.*

Wine burns up beauty, and haſtens age

Exceſs is the work of ſin, and drunkenneſs the effect of riot. *Solon.*

Thoſe things which are hid in a ſober man's heart, are oft-times revealed by the tongue of a drunkard.

Drunkenneſs is a bewitching vice, a pleaſant poiſon, and a ſweet ſin *Aug.*

Drunkenneſs maketh man a beaſt, a ſtrong man weak, and a wiſe man a fool. *Origen.*

Plato bade drunken and angry men, to behold themſelves in a glaſs.

The *Scythians* and the *Thracians* contended, who ſhould drink moſt.

A, on the King of *Illyrium* fell into a ſickneſs of the ſides called the Pleuriſie, by reaſon of his exceſſive drinking, and at laſt died thereof

Sobriety is the ſtrength of the ſoul *Pyth.*

Where drunkenneſs is miſtreſs, there ſecrecy beareth no maſtery.

Wine and Women cauſe men to dote, and many times put men of underſtanding to reproof.

Cleo,

Cleo, a woman, was fo practifed in drinking, that fhe durft challenge all men or women whatfoever, to try mafteries who could drink moft, and overcome the reft.

The Vine bringeth forth three grapes; the fiift of Pleafure, the fecond of Drunkennefs, the third of Sorrow.

Philip King of *Macedon,* making war upon the *Perfians,* underftood that they were a people which abounded in all manner of delicate wines, and other wafiful expences, whereupon he prefently retired his aimy, faying, it was needlefs to make war upon them who would fhortly overthrow themfelves.

Nothing maketh Drunkennefs to be more abhorred than the filty and beaftly behaviour of thofe men whofe ftomachs are overcharged with excefs

Steel is the glafs of beauty, Wine the glafs of the mind. *Eurip.*

Intemperance is a root proper to every difeafe. *Plato*

Sicknefs is the chaftifement of Intemperance *Seneca.*

A drunken man, like an old man, is twice a child. *Plato*

Drunkennefs is nothing elfe but a voluntary madnefs.

The Glutton and the Drunkard fhall be poor.

Wine hath drowned more men than the fea. *Pub*

The firft evil in Drunkennefs is danger to Chaftity. *Arb.*

The *Lacedæmonians* would often fhew their Children fuch as were drunk, to the end they fhould learn to loath that vice.

Romulus made a Law, that if a woman was found overcome with drink, fhe fhould die for her offence; fuppofing that this vice was the foundation or beginning of difhonefty and whoredom

Callifthenes

Callifthenes being urged by one to drink as others did at *Alexander*'s feaft, anfwered, that he would not for, faith he, who fo drinketh to *Alexander*, hath need of *Æfculapius*, meaning a Phyfician.

The Leopard, as many write, cannot be fo foon taken by any thing as by Wine, for being drunk, he falleth into the toils.

Drunkennefs is attended with many evils, as filthy talk, fornication, wrath, murther, fwearing, curfing, and fuch like

There are two kinds of Drunkennefs. one kind above the moon is a celeftial drunkennefs, ftirred up by drinking of heavenly drink, which maketh us only to confider things Divine. The reward of vertue is perpetual drunkennefs. *Mufeus.*

Another kind of Drunkennefs is under the moon, that is, to be drunk with an excefs of drinking· which vice ought of all men carefully to be avoided.

Wine is the blood of the earth, and the fhame of fuch as abufe it

Wine enflameth the liver, rotteth the lungs, dulleth the memory, and breedeth all ficknefses

The *Nazarites* abftained from drinking of any Wine or ftrong Drink

Quid non ebrietas defignat ? operta recludit ;
Spes jubet effe ratas, in prælia trudit inermem ·
Sollicitis animis onus eximit, ac docet utes.
Fæcundi calices quem non fecêre defertum ?
Contracta quem non in paupertate folutum ?

Of Gluttony.

Defin. *Gluttony or Surfeiting is the fworn enemy to Temperance, daughter to excefs and immoderate appetite fhe is health's bane and humility's blemifh, life's enemy, and the foul's everlafting torment, except there follow a true refipifcence, and mercy wipe out the remembrance of fo great a guilt.*

Suffice

SUffice nature, but furfeit not , fupply the bodys need, but offend not.

Moderate diet is the wife man's cognizance, but furfeiting Epicurifm is a fool's chiefeft glory.

To live well and frugally, is to live temperately, and fhun furfeiting . for there is great difference between living well, and living fumptuoufly , becaufe the one proceeds of Temperance, Frugality, Difcipline, and Moderation of the foul, contented with her own riches, and the other of Intemperance, Luft, and contempt of all Order and Mediocrity. but in the end one is followed with fhame, the other with eternal praife and commendation. *Plato.*

It is not the ufe of meat, but the inordinate defire thereof ought to be blamed. *Aug.*

Continency in meat and drink is the beginning and foundation of skill. *Socrat.*

We cannot ufe our fpirits well when our ftomachs are ftuffed with meat. neither muft we gratifie the body and entrals only, but the honeft joy of the mind. *Cicero.*

The *Hebrews* ufed to eat but once a day, which was at Dinner , and the *Grecians* in like manner had but one meal, and that was at Supper.

Sobriety retaineth that in a wife man's thoughts, which a fool without difcretion hath in his mouth.

The belly is an unthankful beaft, never requiting the pleafure done, but craving continually more than it needeth. *Crates*

When we eat we muft remember we have two guefts to entertain, the Body and the Soul: whatfoever the Body hath departs away quickly, but what the Soul receiveth abideth for ever.

The wicked man liveth to eat and drink, but the good man eateth and drinketh to live. *Plut*

A rich man may dine when he lift, but a poor man when he can get meat. *Diog.*   The

The belly is the commanding part of the body. *Homer*.

It is a great fault for a man to be ignorant of the meafure of his own ftomach. *Sen c.*

As meat and drink is food to preferve the body . fo is God's Word the nourifhment for the Soul *Gleg.*

A vertuous Soul hath better taft of godly difcour-fes, than the Body hath of well relifhed meat

The firft draught that a man drinketh ought to be for thirft, the fecond for nourifhment, the third is for pleafure, and the fourth for madnefs. *Anacharfis*

Then is the mind moft apt to comprehend all good reafon, when the operations of the brain are not hin-°a by vapours, which excefs of feeding diftempers withal.

King *Cyrus* being asked by *Artabanus* (as he mar-ched one day in War) what he would have bought him for his Supper , Bread, (quoth he) for I hope we fhall find fome Fountain to furnifh us with drink.

Wifdom is hindred through Wine, and under-ftanding darkned. *Alphonf.*

Nothing can be more abject and hurtful, than to live as a flave to the pleafure of the mouth and belly. *Saluft.*

Difeafes gather together within our bodies, which proceed no lefs of being too full than being too emp-ty , and oftentimes a man hath more trouble to digeft meat than to get meat

How hard a matter is it to preach abftinence to the belly, which hath no ears, and which will take no denial, however the cafe ftandeth?

By Gluttony more die than perifh by the Sword

Gluttony ftirieth up luft, anger, and love in ex-tremity, extinguifhing underftanding, opinion and memory. *Plat*

Gluttony fatteth the body, maketh the mind dull and unapt, nay, which is worfe, undermineth reafon.

Wine

Wine hath as much force as fire so soon as it overtaketh one, it difpatcheth him, it difclofeth the fecrets of the Soul, and troubleth the whole mind.

Homer proving that the Gods die not, becaufe they eat not, alludeth, that eating and drinking do not only maintain life, but are likewife the caufe of death.

We are fick of thofe thing wherewith we live : for there is no proper and peculiar feed of difeafes, but the corruptions of thofe things within us which we eat, and the faults and errours we commit againft them. *Plut.*

Socrates inviting certain of his friends to a Feaft, was reproved for his flender provifion whereunto he anfwered, if they be vertuous, there is enough, but if they be not, there is too much

They which are addicted to belly-fervice, not caring for the food of the mind, may well be compared to Fools, that depend more upon Opinion than Reafon.

It is an old Proverb, much meat, much malady.

Intemperance is a root proper to every difeafe.

He that too much pampereth himfelf is a grievous enemy to his own body

Veffels being more fully frought than they are able to carry do fink, fo fareth it with fuch as eat and drink too much.

By furfeit many perifh, but he that dieteth himfelf prolongeth his life.

Excefs came from *Afia* to *Rome* Ambition came from *Rome* to all the world.

Gluttony caufeth innumerable maladies, and fhortens man's life. *Horace*

Surfeiting is the readieft means to procure ficknefs, and ficknefs is the chaftifement of intemperate diet.

Gorgias

Geo gias being demanded how he attained to the number of an hundred and eight years, anfwered, By never having eaten or drunken any thing through pleafure.

Omne nocet nimium, med ocriter omne gerendum.
Tantum cibi & jotionis adhibendum eft, ut reficiantur vires, non opprimantur. Cicero.

Of Concupifcence.

Defin. *Concupifcence or Luft is a defire againft reafon, a furious and unbridled appetite, which killeth all good motions in man's mind, and leaveth no place for vertue.*

LUft is a pleafure bought with pain, a delight hatcht with difquiet, a content paffed with fear, and a fin finifhed with forrow. *Demorax*

Luft by continuance groweth into impudency.

Shame and Infamy wait continually at the heels of unbridled Luft.

Luft is an enemy to the purfe, a foe to the perfon, a canker to the mind, a corrofive to the confcence, a weakner of the wit, a befotter of the fenfes, and, finally, a mortal bane to all the body, fo that thou fhalt find pleafure is the path-way to perdition, and lufting love the load-ftone to ruth and ruine *Pliny.*

Luft in age is loathfome, in youth excefs, howfoever it is the fruit of idlenefs

Luft inforceth us to covet beyond our power, to act beyond our nature, and to die before our time.

Senfual Vice hath thefe three companions the firft Blindnefs of underftanding, the fecond hardnefs of Heart, the third Want of grace.

Draco wrote fuch laws againft Incontinency, that he is faid not to have writ them with ink, but rather to have figned them with blood.

The

The chanels, which rivers long time have maintained, are hardly reftrained from their courfe, and luft wherein we have been long plunged is hardly purged.

Such things as maintain us in evil, or change our goodnefs to wickednefs, are either nourifhed or begun by Luft.

Pleafure is the end of fuperfluity. *Plato.*

Adultery is called the injury of nature.

Concupifcence is infeparably accompanied with the troubling of all order, with impudency, unfeemlinefs, floth and diffolutenefs. *Plato.*

Our tongues moft willingly talk of thofe things which our hearts moft defire.

Chaftity is a punifhment to the incontinent, and labour to the flothful. *Sen.*

Adultery defireth no procreation, but pleafure. *Anfelm.*

Luft maketh a man to have neither care of his own good name, nor confideration of the fhame which his pofterity fhall poffefs by his evil living

This monftrous fin altereth, marreth, and drieth the body, weakning all the joynts and members, making the face bubbled and yellow, fhortning life, diminifhing memory, undeiftanding, and the very heart.

Adultery is unlawful Matrimony.

Adultery is hated even among beafts.

Luft is a ftrong tower of mifchief, and hath in it many defenders; as needinefs, anger, palenefs, difcord, love, and longing *Diog*

Concupifcence doth injure, profane and defile the holinefs of the foul.

The *Corinthians* for their incontinency have been evil-fpoken of, for they were fo unchaft, that they proftrated their own daughters to enrich themfelves. Hence came the Proverb, It is not fit for every man

to go to *Corinth:* for they paid well for their pleasure.

The *Babylonians,* *Tyrrhenians,* and *Meffalians,* were
greatly fpotted with this vice, abufing their bodies
in fuch monftrous fort, that they were reputed to
live rather like beafts than Men

Meretrix non diffimilis mari. quod dat, devorat :
nunquam abundat.

Hoc'unum in ore perpetuo habent meretrices, Da mihi,
atque Affer mihi.

Of Sloth.

Defin. *Sloth is a fear to endure labour, a defifting from*
the neceffary actions both of body and mind. it is the
fink which receiveth all the filthy chanels of vice,
and with that poifonous air infecteth and fpoileth the
foul.

A Man being idle hath his mind apt to all unclean-
nefs , and when the mind is void of exercife,
the man is void of honefty.

Sloth rifeth fometimes of too much abundance.

Profperity engendreth floth.

Sloth turneth the edge of wit, but ftudy fharpeneth
the memory

That which is moft noble by nature is made moft
vile by negligence. *Arift.*

Idlenefs is the only nurfe and nourifher of fenfual
appetites, and the fole maintainer of youthful affections

Travel is a work that continueth after death.

Be doing always fomewhat, that the Devil find
thee not idle. *Hierom.*

Idlenefs is the fepulchre of a living man.

Sloth is the Devils cufhion or pillow. *Origen*

Idlenefs teacheth much wickednefs. *Eur.*

They

They that do nothing learn to do ill. *Cic.*

Idleneſs infecteth the mind with many miſchiefs.

Idleneſs is againſt nature. *Cicero.*

The ſlothful man ſleepeth in his own want. *Cicero.*

It is hard for him that will not labour to excel in any Art.

Idleneſs is the enemy of vertue, and the very train of all wickedneſs.

Sloth loſeth time, dulleth the underſtanding, nouriſheth humours, choaketh the brain, hinders thrift, and diſpleaſeth God. *Galen.*

Sloth is the mother of poverty. *Sen.*

The ſluggard being neſtled in ignorance, ſooneſt falleth into Atheiſm.

The man that paſſeth his life ſlothfully without profit, ought to loſe it without pity.

Idleneſs maketh of men women, of women beaſts, of beaſts monſters. *Homer.*

Study begetteth ſtudy, and ſloth increaſeth ſloth. *Ambi.*

Pythagoras gave his diſciples this Precept, Take good heed that thou ſit not upon a Buſhel. meaning, that idleneſs ought eſpecially to be eſchewed.

Luſt is quenched by labour, and kindled through idleneſs.

The idle heart is moved with no prayers. *Curtius.*

The rich man, if he wax idle, will be quickly poor.

Idleneſs is ſecurity, and labour is care.

In doing nothing men learn to do ill. *Columella*

That kind of contemplation, tending to ſolitarineſs, is but a glorious title to idleneſs. *S. P. S.*

Sloth is a fear of labour to enſue.

It

It is not for a man of authority to sleep a whole night. *Hom.*

In idleness beware of idleness.

Sloth is the Step mother of Wisdom and Science. *Anacharsis.*

Men are born to good works, whereof our soul may serve for a sufficient and invincible proof, seeing it is never still, but in continual motion and action. *Cicero.*

Idleness decayeth the health of the body, and no man ought to hide his life. *Plut.*

Where nature hath been friendly, there is a certain vain opinion which causeth slothfulness. *Plato.*

The Bees can abide no Drones among them ; but as soon as any begin to be idle, they kill them. *Plato.*

The wise man's idleness is continual labour. *Bern.*

Carthage was overcome, and *Rome* by Idleness came to ruine. *Aug.*

——*Vanam semper dant otia mentem*

Ignavia vitium est animosæ partis, quæ consternitur periculis, præsertim mortis. Ar.st.

Otium summopere fugiendum est, quia multorum malorum causa est.

Otium moderatum corpori & animo prodest, immoderatum vero nocet.

Of Presumption.

Defin. *Presumption is a violent passion of the will, and an utter foe to prudence : it is that affection which thrusteth and exposeth the body to dangers, presuming only upon vain hope and imagination, without either ground or reason*

HE that vaunteth of victory before he hath won the field, may be counted more foolish than valiant. *Bias.*

Vain and light men love commonly that which is forbidden by reafon, and love nothing more than to follow their fenfual appetites.

He that prefumeth of his own ftrength is foon overcome. *Aug.*

A fault wilfully committed ought not to be forgiven.

To flie from that we fhould follow, is to follow our own deftruction.

Hardinefs without fear is the fifter of folly.

Prefumption is the mother of all vices, and is like unto a great fire, which maketh every one to retire back. *Aug.*

It is a great prefumption to look for reverence of our elders, and to enjoin our betters filence. *Greg.*

To prefumption belongeth correction, to correction amendment, and to amendment reward. *Ber.*

There is more hope of a Fool than of him that is wife in his own conceit. *Solon.*

Take heed of rafhnefs in refolution, and cruelty in conqueft, for the one is wilful, and the other wicked, and as the firft wants it, fo the other fhews as little grace, whofe fruits are pernicious to reafon, and torment to the confcience

He that prefumes on that he knows not, may lofe an honour for an humour. *Curtius*

Prefumptuous attempts bring bad ends.

A feftered fore muft have a fearching falve, and a fhamelefs fmile an open frown.

It is an impudent and prefumptuous part, to commit any thing to the judgment of him that wanteth knowledge

Ill fuccefs comes of rafh beginnings.

He that fpeaks of high things, having no experience of them, is like unto a blind man that would lead and teach him the way which feeth better than himfelf. *Bern.*

O   It

It is a troublesome, dangerous, insolent and proud enterprise, for a man to take upon him with a Pen to govern a Common-weal, and with a Prince to reason of his life.

He is not wise, but arrogant, that dares presume unasked to give a Prince counsel.

He that presumeth to understand every thing, is thought to be ignorant in all things.

Every man presumeth on his own fancy, which maketh divers to leap short through want of good rising, and many shoot over for want of true aim.

He is very obstinate whom neither reason nor experience can perswade. *Chilo.*

Aspiring thoughts, as they are lofty, so are they perillous.

To strain farther than the sleeve will stretch maketh the arm bare . and to skip beyond a man's skill, is to leap, but not to know where to light.

The man that presumes to be wise, let him not contend with him that is inflamed with wrath : for if he fail to follow counsel herein, he shall either have his head broken by the furious, or his heart galled by the detractour.

Where men do all that they will, they indeed presume to do that which they should not. *Cicero.*

Presumption is the chief ground and cause of all variance, hatred and mischief.

Among the ambitious men of the world presumption is a fury, and a continual tempter.

The occasion why Leven was forbidden unto the Jews at the Feast of *Easter,* was, to teach them to have a great care to keep themselves from Pride and Presumption, into which they fell that held any good opinions of their own selves, and puffed themselves up therewith, as the dough is puffed with the Leven. *Philo.*

Men

Men ought not to defer the amendment of their life to the laft hour, becaufe the thief was faved. for, as that was a precedent, that none fhould defpair; fo was it but one example, becaufe none fhould prefume.

He is too much prefumptuous that ftriveth to go where another hath fallen, and too much unbridled that fearcheth not at all when others have perifhed before him.

Let him that thinketh he ftandeth take heed left he fall.

Nulla præfumptio perniciofior quàm de propria juftitiæ aut fcientia fuperbire. O fuperba præfumptio! O præfumptuofa fuperbia! Aug.

Cùm non fit noftrum quod fumus, quomodo noftrum eft quod habemus?

Stultitiæ genus eft, ut cùm aliis debeas vitæ beneficium, tibi adfcribas ornamenta virtutum.

Of Treafon.

Defin. *Treafon is that damned vice, hated of God and Man, wherewith perjured perfons being bewitched, fear not to betray themfelves, fo they may either betray others or their Country: it is the breach of faith and loyalty with God, their Governours, and Country.*

THey are deceived that look for any reward for treafon *Curtius*

The conflict with Traitours is more dangerous than with open enemies. *Livius.*

Traitours are like Moths, which eat the cloth in which they were bred, like Vipers, that gnaw the bowels where they were born, like Worms, which confume the wood in which they were ingendered. *Agefil.*

Treachery

Treachery hath always a more glozing shew than the Truth, and Flattery displays a braver Flag than Faith.

No place is safe enough for a Traitour. *Amb.*

Once a Traitour, and never after trusted *Liv.*

Who will not, with *Antigonus*, make much of a Traitour, going about to pleasure him? but having his purpose, who will not hate him to death?

Such as are Traitours to their Prince, and perjured to God, deserve no credit with men.

Treachery ought not to be concealed, and friends have no privilege no be false

Such as covet most bitterly to betray, first seek most sweetly to intrap. *Philip.*

Traitours leave no practice undone, not because they will not, but because they dare not.

Victory is not so earnestly to be sought, as Treason to be shunned.

A good warriour ought to commit the fortune of his war to the trust of his own vertue, not to the impiety and treason of his enemies.

Many men love the Treason, though they hate the Traitour.

Many conspire valiantly, but end wretchedly

Traitours have continual fear for their Bedfellow, care for their Companion, and the sting of conscience for their Torment. *Men.*

A light head, an ambitious desire, a corrupt conscience, and ill counsel, soon make a Traitour.

Where the people's affection is assured, the Traitour's purpose is prevented. *Bias*

There are many Traitours in Common weals whom it is better to forbear than to provoke

Of rash hopes proceed perillous ends, and of execrable treasons damnable success.

Traitours about the Thrones of Princes are like Wolves about the Folds of Sheep.

One fcabbed fheep will infect a whole flock, and one Traitour fubvert the whole Monarchy.

He is worthily hated of all men that beareth not a faithful heart to his Country.

No wife man at any time will truft a Traitour. *Tully*

Nè in colloquiis de prætextu pacis proditiones urbium tententur, fiántque interlocutores, maximè cavendum eft.

Proditores urbium fæpe nè ipfi quidem proditionem e-vadunt, fed ab hofte trucidantur.

Of Defperation.

Defin. *Defperation is a forrowfulnefs without all hope of better fortune, a vice which falfly fhadoweth it felf under the title of Fortitude and Valour, and tickling the vain humours of the vain glorious, carries them to ignoble, and indifferent actions, to the utter lofs of their fouls and bodies.*

DEfperation is a double fin, and final impenitence hath no remiffion

It is better to be called a daftardly Coward, than a defperate Caitiff

Let no man defpair of Grace, although he repent in his latter age · for God judgeth of man's end, and not of his life paft. *Ber.*

Defperation fpringeth from the ignorance of God. *Aug.*

It is better to prolong our life in mifery, than to haften our own death without hope of mercy. *Lactantius.*

Love wanting its defire, makes the mind defperate and fixed fancy bereft of love turneth into fury.

There

There is no offence fo great but mercy may pardon neither is there any thing fo defperate which time can not cure.

Defpair is the fruit of impatience

The fear of inevitable punifhment is the caufe of defperation. *Stob.*

Nothing doth more torment a man than forfaking hope. *Quint.*

Let no man defpair of that thing to be effected which hath been done already.

Extreme fear and danger make cowards defperately adventurous, and what perfwafion could not make conftant, mifery hath made defperate.

Refolution is grounded on honour, defperatenefs on danger.

Fortune *defperately attained* is as *defperately loft*: and defpair fuddainly entertained is a token of a wretched confcience.

Defpair comes of the feeblenefs of courage, and the lack of wit.

To him that is fubject to paffion defpair is ever attendant.

He that is defperately inclined to his own will, is ever moft near to the wrath of God.

Defpair leadeth damnation in chains, and violence lays claim to the wrath of God. *Ber.*

Defpair and revenge deprive men of the mercy of God, and clean blot out the memory of their former good deeds.

Of all the perturbations of man's mind, Defpair is the moft pernicious. *Livius.*

Many, reading *Plato* his Book of the Immortality of the Soul, have laid violent hands upon themfelves.

He that through the burthen of his fins breaks forth into defperation, wilfully refufeth the mercy of the Almighty.

When

When hope leaveth a man, fear beginneth to conquer him. *Plato.*

The foul's firft comfort is to avoid the fault, the next, not to defpair of pardon.

Defperation is a certain death. *Aug.*

As he which without licence breaketh a Prifon, procureth his own death; fo in the world to come fhall he be perpetually punifhed, which, contrary to the will of God, will fet his foul at liberty. *Plato.*

Vincitur haud gratis jugulo qui provocat hoftem.

Qui nil poteft fperare, defperet nihil.

Non eft defperandum in adverfis.

Non læta extollant animum, nec trifta frangant.

Of Herefies and Hereticks.

Defin. *Herefie is a wilful and obftinate opinion grounded in the mind, the fifter of ignorance, a profeffed enemy to all truth, prefumptuoufly oppofing it felf againft the Principles of Faith and true Religion.*

AFter the afcenfion of *Chrift* into Heaven, divers, by the inftigation of the Devil, did, as *Simon* the *Samaritan* and others, who fought to feduce the people from the true faith they embraced, teaching and preaching Herefies. *Juftin.*

Herefie ftreweth the plain and open way of truth with thorns and brambles.

If we follow our own imaginations, neglecting the truth, we renounce our falvation, and yield our felves fubjects to Satan.

Antioch was never without Hereticks: and within the feventh year of *Julius*, the greater part thereof was confumed with fire from Heaven, the other deftroyed by an Earthquake.

Neftorius denied *Mary* to be the mother of *Chrift*; after he was banifhed, his tongue was eaten up with worms, and he died miferably. *Euag.*

Q 4

They

They which through the dimness of their mind, and want of understanding, do contemn the true and living God, do please themselves with all manner of pestilent errours *Amb.*

Some not considering that clear and heavenly light which cometh from God, do fall into the gulf, and sink to the bottom of that most foul and filthy puddle of all false Opinions, Errours, Heresies, and worshipping of false gods. *Amb.*

An Heretick doth corrupt the sincerity of the Faith and Doctrine of the Apostles *Aug.*

A Schismatick, although he sin not at all against the pure Doctrine and sincere Faith, yet he rashly separateth himself from the Church, breaking the bond of unity *Aug.*

If Cockle appear in the Church, yet ought neither our faith nor charity be letted, we must rather learn to be good Corn. *Cyp*

While some men always take to themselves a farther dominion than peaceable justice requireth, they perish from the Church and while they proudly lift up themselves, blinded with their own presumption, they are bereft of the light of the truth. *Greg.*

The Church oft placed amidst much Chaff and Cockle, suffereth many things, and yet whatsoever is either contrary to faith or good life she alloweth not, neither holds she her peace, neither doth she it.

De nucleo olivæ, intus optimæ & suavissimæ, ventosa & vana caprificus exsurgit: ita & hæreses de nostra fructificaverunt religione, degeneres à veritatis grano, mendaces & sylvestres Tertul.

Omnia hæreticorum dogmata inter Aristotelis & Chrysippi *spineta sedem sibi & requiem repererunt.* Hieronymus.

Of Devils.

Defin. *Devils are our tempters to sin, blasphemy, and all other evils : they that stand in fear of God, take pleasure in that which displeaseth them.*

THE Devil labours to deceive man, and greatly envies that any should be saved.

Satan useth great cunning to draw men from Christ, and he is undone for ever, that is deceived by him.

Through the envy of the Devil sin entred into the world.

The Devil was the first author of lying, the first beginner of all subtile deceits, and the chief delighter in all sin and wickedness. *Philo.*

The Devils, not able to oppose God in himself, assault him in his members. *Aug.*

The Devil intangleth Youth with beauty; the Usurer with gold, the Ambitious with smooth looks, the Learned by false doctrine.

The Devils oft times speak truth in Oracles, to the intent they might shadow their falshoods the more cunningly. *Lactan.*

The Devils (as being immortal spirits, and exercised in much knowledge) seem to work many things, which in truth are no miracles, but mere works of nature.

All the great power of Devils proceedeth from the just indignation of God, who by such whips chastiseth the wicked, and exerciseth the good.

The power of God, and not the Devil, is to be feared. *Greg.*

The invisible enemy is overcome by faith.

The Devils have will to hurt, but they want power. *August*

The Devil is overcome by humility.

The

The Devil is ſtrong againſt thoſe that entertain him, but weak againſt thoſe that reſiſt him. *Aug.*

He that giveth his word to the Devil, breaketh his bond with God. *Luther.*

The Devil, Temptation, and Sin, were the occaſion of man's fall.

The Devil in the laſt day ſhall riſe againſt us in condemnation, for that he hath been more careful to get ſouls than we to ſave them. *Bern*

The Devil doth eaſily hit with his arrows the proud man of this world, but the humble he miſſeth.

The Archer ſooner doth hit a great mark than a little one. *Amb.*

The Devil ceaſeth to tempt them whom he hath already won.

The Devil, though he ſeeth not our thoughts, yet by outward ſigns he many times doth know them, as by our words.

The Devil is the father of lyes, and the chief author of all deceit

The Devil tempteth the righteous one way, and the wicked another way. *Greg.*

The Devil preſents before us many vain delights, to the intent he might the better keep our mind from godly meditation.

What ſin ſoever hath been by man at any time committed, was firſt by the Devil invented.

The Devil firſt accuſeth us of our evil words, next of our evil works, laſtly of our evil thoughts. *Greg.*

Chriſtus Leo, dicitur, propter fortitudinem ; Agnus propter innocentiam · Leo. quod invictus ; Agnus, quia manſuetus. Ipſe Agnus occaſu vicit Leonem, qui circumit quærens quem devoret, Diabolus Leo dictus feritate non virtute. Aug.

Of Hell.

Defin. *Hell is in all things contrary to Heaven · It is a place of torment, misery and desolation; where the wicked shall endure the endless judgment of pain for their offences.*

ZEno the Stoick taught, That the places of the Reprobates were separate from the righteous; the one being pleasant and delectable, the other darksome and damnable.

Hell is the hold of horror, distress and misery, the cell of torment, grief and vexation.

The loss of Heaven is to the damned more grievous than the torment of Hell. *Chryf.*

Hell is the land of darkness.

Woe be to him that by experience knoweth there is a Hell. *Chryf.*

Hell is the place of punishment which God hath reserved for the Reprobates.

In Hell is no order, but a heap and chaos of confusion.

The wretches in Hell have an end without end, a death without death, a defect without defect for their death liveth continually, and the end beginneth always, and the defect can never fail.

Hell is every-where where Heaven is not.

The torture of a bad conscience is the Hell of a living soul. *Calvin.*

Good men have their Hell in this world, that they may know there is a Heaven after death, to reward the vertuous and wicked men escape torments in this world, because they shall find there is a judgment to come, wherein the wicked shall have punishment according to the number of their offences. *Lactantius.*

They that believe in *Chrift* have already overcome sin and Hell.

To

To them that are enamoured of the world, the re membrance of Hell is bitter.

The image of our fins reprefents unto us the picture of Hell

Hell, like death, is moft uncertain, and a place of punifhment moft affured.

Hell is compared to the Labyrinth which *Dædalus* made, whofe entrance is eafie, but being once in, it is not poffible to return.

He that tempted *Chrift* will never fpare men. *Bernard*

If thy mind be not moved with the fire of Heaven, take heed left thy foul feel the flames of Hell.

Hell, though now never fo private, yet in the end it will be moft publick.

Envy is a picture or refemblance of Hell.

Death holdeth his Standard in Hell, which is called the Land of death.

Infernvs locus eft fine menfura, profunditas fine fundo, plenus ardoris incomparabilis, plenus fœtoris intolerabilis, ibi miferiæ, ibi tenebræ, ibi horror æternus, ibi nulla fpes boni, nulla defperatio mali

Inferni pœna æterna eft.

Horáque erit tantis ultima nulla malis. Ovid.

F I N I S.

THE NAMES

Of all the Christian and Heathen

Author's in this Book.

A Uguſtine
Ambroſe
Appian
Archimedes
Ælianus
Ariſtotle
Ariſtippus
Anaxagoras
Alex. Severus.
Anſelm

B
Baſil
Bernard
Bonaventure
Boet us
Bullinger
Bodinus
Bias
Bacon
Beza
Bion

C
Chryſoſtome
Cyprian
Clemen Alex
Caſſiodorus
Columella

Cor. Agrippa
Chryſippus
Chilo
Calvin
Cicero
Curtius

D
Diogenes
Diog Laert.
Demoſthenes
Dionyſius

E
Euſebius
Evagoras
Eraſmus
Ennius
Epictetus
Euripides

G
Gregory
Guevara
Galen
Guicciardine

H
Hierome
Horace
Hermes
Hippocrates

Homer

I
Joſephus
Iſidorus
Irenæus
Juſtin
Juſtinian
Iſocrates
Jamblichus

L
Luther
Lactantius
Lud. Vives
Livius
Lucretius
Lycurgus

M
Macrobius
Muſonius
Marc. Aurel.
Muſæus
Menander
Martial

N
Arphus

O
Origen
Olaus

Oſo.

The Authors Names

Oſerius

P

Polycarpus
Petrarch
Publius
Plautus
Plato
Philo
Pontanus
Pacuvius
Phocion
Periander
Pythagoras
Plotinus
Plutarch
Pittacus
Pindarus
Petronius

Plinius
Pſellus

Q

Quintilianus

R

Ramus

S

Sirach
Solon
Socrates
Stobæus
Saluſt
Suetonius
Silius Italicus
Sophocles
Seneca
Sir Thomas Moor
Sir Philip Sidney

T

Thomas Aquinas
Theodorus
Thales
Terence
Tertullian
Theopompus
Theophraſtus
Theocritus

V

Vegetius
Virgil

X

Xenocrates
Xenophon

Z

Zeno

A Table

A

TABLE

Of all the

Principal Matters

CONTAINED

In the Former Treatife.

The Table

The Table

The Table

THE END

Some

Some Books Printed for W. Freeman,
in Fleetſtreet.

ERaſmi Colloquia, 8*vo.*
Tropoſchematologia Rhetorica, cum Etymolo-
gica Troporum Figurarumque explicatione lucu-
lenter illuſtrata, atque in Uſum Scholæ Grammá-
ticalis apud *Pontem Uxinum* adornata. *Price* 4 d.

Titi Livii Patavini Hiſtoriarum Decades quæ
ſuperſunt, Juxta Editionem *Gronovianam* diligen-
ter recenſitæ: Lemmatibus Hiſtoricis ad paginarum
oras ornatæ. Adjiciuntur *Tabulæ Geographicæ* Hiſto-
riam Romanam egregie illuſtrantes Tomi Duo.
In 8*vo.*

The *Roman Hiſtory,* Deſign'd as well for the
Underſtanding of the *Roman* Authors, as the *Roman* Affairs. In Four Vol. Compleat: The Two
Firſt done by *L. Echard,* A. M. of *Chriſt College*
in *Cambridge.*

The Elements of *Euclid,* explain'd in a *New,*
but moſt *Eaſie* Method: Together with the Uſe
of every Propoſition through all parts of the Mathematicks. Written in *French* by that Excellent
Mathematician, *F. C. F. Milliet de Chales* of the
Society of *Jeſus.* Now made *Engliſh,* and a
Multitude of Errors corrected, which had eſca-
ped in the Original. *Price* 4 s. The

A Catalogue of Books.

The *New Method of Fortification*, by Monſieur *de Vauban*, Engineer General of *France*. The Third Edition, carefully Reviſed and Corrected by the Original To which is now added, a Treatiſe of *Military Orders*, and the *Art* of Gunnery, or Throwing of *Bombs*, *Balls*, &c. By *W. Alingham*, Maſter of the Mathematical School in *Channel-Row*, *Weſtminſter*. Illuſtrated with 32 Copper Plates. In 8*vo*. *Price* 6 s

Arithmetick Or, *The Ground of Arts* Teaching that Science both in whole Numbers and Fractions, Theorically and Practically applied in the Operation and Solution of Queſtions in Numeration, Addition, Subſtraction, Multiplication, Diviſion, the Rules of Proportion, Fellowſhip, Barter, the Rules of Practice, Exchange of Coin, Loſs and Gain, Tare, Trett, and other Queſtions relating to Weights and Meaſures, Lengths and Breadths, Equation of Payments, Commiſſion to Factors, &c. Originally compoſed by Dr. *Record* and others. And now peruſed, Corrected, new Methodized and much Improved And thereto added, 1. A new Treatiſe of Decimals, with the Demonſtration of each Rule, &c. 2. Tables of Simple and Compound Intereſt, &c. Dedicated to his Highneſs *William*, late Duke of *Gloceſter* By *E. Hatton*, Philomercat. *Price* 5 s.

The *Devout Communicant* Exemplified in his Behaviour, Before, At, and After the Sacrament of the Lord's Supper, Practically ſuited to all the Parts of that ſolemn Ordinance. The Ninth Edition *Price* 1 s. 6 d.

A Catalogue of Books.

An Infallible Way to Contentment, in the midſt of *Publick* or Perſonal Calamities. The Fourth Edition, Corrected. And thereto added a ſecond Part, Entituled, *The Peace and Joy of the Soul Procured and Preſerved.* By the Author of the Devout Communicant *Price* 2 s

The whole Duty of a Chriſtian; containing all things neceſſary both as to what he is to *Know* and *Do*, for the obtaining a Happy Eternity. To which is added more particular Directions, *How to prepare for a Comfortable Death.* Price. 1 s 6 d

An *Expoſition of the Church Catechiſm*, with Scripture Proofs in Words at Length. The Second Edition. *Price* 1 s. 6 d.

The *Church of England's Communicant*, Directed and Aſſiſted by the Publick Liturg. In 24° *Price* 6 d

The *Terrible Stormy Wind* and *Tempeſt*, which hapned *Nov.* 27 1703 Conſider'd and ought *to be had in Everlaſting Remembrance* ‧ To which is added *Fair Warning* to a *Careleſs World.* Pr. 6 d. Theſe ſix were all Written by the Author of the *Devout Communicant.*

Syſtema Horti-culturæ, Or, *The Art of Gardening* In Three Books. Treating of the Excellency, Situation, Soil, Walks, &c. and other Ornaments of *Gardens*, With many Rules and Directions concerning the ſame Of Winter-Greens, Flowers, &c. of the Kitchen-Garden; with Inſtructions for making Hot-Beds, altering and enriching

ing

ing any fort of Garden-Ground, &c. to a very great Improvement of every fort of Land for Ufe and Profit, Ornament and Delight. Illuftrated with Sculptures. The Fourth Edition: By *J. Worlidge*, Gent. *Price* 2 s. 6 d.

A *Manual of Private Devotions*, with Directions for the Sick: By the Right Reverend Father in God, *L. Andrews*, Late Bifhop of *Winchefter*. Price 1 s. 6 d.

New *Obfervations* on the Natural Hiftory of this World of Matter, and this World of Life; Being a Philofophical Difcourfe, grounded upon the *Mofaick Syftem* of the *Creation* and the *Flood*; With fome Thoughts concerning *Paradife*, the *conflagration of the World*, a Treatife of *Meteorology*, and fome Occafional Remarks upon fome late *Theories, Conferences* and *Effays*. Price 2 s. 6 d.

The *Anatomy of the Earth*. In 4to. Price 6 d. Thefe Two were Written by *Tho. Robinfon*, Rector of *Ousby* in *Cumberland*.

A Difcourfe of *Natural* and *Reveal'd Religion*. By Mr. *T. Nourfe*, in 8vo. *Price* 2 s. 6 d.

The *Law* of *Nature* and *Nations:* Written Originally in Latin, by *S. Puffendorf*, Counfellor of State to the late King of *Sweden*. Done into Englifh by Mr. *Kennett*. In *Folio*. Price 1 l.

A *Compleat Hiftory of England*, from before the Conqueft to the Death of King *William* the IIId. With the *Effigies* of all the Kings and Queens; Curioufly done by the beft Hands. In Three Volumes, *Folio*.

The

A Catalogue of Books.

The Whole *Critical* Works of Monſieur *Rapin.* In Two Volumes: Done into Engliſh by ſeveral Hands. *Price* 12 *s.*

The *Compleat Body of Surgery* by *Vaugion.* In 8*vo.* Price 6 *s.*

The *Compleat Surgeon,* with a Treatiſe of Bandages, and many Copper-Cuts: By Monſieur *Le Clerc.* Price 4 s. 6 *d.*

The *Anatomy* of *Humane Bodies* Improv'd, according to the *Circulation* of the *Blood,* and all the Modern Diſcoveries: By Monſieur *Dionis,* Chief Surgeon to the late *Dauphineſs,* and the preſent Dutcheſs of *Burgundy.* Done into Engliſh, and Illuſtrated with Figures. *Price* 6 s.

Charron of *Wiſdom:* Done into Engliſh by the Reverend Dr. *Stanhope,* Dean of *Canterbury.* In Two Volumes.

Quarles's Emblems, a Curious Edition thereof. *Price* 5 s.

Steps of Aſcenſion to God: By the Famous Cardinal *Bellarmine* Done into Engliſh and Reformed, by the Reverend Mr. *Hall* of *Hampſtead.* Price 2 *s.* 6 *d.*

A *New Voyage* to the *Levant.* Price 5 *s.*

A *New Voyage* to *Italy.* In Two Volumes. *Pr.* 12 s.

A New *High German Grammar.* By Mr. *King,* Maſter of that Language in *London.* Price 2 *s.*

Miege's Laſt and Beſt *French Grammar.* In 8*vo.* Price 2 *s.*

------His Grammar for Foreigners to Learn Engliſh. *Price* 2.

Ordi-

A Catalogue of Books.

Ordination, by *Meer Presbyters*, proved *Void* and *Null*. In a *Conference* between Philalethes a *Presbyter* of the *Church* of England, and Pſeudochœus a *Diſſenting Teacher*. By *John Jacques*, M. A. Rector of *Cowley*, and Miniſter of *Uxbridge* in *Middleſex*. In 8vo. Price 2 s 6 d.

Theſaurarrum Mathematicæ : Or, *The Treaſury of the Mathematicks* ; containing Variety of uſeful Practices in *Arithmetick*, *Geometry*, *Trigonometry*, *Aſtronomy*, *Geography*, *Navigation* and *Surveying*. As alſo the Menſuration of *Board*, *Glaſs*, *Tiling*, *Paving*, *Timber*, *Stone* and *Irregular Solids*. Likewiſe it teacheth the Art of *Gauging*, *Dialling*, *Fortification*, *Military Orders* and *Gunnery* Explains the *Logarithms*, *Sines*, *Tangents*, and *Secants* · Sheweth their uſe in *Arithmetick*, &c. To which is annex'd a Table of 10000 *Logarithms*, *Log-Sines* and *Log-Tangents*. Illuſtrated with ſeveral *Mathematical Sculptures* on Copper-Plates. Originally compos'd by *John Taylor*, Gent. And now carefully Revis'd and Corrected. To which is added, the Uſe and Practice of ſeveral *Propoſitions* and *Problems* throughout the whole Work, as alſo the Deſcription and Uſe of both *Globes*, and ſome of the chiefeſt *Mathematical Inſtruments* both for Sea and Land With many other conſiderable Additions and Improvements. By *W. Alingham*, Teacher of the *Mathematicks*. In 8vo. Price 6 s. 6 d.

A Diſcourſe concerning the *Certainty* of a *Future* and *Immortal State*. In ſome Moral, Phyſiological and Religious Conſiderations. By a *Doctor of Phyſick*. Price 2 s. 6 d.